D1547840

RITES OF RETURN

RITES OF RETURN

Diaspora Poetics and the Politics of Memory

edited by
Marianne Hirsch
and Nancy K. Miller

Columbia University Press   New York

Columbia University Press

Publishers Since 1893

New York   Chichester, West Sussex

Library of Congress Cataloging-in-Publication Data

Rites of return : diaspora poetics and the politics of
memory / edited by Marianne Hirsch and Nancy K.
Miller.

   p.   cm. — (Gender and culture)

  Includes bibliographical references and index.

  ISBN 978-0-231-15090-3 (cloth: acid-free paper)—
ISBN 978-0-231-15091-0 (pbk.: acid-free paper)—
ISBN 978-0-231-52179-6 (e-book)

  1. Return in literature. 2. Feminist literary
criticism. 3. Collective memory and literature.
4. Discourse analysis, Narrative. 5. Poetics.
I. Hirsch, Marianne. II. Miller, Nancy K.,
1941– III. Title. IV. Series.

PN56.R475R58 2011

306—dc22

                    2011010557

For our students

Contents

Preface

The twenty-first century seems strangely attached to the past. The losses suffered in the last century and the atrocities that have dominated its history continue to preoccupy our imaginations. A long-standing legacy of violence, compounded by new disasters, has engendered a set of rites—both individual and collective—that have taken many forms: the reconstruction of past histories, the retrieval of lost communities, the activation of historic sites, and a quest for origins.

In the first decade of the century, the turn to roots has been supported and stimulated by the vast resources of the Internet and other new or recycled technologies of research. With the decoding of the human genome in 2000, the science of genetics seemed to offer a reliable way to decipher difference through the language of genes. But, through a perhaps predictable feedback loop, the desire to recapture the past and to retrieve its stories also led to the creation of new products, like Macintosh's Reunion software, designed to organize family history into genealogical trees, or readily accessible DNA test kits to establish and prove lineage. These consumer products, in turn, enable, and underwrite, the quest and feed nostalgic fantasies about homecoming.

As both a record and interpretation of this complexly intertwined phenomenon, *Rites of Return* offers a set of critical approaches to our contemporary obsession with the past that entails a simultaneous commitment to acknowledgment and repair. Cutting across disciplinary boundaries, our project takes shape in the face of a worldwide refugee crisis, ongoing wars, natural disasters caused by human neglect, political upheavals, and the displacements caused by economic globalization.

Rites of Return emerges from several years of conversation between the two of us and our shared meditations on the question of return. Wanting to find a concrete expression to our joint preoccupation, we experimented first with a conference, "Rites of Return: Poetics and Politics," held at both our institutions—the Graduate Center of the City University of New York and Columbia University—in the spring of 2008. Thanks to the support of Aoibheann Sweeney, executive director of the Center for the Humanities at the Graduate Center (CUNY), and to Laura Ciolkowski, associate director of the of the Center for the Critical Analysis of Social Difference at Columbia, we were able to bring together scholars, writers, artists, photographers, and legal scholars for two days of intense exchange.

The success of this event led us to want to think further about the feminist implications and contributions to an expansive, reimagined scholarship on diaspora and the new genealogy, cultural memory, and the paradoxes of nostalgia. The present volume builds on the conference by expanding its historical, geographical, and conceptual range. What began as a conversation between two feminist literary and cultural critics preoccupied with acts of return in our own lives and writing has morphed into a broader inquiry into the preoccupation with return and its vicissitudes that we share with the contributors to these pages.

As we enter the second decade of the twenty-first century, with the fallout from the greatest man-made environmental disaster of U.S. history, the Gulf of Mexico oil spill, and legislation easing immigration into the United States still being debated, we hope to engage these difficult, often intractable issues through personal, scholarly, and artistic contributions. *Rites of Return* confronts the responsibilities and ethics of the Janus-like effort entailed in looking back to the past and forward to the future at the same time.

We are indebted to a number of colleagues who joined us at various stages of this project. Aoibheann Sweeney deserves special thanks for her guidance in the planning and execution of the "Rites of Return" conference, as well as her intellectual rigor. The conference also served as the inaugural event of the newly formed Center for the Critical Analysis of Social Difference, and we are grateful to Columbia president Lee Bollinger for his support. Saidiya Hartman and Jean Howard, co-conveners with Marianne Hirsch of the CCASD working group on "Engendering Archives," offered valuable advice and inspiration.

At various stages of the book's evolution, we benefited from the wisdom, time, and extraordinary talents of several young scholars to whom we are deeply grateful: Marta Bladek, Jenny James, Sherally Munshi, and Sonali Thakkar helped us to think further by offering constructive editing and critique of the project from its inception, as did Cat Bohannon and Mikhal Dekel in their reading of the introduction. Vina Tran's artistic and editorial abilities helped create our beautiful conference program and brought the manuscript to its final form.

The Columbia University Seminar on Cultural Memory provided a forum for a critical discussion of our project and its introduction, and we especially want to recognize the support of the Schoff Fund for its generous assistance.

We are also grateful to Jennifer Crewe, editorial director, Columbia University Press, and Victoria Rosner, coeditor of the Gender and Culture Series, for their support of this book and for the critical perspective of the anonymous readings of the manuscript. Most of all, we want to acknowledge our contributors. Thanks to them, we continue to believe—in good feminist tradition—that some topics are best explored through the collaborative genre of the conference and the edited volume.

RITES OF RETURN

Introduction

MARIANNE HIRSCH AND NANCY K. MILLER

"To be rooted is perhaps the most important and least recognized need of the human soul," philosopher Simone Weil declared in the chapter "Uprootedness" of her famous 1949 essay, *The Need for Roots*. Emerging from the European aftermath of World War II, Weil's belief has not ceased to resonate in popular consciousness as well as in theoretical reflections on displacement and dispossession that have come to characterize our modernity. But, Weil also argued, "Every human being needs multiple roots."[1]

In the United States, Alex Haley's *Roots* gave a name and shape to the longing for a verifiable identification of personal and cultural beginnings. The tremendous success of Haley's 1976 Pulitzer Prize–winning book and television miniseries attested to the fact that that identification needed more than research into the group genealogy of displaced peoples: it required the hook of a personal journey to an ancestral homeland. *Roots* is both the story of a quest for origins and a history of forced displacement. As a quest narrative, it exposes its research methods: travel to the village of Juffure in Gambia where Haley believed his slave ancestor Kunta Kinte was born, the collection of oral accounts of the capture and enslavement of his forebear, and the consultation of the manifest of *The Lord Ligonier,* the slave ship on which Kunta Kinte was thought to have crossed the seas to the United States. Using this evidence to construct a history of Kunta Kinte's representative life story, Haley set the stage for the performance of roots seeking and the climactic moments of recovery that have become common features of American collective self-fashioning.[2] For example, the 2006 public television series *African American Lives* and its sequels, hosted by Henry Louis Gates Jr., updated and supplemented Haley's roots-seeking quest with the use of DNA technologies, as well as user-friendly Internet guidance to help interested viewers research their familial past, construct their family tree, and locate their cultural origins in Africa. Although the DNA tests remained inconclusive for most of Gates's celebrity guests, and mostly dispelled their imagined origins (Gates himself is found to be 50 percent European), the trajectory of *African American Lives* culminates in the "return" journey of well-known actor Chris Tucker to an authentic-looking village in Angola—not the village where his ancestors probably originated, the program assures us, but one "like it." There, dancing around the ancestral baobab tree, villagers welcome Tucker as he cheerfully exclaims that "I'm happy to be back."

The vast appeal of *African American Lives* and its spinoffs to U.S. audiences, along with the success of Web sites like www.africanancestry.com and www.jewishgen.org, attest both to the seduction of the quest for a direct link to deep roots and family bloodlines, and to what appears to be a widespread longing that crosses the boundaries of ethnicity, gender, and social class.[3] But Saidiya Hartman challenges these longings in *Lose Your Mother: A Journey Along the Atlantic Slave Route*: "Neither blood nor belonging accounted for my presence in Ghana . . . only the path of strangers impelled toward the sea. . . . I wasn't seeking the ancestral village but the barracoon."[4] Unlike Haley or Gates, Hartman is impelled not by a desire to recover a lost homeland but to witness, record, and repair a history of injury through which lives are undone and humans are transformed into commodities. And yet, even as she resolutely embraces the identity of the "stranger" rather than the returnee, Hartman searches for her own beginnings, for how the spaces and traces of enslavement "had created and marked me."[5]

Mutual imbrication rather than clear opposition between a desire for roots and an embrace of diasporic existence is symptomatic of our post-millennial moment. In his classic 1984 essay "Reflections on Exile," Edward Said observed that our age "with its modern warfare, imperialism, and the quasi-theological ambitions of totalitarian rulers—is indeed the age of the refugee, the displaced person, mass immigration." But, despite his recognition of the pain and sadness of exile, Said, in the mid-1980s, warned against the equally powerful implications of the quest for rootedness—defensive nationalism, territorialism, cultural chauvinism, so many variants of "triumphant ideology."[6] Said gave voice here to the dominant postmodern discourses of hybridity, frequently heard across U.S. campuses throughout the 1980s and 1990s: the embrace of marginality, the border, and diasporic existence as a corrective to both the essentialist identity politics of the 1970s and insidious nationalist orthodoxies.

In his landmark essays on the meanings of diaspora, James Clifford added the now familiar homonym *routes* to *roots* so as to emphasize the ways in which every form of rootedness and dwelling already presupposes travel, cultural exchange—routes. Opposed to colonialism and war, moreover, diaspora came to appear, in Clifford's terms, as a "positive transnationalism," a fruitful paradigm capable of disrupting identity-based conflicts.[7] In the language of diaspora, originary homelands are not simply there to be recovered: already multiply interconnected with other places, they are further transformed by the ravages of time, transfigured through the lenses of loss and nostalgia, constructed in the process of the search. "Root-seekers," Alondra Nelson argues, "also become root-makers."

The very definition of diaspora depends on attachments to a former home and, typically, on a fantasy of return. At the same time, diaspora's classic writings tend to defer that fantasy in favor of a practice of "dwelling (differently)" in a global network of interchange and circulation.[8] Far from waning, however, in the twenty-first century, the desire for return to origins and to sites of communal suffering has progressively intensified. The cumulative effects of multiplying disasters at the end of the twentieth century and the refugee crises many of them unleashed have contributed to these desires—as do anxieties about belonging and concerns about the violence and inequities faced by refugees and illegal immigrants here in the United States, as well as in Europe and other parts of the globe. The ability to travel after the end of the cold war and the fall of the iron curtain, however, in combination with specialized Web-based technologies, have rekindled desires for reconnection with lost personal and familial pasts.

As academic feminist critics in the United States, we lived through and participated in critical and sometimes bitter conversations about the conflicting claims of identity animating the phenomenon of return. It is from this vantage point that we ask: What links the ostensibly postmodern individual to the community from which she has been severed by accidents of history? How, in particular, does a feminist subject negotiate the intensities and contradictory impulses of diasporic return?

Rites of Return stages a dialogue between feminist and diaspora studies, offering a multifaceted paradigm of community that acknowledges longings to belong and to return while remaining critical of a politics of identity and nation.

Simone de Beauvoir's famous statement "One is not born, but rather becomes a woman" inspired generations of postwar, second-wave feminist scholars to understand gender identity as an existential construction rather than an inherited essence.[9] Recast in new language for the 1990s by Judith Butler, the idea of cultural self-construction emerged as a performative process and a reinterpretation of sexual codes and gender norms. In the first decade of the twenty-first century, however, the elaboration of new identities secured by the evidence of science and genetics has posed an intriguing challenge to constructionist models.

An attention to roots annd identity-based origins does not necessarily mean an appeal to a biological essentialism, shored up and masked by innovative technology. Like most cultural theorists working during the years of poststructuralist and postcolonial debate, we are suspicious of origins and, as feminists, we are committed to challenging idealizations of home. We have embraced the commitment to contingent, ambiguous definitions of self. But, as our own essays here reveal, each of us, along with many other American Jews of our generation, has also devoted the last several years to the recovery of our own family stories and the search for lost Jewish worlds in Eastern Europe. Throughout this past decade, we have been actively engaged in the emerging fields of memory and trauma studies and particularly have come to appreciate the confluences and the commitments these theoretical projects share with feminism. Indeed, the notion of *postmemory* elaborated by Marianne Hirsch emerges from feminist insights into the mediated structuring of identity and the intersection of private and public forces in its formation. Thus the legacies of the past, transmitted powerfully from parent to child within the family, are always already inflected by broader public and generational stories, images, artifacts, and understandings that together shape identity and identification. While the idea of postmemory can account for the lure of second-generation "return," it also underscores the radical distance that separates the past from the present and the risks of projection, appropriation, and overidentification occasioned by second- and third-generation desires and needs.

In an analogous formation, Nancy K. Miller's term the *transpersonal* builds on the feminist understanding that the personal is necessarily political, which is to say shared with others. The transpersonal emphasizes the links that connect an individual not only backward in time vertically through earlier generations but also in a horizontal, present tense of affinities.[10] The transpersonal is a zone of relation that is social, affective, material, and inevitably public.

Taken together, the essays in *Rites of Return* bring to diaspora studies an articulation of the complex interaction between the affects of belonging and the politics of entitlement in a diasporic world, rethinking and retheorizing the complex interactions between loss and reclamation, mourning and repair, departure and return. The readings of diaspora and rites of return offered by this volume propose alternatives to the celebration of rootlessnesss and diasporism by making space for the persistent power of nostalgia, and the magnetism of the idea of belonging, even while casting a critical eye on the obsession with roots. This dual vision can combine the desire for "home," and for the concreteness and materiality of place and connection, with a concomitant, ethical commitment to carefully contextualized and differentiated practices of witness, restoration of rights, and acts of repair.

Three special issues of feminist journals were recently devoted to thinking diaspora and gender together in the context of transnational feminism. In their introduction to "The Global and the Intimate," geographer Geraldine Pratt and literary critic Victoria Rosner argue for the productive consonance of two paradigms: "The global and the intimate," they write, "may seem an unexpected combination, yet our pairing draws on a central strand of feminist practice, one that challenges gender-based oppositions by upending hierarchies of space and scale."[11] Emerging from African diaspora studies and an interdisciplinary project on "Gendering Diaspora," the 2008 issue of *Feminist Review*, edited by Tina Campt and Deborah Thomas, also focuses on such experiential specificities, applying the lens of feminist critical analysis, if not always a primary focus on women and gender, to the study of diaspora.[12] Both "The Global and the Intimate" and "Gendering Diaspora" situate themselves against the backdrop of the differential effects of globalization on diverse populations, the new hegemonies and power structures that are formed within diasporic communities, and gendered and raced conceptions of the relationships between routes and roots in the self-conceptions of displaced peoples.

In her introduction to the 2009 special "Diaspora" issue of the new journal *Contemporary Women's Writing*, Susan Stanford Friedman aims to show "how gender—particularly the experience of women—is the flashpoint of complexity exploding at every step reductionistic readings of the 'new migration.'" Women's narratives, Friedman writes, "suggest that the displacement of diaspora begins *before* the journey from home to elsewhere, begins indeed within the home and homeland and travels with the women as they face the difficulties of negotiating between new ways and old ways of living."[13] Several of the essays in *Rites of Return*, like the essays in these special issues, account for the differential diasporic experiences of women and for women's gendered oppression at home as well as abroad.

As early as the 1990s, queer theorists challenged the notion of diaspora by pointing out its masculinist, patriarchal, and heteronormative assumptions. At the same time, as Jarrod Hayes shows in this volume, an ever growing body of scholarship in queer diaspora studies has found the concept of diaspora surprisingly generative for theoretical elaborations of postcolonial thought that focus on the multiplicity of roots and the lateral, extrafamilial connections queering structures of kinship.[14]

Sharing the feminist and queer methodology of this recent work, *Rites of Return* shifts the focus from *diaspora* to *return*, to the practices that take place between routes and roots. Throughout, we emphasize the links between private experience and national and global crises as well as the role of generational histories and genealogies in acts of memory as well as fantasies of return. This accent on the personal, the familial, the affective, and the intimate has long been constitutive in feminist theory, trauma theory, and psychoanalysis. Here we bring these same pressures to bear on the paradigms of place and displacement that shape the field of diasporic studies.

It has been instructive to return to the genealogy of feminist thought that underpins our current reevaluation of diasporic canons. In its desire to mark the places of connection between intimate values and a wider world of conflict, this volume in fact returns to a force that has animated feminist theory since at least the mid-1980s. In her 1984 "Notes Toward a Politics of Location," for instance, Adrienne Rich revisits her earlier conviction that seeing the politics in women's individual personal experience is key to a collective political vision. And she worries about looking back to a lost female utopia for inspiration: "I've been thinking a lot about the obsession with origins," Rich admits. "It seems a way of stopping time in its tracks." As she ponders the history of racism, she reflects: "Don't we have to start here, where we are, forty years after the Holocaust, in the churn of Middle East violence, in the midst of decisive ferment in South Africa—not in some debate over origins and precedents, but in the recognition of simultaneous oppressions?"[15]

To some extent the desire for return always arises from a need to redress an injustice, one often inflicted upon an entire group of people caused by displacement or dispossession, the loss of home and of family autonomy, the conditions of expulsion, colonization, and migration. When we examine the detail, the case studies of individual and collective return, attentive to hierarchies of gender and sexuality and the power dynamics of contested histories, we find that hidden within what appears to be a universal narrative of rights are uneven and gendered smaller stories, forgotten and submerged plots of the kind that feminist theory has taught us to bring to light.

Rites of Return is organized around four overlapping nodes that map a present moment in which return has become a generative practice and paradigm. Part 1, "Tangled Roots and New Genealogies," explores at once the social effects of digital and biological technologies that have produced new possibilities in genealogical research and identity constructions and recent literary and artistic contestations of biological and essentialist conceptions of identity and genealogy. The essays in part 1 illuminate Simone Weil's belief that every "human being needs to have multiple roots."[16]

Part 2, "Genres of Return," analyzes different aesthetic modes and genres—memoir, photography, music—as well as different forms of cultural engagement, like travel and activism, that have been mobilized by and expressed through a variety of acts of return. The first-person voice of these and many of the other essays in the volume underscores the emotional stakes of familial and national legacies, the cost of return, and the necessary interrelatedness of memorial projects occurring in dramatically different cultural contexts.

But *rites* of return always invoke the question of *rights*, and part 3, "Rights of Return," explicitly examines the fundamental tensions between acts and claims. Whatever the location or political history, the effects of these complexities emerge with equal force in the analyses of novels and memoirs, legal and humanitarian documents, and impassioned testimonial essays that appear in this third section.

The volume ends with part 4, "Sites of Return and the New Tourism of Witness," which focuses on the transformation of sites and the kinds of travel that have arisen in response to the civic needs generated by catastrophic events across the globe. At their best, the museums, memorials, and "modes of memory tourism" discussed in these essays combine the powerful affects of return with a critical and political form of witness.

How can such radically different sites of return be thought together, in one volume, without blurring the distinctions between the historical, political, and personal circumstances of African Americans, Jews, Aboriginal and indigenous peoples, South Asians, and Palestinians? In placing their stories alongside each other, we are putting forward a *connective* rather than *comparative* approach that places the claims, responses, and strategies of redress emerging from different contexts in conversation with each other. The performance of return crosses cultural divides and reveals both commonalities and differences among diverse groups with divergent histories. Such *connective* work in memory studies is meant as a corrective to the nationalist and identity-based tendencies at work in some of the memorial projects described in the volume.[17]

The essays in *Rites of Return* focus on small, ordinary stories, on objects and images, on local and familiar sites of longing and belonging. But they always reveal the political dimensions of the private and familial as well: the family becomes not only the site of memorial transmission and continuity across generations but also a trope of loss, longing, and the desire for home. From a feminist and queer perspective, however, the family often becomes the site of critique—sometimes of rejection and abjection. Thus, in "Queer Roots for the Diaspora," Jarrod Hayes suggests that "the family tree that typically structures return narratives" tends to be heterosexual and that "whereas a return to roots attempts to remedy the alienation resulting from a historical uprooting, an assertion of roots can just as easily justify oppression by excluding those considered not to share them." The African and Caribbean writers on which his argument focuses instead propose "alternative, multiple roots that ground an identity based on not only sexual diversity, but also diversity in general."

Similarly, Sonali Thakkar's "Foreign Correspondence" shows the difficult yet seemingly inevitable return of a young Ghanaian woman from 1970s Western Europe to postindependence Africa, as narrated in Ama

Ata Aidoo's prose poem *Our Sister Killjoy*. Family offers the protagonist only the limiting role of "Sissie," but the queer kiss by a German woman cannot provide an alternative form of affiliation. Ultimately, "Sissie must return home, not just because her loyalties demand it, but also because she feels herself unwelcome and unwanted elsewhere." If injury can spur the original departure, for today's foreign immigrants and refugees, injury can spur the need to return, often leaving would-be returnees amid impossible alternatives.

This dilemma, and the powerful forces of family and the maternal, emerge most clearly in a distinctly contemporary roots-seeking phenomenon, a practice, as Margaret Homans shows, that is common to a cohort of transnational adoptees: young women who decide to undertake a journey to their country of origin—in this case Korea—in order to come to terms with their severance from originary homeland and maternal attachment. What they long for from their biological mothers is perhaps the fantasy of every daughter, biological or adopted: to be embraced, accepted, seen, and understood, even beyond language. By definition, however, fantasies are rarely satisfied in reality, and it is not surprising that the young women are often disappointed and reinjured by their return to what they think of as their lost home. For many, what Homans terms "scopic sexism" and the prevalent racism of the U.S. communities in which the girls grow up are sadly matched by the patriarchal beliefs of the Korean family with which they reconnect.

Nevertheless, the encounter with the realities of reunion has productive effects on the level of writing. In their memoirs the adopted daughters convert their suffering into a document through which their stories are preserved as history, and the "ambiguous maternal legacies" become "strong assertions of creative futures." As home becomes a textual effect of the journey and a figure of writing, the memoirists reverse the traditional sequence between roots and routes, thus complicating or, in Jarrod Hayes's terms, queering, the conception of origin itself.

In the literature of return, a painful past can sometimes be reframed through writing. When suffering is translated into fictional narrative and art, it becomes a way to counter the history of violence through an aesthetics of reattachment. This is Rosanne Kennedy's argument in her study of Aboriginal responses to the disruption of biological family and exile from homeland in Australia. What this would mean, for any disinherited group, might be thought of as an adaptation of what Adrienne Rich called, several decades ago, "writing as re-vision," a gesture with powerful implications. For women, Rich famously declared, re-vision is "more than a chapter in cultural history: it is an act of survival."[18] In much the same way, Kennedy shows, indigenous writers and artists refuse the silence surrounding the violence done to bloodlines and generational descent through work that seeks to "represent and commemorate the trauma of dispossession and bring that experience into visibility." When artist Judy Watson resorts to the "perverse archives" of the colonizers and resignifies the documents that record the injuries inflicted on Australian Aboriginal peoples by subjecting them to "blood marks," she creates a new way of reading the past that brings oppressions into a forum that can begin to acknowledge injustice and lay the groundwork for redress.

The emotional effects of diasporic dislocation and relocation also have led many of us in the twenty-first century to recapture, in writing, family memories and stories, in order to rescue lost legacies, to restore connections suspended by time, place, and politics. This is especially true of descendants of groups that have been subjected to extermination or expulsion. Memoir, a literary genre reinvigorated and reinvented in the 1990s, has become an increasingly productive form for exploring the meaning of family, generational identity, and ethnicity, as well as one for researching a past marked by historical calamity—the losses caused by the vicissitudes of violence, war, and genocide. The success of the memoirs of return by three writers we have placed in conversation, Saidiya Hartman, Eva Hoffman, and Daniel Mendelsohn, attests to the power of the personal voice and of the family as vehicle in the transpersonal writing of historical return.

The return to family through acts of memory is a journey in place and time. In the most common form of the genre, the returning son or daughter seeks connection to a parent or more distant ancestor and thereby to a culture and a physical site that has been transformed by the effects of distance and the ravages of political violence. They wish to see, touch, and hear that familial house, that street corner, the sounds of the language that the child often does not speak or perhaps never did. Never straightforward, the return to the generational family is always dependent on translation, approximation, and acts of imagination.

In his meditation on his family's complicated roots, Jay Prosser attempts to connect to his mother's past, writing *her* memoir *for her*, by reconnecting her memory to that of her father—his grandfather—through the pathways of music. Prosser returns to the family's diasporic history through physical journeys, his and his mother's, but most effectively and poignantly by replaying a cassette, recorded in the 1970s, of the voice of his grandfather, "a Baghdadi Jew living in Singapore . . . born in Bombay." Thanks to the tape, the grandson can hear and repossess the complex linguistic legacy that held his family together over the distances of dispersion. "Singing is what I remember about my grandfather," Prosser writes, "not his stories, for which I was neither old nor geographically close enough." In this autobiographical return through music, it becomes possible to override the spaces of geographical separation and to restore some of the lost dimensions of a scattered family with sharing and collaboration. Again, a postmemorial aesthetic of reattachment creates a new way of bringing historically inflected meaning to intergenerational transmission.

In Prosser's multicultural musical archive, the emotional, bodily longing to recapture lost time is unmistakable. And it is his belief in the power of music to cross borders that connects the affect of familial return to a future politics, one not stymied by bitter histories of exclusion and repression. This hopeful vision, embodied in the West-Eastern Divan Orchestra cofounded by Edward Said and David Barenboim, is moving in its optimism, but optimism in the Middle East is always lined with a pessimism lived on the ground, in struggle.

This entwined awareness of history, injustice, and responsibility is embedded in Amira Hass's "Between Two Returns: A Meditation from Palestine." Writing autobiographically, Hass both acknowledges the sense in which she is "split at the root," not biologically, in her case, but historically: both as the daughter of Holocaust survivors, born in Jerusalem, and as a journalist deeply committed to Palestinian rights of return.[19] Hass protests the ideology underwriting the Israeli Law of Return that concretizes "the alleged blood links supposedly shared by Jews all over the world and tie them all to the soil of the Holy Land." She constructs her meditation in part from the complicated details of the diasporic journeys of her parents, citing the example of her mother who, by her own practice of dwelling, voted "for the right of Jews to live in the Diaspora of their choice, not necessarily the Diaspora of their birth." But she ends on a note that emerges from the language of a poem by Palestinian poet Mahmoud Darwish, hoping for another iteration of a long-deferred return: "Perhaps, because it is trans-temporal, the Palestinians' return will possibly materialize one day, and their exile will have become one of choice, not of coercion."

In these and other feminist accounts of return, the memory strands of inheritance are intimately intertwined—the domestic and the political, the familial and the global. If Prosser's Baghdadi grandfather handed down the emotion of warmth and attachment of his diasporic legacy through song, Lila Abu-Lughod's Palestinian inheritance was passed on through her father's stories. "My father was a talker and a storyteller," Abu-Lughod begins her meditation on her father's return to Palestine. "Because of this, there was no time when we, his children, did not know we were Palestinian." For a Palestinian to say return to Palestine is also to come to grips with the expulsion that preceded it. But what does it mean for the American-born daughter of a Palestinian-born father to invoke the trauma of this past history? As in many autobiographical accounts of return to a geography one has inherited through familial memory as a "wounded identification," the writer must grapple with two levels of return: her entrance into a world by way of another's story and her own political views of that world's history from another location and its politics. Those two levels of return are necessarily related to each other, but never identical, particularly after the parent's death: "I had heard my father's stories all my life, but it is different to walk, orphaned, through a hot dusty checkpoint dragging your suitcases because they won't allow any Palestinian vehicles to cross." The trauma of the daughter's return remains doubly layered: a daughter's loss of her father, a daughter, who is also a writer, for whom the father's past continues to be a brutal present.

The doubleness of inherited trauma as it is expressed in the act of return haunts memoirs, as does, in fact, the double frame of return itself. For the generation of descendants for whom the world of the parents and grandparents is not a world they shared in the same fold of time, going back to the city of origin, however, is a way of coming to grips with the mythic dimensions of a place they would have to apprehend on new terms. The experience of return to an earlier generation's lived places is mediated by story, song, image, and history. But now it is also powerfully mediated by the parallel reality of the digital. In fact, it could be argued, as Hirsch and Spitzer do, that it is the very immateriality of the virtual landscape that compels the return to the actual, the three-dimensionality of the vanished or, at least, irrevocably transformed place itself.

Some return journeys, like Daniel Mendelsohn's in *The Lost* and Eva Hoffman's in *After Such Knowledge*, may begin with individual and familial loss, but when family history is intimately bound up with momentous historical events, individual stories become communal and generational and family histories become representative. New technologies have fostered such a sense of community, the formation of groups based on presumed shared desires and needs. In the case of the Czernowitz reunion group described by Hirsch and Spitzer, the trip itself emerged from a need for making community on the basis of a common history. The group had shared knowledge and memories with each other on the Web site. But is it possible to become a group in the present on the basis of overlapping but distant histories, intersecting memories, familiar stories, and the seduction of a place known for its seductiveness, without erasing differences and disagreements? Hirsch and Spitzer reveal the pitfalls of Web-based intimacy and group affiliation that always lurks in the fascination with genealogy and allure of origin.

Place and a shared past may offer no more than illusory forms of group connections, no less problematic than a return to familial origins. But the increasing popularity of the use of population DNA tests to determine group belonging attests to a need for group identity certified through new forms of evidence. In "The Factness of Diaspora" Alondra Nelson shows that while African American root seekers tend to embrace the findings of genetic genealogy that locate family origins in specific places and with specific ethnic groups on the African continent, the experience of "self-making" does not end there. Rather, the technoscientific evidence of identity serves as a first step in a more expansive and complicated process that she calls "affiliative self-fashioning." Unlike the new historicist trope of self-fashioning at the heart of Stephen Greenblatt's famous argument about self-construction in the Renaissance, in which the emphasis was on an individual's self-creation through literature and art, Nelson's concept entails an identification with a diasporic group and with that group's ethnic and cultural profile. In other words, while the fact of genealogical material puts a name on a lineage, the outcome of the quest takes on meaning only when the root seeker acts on the desire for a communal affiliation.

What seems productive and interesting about this concept is that while the scientific component of the new identity points toward the power of bloodline, the outcome of the genealogical quest is not simply a label. Motivated by the principles of constructedness that seemed to be lost in the rush to a simple evidentiary truth model, and seen through the paradigm of "factness" rather than fact, the desire for bonds and relations based on what might have once been a shared history leads to the imagining of another kind of community. Root seekers selectively reimagine their lives with the idea of a group and its cultural legacies. "Affiliative self-fashioning" thus becomes a useful tool for creating alternative, transpersonal models of selfhood that take on meaning in relation and in what we might think of as a diasporic kinship based on shared desires. In the case of African American communities, the stakes of this remaking are high, for they represent an avenue of future repair, a way to counter the pain of slavery's history of displacement through a contemporary politics of acknowledgment.

In the world of biomedecine, the "new genetics," as Nadia Abu El-Haj demonstrates, looking at the meaning of DNA as scientific evidence for group self-image, takes the question of identity both backward in time and forward into the present. Abu El-Haj interprets the project of the U.S.-based group Kulanu ("all of us" in Hebrew). Founded in 1994, the organization's stated aim is to bring about the recognition of nonwhite Jews, thus revising the boundaries of the white Jewish world. While the specific example Abu El-Haj examines emerges from an anthropological study of the Lemba of Southern Africa, who see themselves as descendants of the "ancient Lost Tribes of Israel," what is at stake is something broader, the Israeli state's definition of what it means to be a Jew—genealogical descent or religious practice. This combination of biological material and cultural choice resembles the kind of "affiliative self-fashioning" that Alondra Nelson describes in the creative self-remaking of roots-seeking African Americans, but with an important difference. In the final analysis, for the groups protected by Kulanu, the meaning of affiliation is dependent for validation on legal, religious, and governmental authority in Israel, not just the community and its ideal of kinship.

But neither collective affinity, shared cultural history, nor national belonging can guarantee the protection of a community of citizens from disaster when racism is an unspoken but nonetheless powerful force. This was demonstrated by the U.S. government's response to the disaster wrought on home and family by Hurricane Katrina. Seen against the discourse of "homeland security," Patricia Williams poignantly shows, the "simplicity of 'home' becomes a site for nostalgia, the old country before famine, flood, or pogrom, an imaginary geography of tremendous contradiction, of ambivalence and flight, of (up) rootedness and romance, of magic and superstition." Katrina engendered a violent experience of forced departure and impeded, selective return. As Williams puts it, "despite all the talk about rights of return, the only thing that's happened . . . has been the planting of a few strips of grass in front of still empty buildings." Katrina exposed the vulnerability of a discourse of rights in the face of national policy disorganization and an underlying politics of economic and racial discrimination. As evacuees and not refugees—a term rejected as describing the situation of foreign victims of disaster—the American citizens of New Orleans were on the whole unable to invoke any official protection and benefits that would allow them to return to their lost homes, or the sites of former homes, to rebuild and remake community and future. Despite the shocking failure of governmental redress to the poorest of the displaced, New Orleans has spurred a great deal of artistic response as an unofficial site of conscience. The artistic and cultural response to memorializing the catastrophe and conceptualizing possibilities of repair can be understood in relation to forms of site-specific remembrance. Keith Calhoun and Chandra McCormick have documented life in New Orleans's Treme and Lower Ninth Ward for decades. Their studio and their negatives were destroyed by the flood, but the two of them returned to New Orleans and formed the L9 Cultural Center in a small renovated building in the Lower Ninth. The images included here document this mixture of devastation and resilience, the impossibility and stubborn insistence on return and attempted repair. Like Susan Meiselas's "Homecoming," which serves as the cover image of this volume, "L9 Destruction" depicts a woman's return to a devastated home. Looking at her look at the ruin makes palpable the depths of the losses suffered by women, who are so often the unnoted civilian casualties of war and natural or historical disaster, and the courage they will have to muster to rebuild their lives and those of their families.

In our historical moment, much energy is being spent around the world designing museums and memorials that facilitate the process of site-specific remembrance. In its mission statement, the International Coalition of Sites of Conscience, founded in 1999, states that "it is the obligation of historic sites to assist the public in drawing connections between the history of our sites and their contemporary implications. We view stimulating dialogue on pressing social issues and promoting humanitarian and democratic values as a primary function." The coalition, described here by U.S.-based founding director Liz Ševčenko, consists of seven accredited and more than one hundred affiliated sites across the world. Many are sites of former atrocity, like the Gulag Museum in Russia, the District 6 Museum in Cape Town, the Maison des Esclaves in Senegal, or the Terezín Memorial in the Czech Republic; others, like the Eleanor Roosevelt National Historic Site, are memorial and pedagogic sites marking events or conditions of persecution, using them to promote democratic and humanitarian values through historical knowledge and consciousness.

The risks entailed in the effort to create responsive global citizens are articulated by Marita Sturken. What will transform the consumerist gaze of the tourist eager to say she has been there, and who has purchased souvenirs to prove it, into an engagement with the past and a connection to the inequities and injustices of the present? Sturken outlines some of the techniques used in different museums and memorials to promote responsible memory tourism on the sites of former acts of atrocity or suffering.

But some, like Andreas Huyssen, who calls the belief in the aura of place "tropolatry," have challenged the importance of "the place itself" in the work of memory and history.[20] Svetlana Boym shares this skepticism. Nostalgia, Boym writes, is "a longing for a home that no longer exists or has never existed."[21] While "restorative nostalgia" focuses its desire on *nostos*, a home that might be recovered or a past that can be restored, "reflective nostalgia" places the accent on *algia*, longing itself, and the multiple forms of creativity it spurs. Boym's "Eccentric Modernities" begins with the imbrication of homesickness and being sick of home, and it moves not back toward a return to the past but sideways in search of the "off," the chance encounter, the freedom that comes from detours, errors, alternative, and, indeed, multiple genealogies.

The practice of return inevitably consists of such detours and errors in the quest for the place itself. Returnees must come to terms with not just the possibility but often the inevitability of the failure to coincide with the lost object of the quest. At the same time, as Eva Hoffman writes in *After Such Knowledge*, it is also possible to feel "consoled by this near-touching of the time before, this near-meeting of parallel lines that, after all these years, seem to be bending towards each other again."[22] There is something of this consolation in Nancy K. Miller's travel to the last place in Eastern Europe in which her paternal grandparents resided, the place she began looking for under the name Kishinev, the name of the city recorded on the manifest of the ship that brought her ancestors to New York.

The evidence, especially in third-generation returns, is often scant—family letters and inherited objects found, in Miller's terms, "in a drawer." But what, after the ravages of time and the transformations wrought by history and politics, remains to be found? No further evidence of her ancestors' actual residence in Kishinev, no possibility of visiting the exact locations of rape and murder documented in Bialik's famous poem about the 1903 pogrom. If one follows the desire for the place itself, the story can be no more than a record of missed encounters, of unsatisfied long-ing that generates renewed interest in repeated trips and further and ever deeper and more dedicated genealogical and archival research. But, per-haps, as she comes to understand, the exact family story is finally less important than perceiving its relation to the more general history of the community to which it belonged, a transpersonal belonging preserved, in the case of Moldovan Chișinău, through a set of child-sized dolls.

Perhaps places do not actually themselves carry memory, but memory can be activated by the encounter between the visitor and the place. Diana Taylor records such a powerful performance of memory when she accom-panies Pedro Matta, a survivor of torture in Villa Grimaldi, an infamous torture center in Chile and a member of the International Coalition of Sites of Conscience. As she visits the site with Matta, Taylor is left with myriad questions—about Matta, the authenticity of his affect, his willing-ness to relive his trauma repeatedly for her and other visitors. In her act of what Irene Kacandes calls "co-witness," Taylor opens the space for him to tell his story of victimization and survival and she transmits his story to her readers.[23] This encounter, outside the official institution of the memo-rial, testifies to the power of place and to the personal act of engagement through which that power can be activated.

It is such an act of activist engagement that connects Susan Meiselas to Nicaragua and provokes her repeated return there. Having worked in Central America as a photojournalist during the revolution, Meiselas has returned on a number of occasions. Why, she wonders, has Nicaragua been a primary site of return for her as opposed to the many other sites in which she photographed? She thinks of returning to Nicaragua as a "re-turn to hope"—the hope of the revolution that was disappointed but that can, she believes, be remembered and reclaimed—and it is this reparative belief that animates her numerous return journeys, the film she made about bringing her photographs back to the people who were depicted in them, *Pictures from a Revolution*. Meiselas as artist continues to engage with the place in the present. If she returns, it is not to the past she docu-mented, but to the ways in which that past lives on in the present, in part through her images. Her activist return provokes active remembrance and transmission on site.

These acts of witness take return out of the personal and familial to the realm of history and politics. The popularization of return tourism, which has become a familiar activity of our global moment, equally and simultaneously is a matter of rights: who is entitled to return to a home, a homeland, a place to which one once belonged? When is return a claim to resettlement? In his "The Politics of Return: When Rights Become Rites" Elazar Barkan traces international policies and conventions concerning refugees, which, largely spurred by the United Nations, always insist on the right to return. Yet Barkan also shows, when it comes to populations that would constitute minorities were they to return to the lands from which they were evicted, how those rights are never implemented. In his terms, rights thus become mere "rites"—useful as aspirations or speech acts, but actually harmful to refugees in that they impede other possible forms of political settlement.

Even if every return emerges on some level from a desire to map a loss, at the same time, every return inevitably exercises, or attempts to exercise, a right to acknowledgment. For some, return is an act of undoing— a counterfactual effort to imagine a world before disaster and displacement. That act of imagination can also become an act of repair, however tenuous. For others, it is a claim to justice and restitution or, for others still, a form of memory tourism. Return can thus be directed back toward the past, sideways to detours and alternate trajectories, and, as a critique of the present, forward toward the future. In this sense, *Rites of Return* contributes to new thinking about nostalgia, showing that it need not be simply directed toward what is deemed to be a better past in need of restoration.

In its concern with justice, ethics, and repair, and the ways in which those domains are shaped by structures of family, generational identity, and home, *Rites of Return* marks a new moment in the field of gender and cultural studies. Our project illuminates the feminist roots and affiliations at the heart of narratives that seek to account for loss and dispossession, trauma and cultural memory but that have not thus far been recognized as such. Through our emphasis on the connections between the private and public, the intimate and global dimensions of the diasporic world we all now inhabit, *Rites of Return* aims to reenliven debates about how to face an uncertain future without forgetting the lessons of the past—without, in turn, being paralyzed by longing for its lost places.

Notes

1. Simone Weil, *The Need for Roots: Prelude to a Declaration of Duties Toward Mankind* (New York: Routledge, 2001), 43.

2. The year after receiving the Pulitzer Prize, Haley was accused of plagiarism by Harold Courlander, author of *The African*, a novel published ten years earlier. The suit was settled out of court, leaving the authenticity of Haley's research in doubt.

3. In *Roots Too: White Ethnic Revival in Post-Civil Rights America* (Cambridge: Harvard University Press, 2006), Matthew Frye Jacobson locates John F. Kennedy's 1963 "'return' to Ireland" (14), as the inaugural moment of white ethnic revival and the emergence of "roots talk" in American postwar culture (16).

4. Saidiya Hartman, *Lose Your Mother: A Journey Along the Atlantic Slave Route* (New York: Farrar, Straus and Giroux, 2007), 7, 6.

5. Ibid., 130.

6. Edward W. Said, "Reflections on Exile," *Reflections on Exile and Other Essays* (Cambridge: Harvard University Press, 2000).

7. James Clifford, "Diasporas," *Cultural Anthropology*, 9, no. 3 (1994): 302–338.

8. Ibid., 321. See also Paul Gilroy, *Against Race: Imagining Political Culture Beyond the Color Line* (Cambridge: Harvard University Press, 2000).

9. Simone de Beauvoir, *The Second Sex*, trans. H. M. Parshley (New York: Vintage, 1989).

10. For the prominence of the paradigm of return in the Jewish diasporic imagination, see Sidra DeKoven Ezrahi, *Booking Passage: Exile and Homecoming in the Modern Jewish Imagination* (Berkeley: University of California Press, 2000). In the last two decades, numerous writers and academics have returned in their scholarship to lost-family narratives and to sites of past trauma, before, during, and after the Holocaust. See, for example, Leo Spitzer, *Hotel Bolivia: A Culture of Memory in a Refuge from Nazism* (New York: Hill and Wang, 1998) and Susan Rubin Suleiman, *Budapest Diary: In Search of the Motherbook* (Lincoln: University of Nebraska Press, 1996), as well as Omer Bartov, *Erased: Vanishing Traces of Jewish Galicia in Present-Day Ukraine* (Princeton: Princeton University Press, 2007); the epilogue of Bella Brodzki's *Can These Bones Live: Translation, Survival, and Cultural Memory* (Palo Alto: Stanford University Press, 2007); Helen Epstein, *Where She Came From: A Daughter's Search for Her Mother's History* (New York: Plume, 1998); and Claire Kahane, "Geographies of Loss," in Julia Epstein and Lori Hope Lefkowitz, eds, *Shaping Losses: Cultural Memory and the Holocaust* (Urbana: University of Illinois Press, 2001).

On postmemory, see Marianne Hirsch, *The Generation of Postmemory: Visual Culture After the Holocaust* (New York: Columbia University Press, 2012). In "Getting Transpersonal: The Cost of an Academic Life," *Prose Studies* 31, no. 3 (December 2009), Nancy K. Miller shows how a generation of academic memoirs produced in the 1990s reveals the affective commonalities of the authors' journey to their institutional identities.

11. Geraldine Pratt and Victoria Rosner, "Introduction: The Global and the Intimate," in "The Global and the Intimate," special issue, *WSQ* 34, nos. 1–2 (Spring/Summer, 2006): 16.

12. Tina Campt and Deborah A. Thomas, eds., "Gendering Diaspora," special issue, *Feminist Review* 90, no. 1 (October 2008).

13. Susan Stanford Friedman, "The 'New Migration': Clashes, Connections, and Diasporic Women's Writing," *Contemporary Women's Writing* 3, no. 1 (June 2009: 22–23.

14. To cite a few examples of this work: David Eng, "Out Here and Over There: Queerness and Diaspora in Asian American Studies," *Social Text* 52/53 (1997); Cindi Patton and Benigno Sánchez-Eppler, eds., *Queer Diasporas* (Durham: Duke University Press, 2000); Ann Cvetkovich, *An Archive of Feeling: Trauma, Sexuality, and Lesbian Public Cultures* (Durham: Duke University Press, 2003); Gayatri Gopinath, *Impossible Desires: Queer Diasporas and South Asian Public Cultures* (Durham: Duke University Press, 2005).

15. Adrienne Rich, "Notes Toward a Politics of Location," *Blood, Bread, and Poetry: Selected Prose, 1979–1985* (New York: Norton, 1986), 227, 226–27.

16. Weil, *The Need for Roots*, 40.

17. Our approach is related to Michael Rothberg's work on "multidirectional memory": *Multidirectional Memory: Remembering the Holocaust in the Age of Decolonization* (Palo Alto: Stanford University Press, 2009), 3. For more on "connective histories," see Hirsch, *The Generation of Postmemory*.

18. Adrienne Rich, "When We Dead Awaken: Writing as Re-Vision," *On Lies, Secrets, and Silence* (New York: Norton, 1979), 35.

19. Adrienne Rich, "Split at the Root: An Essay on Jewish Identity," *Blood, Bread, and Poetry*, 110.

20. Andreas Huyssen, personal communication.

21. Svetlana Boym, *The Future of Nostalgia* (New York: Basic Books, 2001), 13.

22. Eva Hoffman, *After Such Knowledge: Memory, History, and the Legacy of the Holocaust* (New York: Public Affairs, 2004).

23. Irene Kacandes, *Talk Fiction: Literature and the Talk Explosion* (Lincoln: University of Nebraska Press, 2001).

PART I

Tangled Roots and New Genealogies

1 The Factness of Diaspora

The Social Sources of Genetic Genealogy

ALONDRA NELSON

Family history research is a popular pastime for those seeking to discover unknown ancestors.[1] For many, this pursuit has taken the form of genealogical journeys modeled on *Roots: The Saga of an American Family,* Alex Haley's famous (and now infamously embellished) account of his venture to trace his African American family's African lineage.[2] The book and subsequent award-winning miniseries of the same name were the result of the author's efforts to uncover the mystery of his ancestral origins with clues garnered from Gambian griots, deciphered linguistic retentions, archival research, and his own genealogical imagination. Haley's account became an ur-text of African diasporic reconciliation for a generation of Americans, both black and white.[3] Despite this example, few African Americans are able to fill in the contours of their past as Haley did, owing to the decimation of families (and, thus, the transmission of families' oral histories and traditions) that was a hallmark of the era of racial slavery and to the dearth of records that remain from this period. As a consequence, genetic genealogy testing, which is broadly available and also less taxing and seemingly more authoritative than conventional genealogical research, holds considerable appeal for some root seekers of African descent.

Drawing on sampling techniques and statistical models developed in human population genetics, direct-to-consumer commercial genetic genealogy testing analyzes an individual's DNA in order to infer information about family history, ethnic affiliation, or "biogeographic ancestry."[4] These services are becoming widely used. Some are niche marketed to specific social groups, such as the testing sold by African Ancestry, Inc., of Washington, D.C. Established by geneticist Rick Kittles and his business partner Gina Paige in early 2003, African Ancestry (also, www.africanancestry .com) is promoted among African Americans and "matches" customers to nation-states and ethnic groups on the African continent.[5]

African Ancestry is an information-age business—the exchange of a fee for service takes place online and through the mail. The company mails test kits to customers that contain the implements necessary to secure a DNA sample. The customer returns the sample to the company by mail; it is amplified and sequenced by the company's lab partner Sorenson Genomics of Salt Lake City, Utah. African Ancestry then compares the resulting data to its proprietary DNA biobank—the African Lineage Database (ALD)—that is said to contain more than twenty-five thousand DNA samples from over thirty countries and two hundred ethnic groups in Africa. After several weeks, a customer will receive a results package that includes a printout of the customer's Y- or mt-DNA markers, a "Certificate of Ancestry," and sociohistorical information about the African continent.[6] A hypothetical root seeker employing African Ancestry's services may learn that her mt-DNA traces to the current Mende people of Sierra Leone and that her Y-DNA test, for which she submitted her brother's DNA, traces to the Bubi group of present-day Equatorial Guinea.[7] African Ancestry analyses might thus be regarded as ethnic lineage instruments through which an undifferentiated racial identity is translated into African ethnicity and kinship. By linking blacks to inferred ethnic communities and nation-states of Africa, African Ancestry's analyses offer root seekers the possibility of constituting new forms of diasporic affiliation and identification.

On the surface, both the appeal and most likely outcome of the DNA testing service provided by African Ancestry (and other similar companies) appear to confirm that genetic genealogy is an essentialist practice—that ancestry testing, as a vehicle of identification, amounts to the reduction of transnational affiliation to molecular biology, in the process abetting the "reauthoriz[ation] of race as a biological category" and eliding the historical, political, and economic diversity of black experiences.[8] However, as I describe here using ethnographic vignettes, the experiences of root seek-ers suggest that a more complex dynamic is at play. The genetic facts ren-dered as the outcome of genealogy testing may provide the circumstance for reconfigured social arrangements, yet this potential transformation does not stem solely from these data. Rather, the cogency of genetic gene-alogy testing is derived significantly from social sources that shape how facts are anticipated, interpreted, and mobilized by root seekers.

More specifically, in this chapter I begin to develop the concept of the *factness of diaspora* to describe the particular process of coproduction through which genetic genealogy testing attains value and validation for the root seekers of African descent I have encountered in the course of my ethnographic fieldwork and interviews.[9]

"Factness," as I use it here, means possessing the state, condition, or quality of fact, yet not being only or exactly fact.[10] The factness of dias-pora denotes the imbrication of the "biogenetic facts" of genealogy testing *and* aspirations for African affiliation against the backdrop of histories of forced displacement and through the subsequent enactment of what I term reconciliation projects—practices in which scientific techniques are employed toward the resolution of the injuries of racial slavery.[11] I elaborate the factness of diaspora through a discussion of three signifi-cant points in the interpretive trajectory of African Ancestry's genetic ge-nealogy testing service: the "authentic expertise" of the company's chief science officer, Rick Kittles, which significantly influences root seekers' confidence in its product; the forms of self-making—including *affiliative self-fashioning*, the creation of identity from both facts and desire for con-nection to a community—that may be spurred following the receipt of one's genetic genealogy test results; and, related to this, the extragenetic forms of "kinship" the test outcomes may foster.

In October 2005 I attended the three-day national meeting of the Afro-American Historical and Genealogical Society (AAHGS) for the first time. The conference program consisted of social events, tours of historic sites, invited lectures by prominent figures, and concurrent panels on topics of interest to the genealogists in attendance. Panel topics included ac-counts of hurdles and successes in family history research, how to use the now fully digitized Freedman's Bureau records for family history re-search, how to participate in the Library of Congress's oral history project for veterans, and how to document one's genealogical research in com-pelling narrative form to share with family, friends, and local historical societies. The Saturday morning keynote address, a lecture entitled "Trace Your DNA and Find Your Roots: The Genetic Ancestries of African Americans," was delivered by Rick Kittles, African Ancestry's cofounder and scientific director. I previously attended other public presentations by Kittles and, as on these prior occasions, I watched with wonder as he performed his unique combination of erudition, charisma, and folksiness to a rapt audience comprising over one hundred people—women and some men who, with a few exceptions, appeared to be above age fifty, and many sixty years of age or older.

Kittles discussed how genetics could be used to help blacks trace their roots to African ethnic groups, detailing the scientific assumptions on which African Ancestry's products are based. In addition to educating those in attendance about the technical aspects of MatriClan and Patri-Clan analysis, his presentation was also clearly intended to demonstrate how much Kittles held in common with his customer base, including their concerns about privacy and the unique historical circumstances that inspired their root-seeking pursuits. "African Ancestry is the only [genetic genealogy] company that focuses on people of African descent; it's run by Black folks and it's going to stay that way," Kittles proclaimed. Genetic genealogy research should be "guarded by someone who shares the same sensitivity to the concerns of the community," he continued to applause. The many audience members who cheered in response to Kittles's assertion of community mindedness testified to the effectiveness of the geneticist's claim to cultural authenticity.

This legitimacy was shored up as Kittles continued his pitch, changing registers slightly from man of the people to genealogist colleague. He recalled that he "caught the genealogy bug"—using a phrase common among genealogists who liken their interest in the pursuit of the past to a virus—as a doctoral student in biological sciences at George Washington University. "AAHGS is near and dear to my heart," Kittles said; "I came to this event even before my research interests emerged in this area [of genetic genealogy testing]." Continuing to speak as a fellow traveler, with a PowerPoint slide in the background of the iconic image of the cross-section of a slave ship packed with black bodies, Kittles recounted his personal frustrations with genealogical research and spoke of the challenges facing even the most diligent amateur historians seeking to trace their African roots. He discussed how genetic genealogy testing had helped him discover that his maternal mt-DNA matched to the Mandinka of Mali. His paternal Y-chromosome line traced to Germany, a result he attributed to what he described as "the Thomas Jefferson effect." This characterization doubly signaled the sexual violence of racial slavery and the forensic DNA analysis establishing (along with archival records) that the third U.S. president fathered the children of his slave Sally Hemings.[12]

At the conclusion of his formal presentation, Kittles raffled off a free African Ancestry test and then spoke at turns with thirty or so audience members who stood in a queue, which wound through the aisles of the auditorium, to await their turn to offer questions, comments, and compliments. One African American woman, attired in red, white, and blue clothing adorned with rhinestone American flags and a lanyard for her ID cards embroidered with the acronym DAR (for Daughters of the American Revolution), introduced herself as a member of the "underground railroad of the DAR, called the Daughters of Color," before proceeding to ask Kittles for further interpretation of the genetic genealogy results she had recently received from his company.[13] The great majority of Kittles's audience, however, gathered in the lobby just outside of the auditorium where the lecture had taken place. Here vendors had set up tables arrayed with items for sale ranging from African-themed knickknacks to genealogical research primers. Most merchants sat noticeably idle. But enthusiastic customers surrounded one vendor's table. In the center of this crowd was African Ancestry cofounder Gina Paige, who struggled to stay on top of the many orders being placed for her company's services. Her business partner's presentation, during which Kittles had stressed his shared experience with the audience, had succeeded in persuading many of the AAHGS membership to purchase African Ancestry's genetic genealogy test.

The audience's indisputably positive response to African Ancestry, evidenced both by their reception to the lecture and their purchase of its product, was perhaps preconditioned by the fact that Rick Kittles is among the most well-known molecular biologists in the United States. The authenticity Kittles displayed at the AAHGS gathering was bolstered by scientific authority established through press coverage, scholarly publications, and institutional associations. He has made frequent media appearances over the last several years in his capacity as chief scientist of African Ancestry. For example, he appeared in *Motherland: A Genetic Journey,* a 2003 British Broadcasting Company documentary that aired in the United States on the Sundance Channel, as well as in the PBS documentary *African*

American Lives, in 2006, in which his company's services were employed to trace the roots of black celebrities.[14] Kittles has also been featured on ABC's *Good Morning, America* and *The Morning Show* and *60 Minutes* on the CBS network. Since 2002, scores of newspaper and magazine articles, including those in the *New York Times, Time, New York Daily News, Black Enterprise, Wired, Fortune,* and the *Los Angeles Times,* have cited commentary from Kittles, solidifying his position as an expert on genetic genealogy testing.[15]

Kittles's professional ascent has included the publication of scholarly papers in leading science journals as well as stints at prestigious institutions. He has authored numerous articles in the area of human variation and genetics in notable publications, including the *American Journal of Human Genetics, Science,* the *Annals of Epidemiology,* and the *American Journal of Public Health.* The scientist has also held positions at the National Human Genome Center at Howard University, at Ohio State University, and, presently, at the Cancer Research Center at the University of Chicago. Kittles's "hard" scientific research at prominent institutional settings on the genetic determinants of prostate cancer—a disease that disproportionately afflicts African American men—is concomitant with his investigations into what might be regarded as the "softer" science of the genetic genealogy testing.[16] The geneticist's demonstrated concern for black communities thus covers a spectrum from the prevention of racial health disparities to biological "optimization" of identity.[17]

As the public face of African Ancestry, Rick Kittles draws together cultural and scientific legitimacy into a complex I term authentic expertise. In his guise as a genealogist colleague who shares his customers' desires for ancestral reckoning and their reservations about DNA analysis, Kittles establishes genetic genealogy testing as a legitimate and safe practice for African American root seekers. At the same time, his renown as a scientist and his involvement with cutting-edge medical genetics research lend authority to his commercial genetics enterprise. Thus, many root seekers are as compelled by Kittles as they are convinced by genetic science. "I trust Dr. Kittles," a root seeker named Pat explained to me when I asked if she had any apprehensions prior to purchasing the MatriClan test that linked her to the Akan of Ghana and Côte d'Ivoire.[18] Although Alicia, another informant, had reservations about the genetic genealogy results she received from African Ancestry because they were inconsistent with those from another company, she took great pride in telling me that she had been in contact with Kittles by both telephone and e-mail. Her misgivings were subsequently assuaged through her interactions with him. Kittles's authentic expertise is an unmistakably important aspect of the appeal of African Ancestry's genetic genealogy testing and of consumers' faith in the genetic facts it supplies to its customers. This symbolic capital produces value around genetic genealogy tests that extends beyond the presumed capacity of DNA to assign identity and subsumes yearnings for African diasporic affiliation.

Back at the AAHGS conference, the society's annual "sharing dinner" took place in a large ballroom of the on-campus hotel of Gallaudet University in Washington, D.C. All the genealogists at my table were women, as were the large majority of conference attendees. The gendered nature of this space is unsurprising if we appreciate the genealogists as "kin keepers." Kin keeping refers to the maintenance of familial links, the circulation of information and traditions through the familial network, and the provision of financial and emotional support to kin that is predominantly performed by women and often passed intergenerationally between grandmothers, mothers, and daughters.[19] The genealogical practices in which these women are engaged surely solidified kinship ties. At the same time, the genealogists drew upon new techniques, uncovering and also establishing family history with archival research and through the use of forms of genetic analysis.

During the meal, genealogists were invited to stand and share highlights of their experiences as family history researchers, if they were so inclined. Although none at my table availed themselves of this opportunity, we spoke amongst ourselves about our respective genealogical research projects. I struck up a conversation with Bess, an African American woman in her fifties who lives near Baltimore, Maryland seated next to me. I told her about my ethnographic study of conventional and genetic root seeking, including my preliminary foray into my own family's history, which had brought me to the AAHGS meeting. Bess confided that she had been conducting genealogical research on her family for about a decade and had also recently received genetic genealogy test results from African Ancestry.

The next morning, I ran into Bess in the hotel lobby, where merchants, including Gina Paige, were setting up their tables for the day. Bess said to me, "I have something for you." We sat together on the edge of a water fountain in the hotel atrium, and she showed me the results of her genetic genealogy test, which she had arranged in a binder. A letter from African Ancestry indicated that mtDNA analysis had linked Bess to the Kru of

Liberia "plus/or Mende-Temne of Sierra Leone." Her result package also contained a "Certificate of Ancestry" signed by Rick Kittles, a printout of the genetic markers from which Bess's African ethnicity was inferred, a map of the African continent with Liberia foregrounded, and a flier advertising Encarta Africana, a CD-ROM encyclopedia, at a discounted rate.

Bess explained to me that she wants to "do something" with her results, like perhaps "travel to Africa." Curious as to which of the two possible ethnicities suggested by African Ancestry was most compelling to Bess, I asked whether she planned to visit Liberia, neighboring Sierra Leone, or both countries in the future. "My sister was married to a man from Sierra Leone; his name was Abdul," she replied obliquely, intimating that she would likely travel to the natal home of her deceased brother-in-law. "When will you be ready to travel to Africa?" I asked. "After I get back further in time [with my genealogical research]," she responded. As is common with other root seekers who make use of genetic ancestry tracing, Bess assumed a role in determining her test's significance and its potential import to her life. Her intention to engage in practices motivated by the findings she received from African Ancestry *after* she advanced with conventional genealogy underscores how the interpretative work that commences following the receipt of genetic genealogy results can involve consumers' efforts to "align" genetic DNA analysis with other evidence of their ancestry as well as with their genealogical aspirations and with prior experience or extant relationships.[20]

The conduct by which root seekers decide to accept or jettison genetic genealogy test results in the constitution of African diasporic connection and identity can be described as "affiliative self-fashioning."[21] Writing about the interface of brain imaging techniques and social identity, Joseph Dumit employs the phrase "objective self-fashioning" to explain how subjectivity can be "fashion[ed] and refashion[ed]" from the "received-facts of science and medicine."[22] By extending this useful analytic from objective self-fashioning to affiliative self-fashioning, I seek to emphasize that root seekers' aspirations to be oriented on the African continent and/or within its diaspora mediate how technoscience becomes incorporated into self-making. Affiliative self-fashioning accounts for how identities culled from genetic genealogy are shaped not only by "received facts" but also by desires for diasporic connection—a confluence that impacts root seekers' evaluations of genetic genealogy testing and, in turn, the way that the data it provides is incorporated into their lives. Affiliative self-fashioning thus reflects, on subjective and interpersonal levels, an aspect of the interpretive arc of ethnic lineage testing that I term the factness of diaspora.

Purveyors of genetic genealogy testing claim that their services trace or reveal otherwise unavailable information about ancestry and ethnicity. However, at present, matching a consumer's DNA against proprietary genetic databases comprised of samples from contemporary populations, as African Ancestry and other genetic ancestry tracing companies do, cannot establish kinship with any certainty; ethnic lineage analysis does not associate a root seeker with specific persons at precise spatiotemporal locations. Also, owing to both technical limitations and historical dynamics, the associations inferred through the use of genetic genealogy are necessarily provisional.[23]

By supplying associations that are underspecified, genetic genealogy tracing presents consumers with the paradox of *imprecise pedigree*. Root seekers' awareness of this paradox is indicated by their use of ostensibly redundant phrases such as "DNA cousins" and "genetic kin."[24] These composite descriptors, of course, acknowledge DNA analysis as the medium of affiliation. However, because the words *cousin* and *kin* are already commonly understood to connote "biogenetic ties," the placement of the adjectives *DNA* and *genetic* before these words therefore should be unnecessary.[25] Thus the circulation of these phrases also seems to suggest that the associations supplied through genetic genealogy are qualified and, therefore, must be rhetorically set apart from "natural" kinship or, in other words, that genetic genealogy testing is categorical yet imprecise. It is this space of indeterminacy that factness of diaspora unfolds. Root seekers forge "cultures of relatedness"—relationships, experiences, and narratives—that have some basis in molecular-level analysis but are also extragenetic.[26]

The recent family reunion of Marvin, a genealogist from the southern U.S., featured an appearance by someone he described as a "genetic kinswoman." Some months prior, Marvin had purchased a genetic genealogy test from African Ancestry that associated him with the Mbundu people, the second largest ethnic group in the south-central African country of Angola. Marvin shared his results with a friend who subsequently put him in touch with Gertrudes, an Angolan immigrant neighbor of Mbundu ethnicity. At their first meeting, Marvin recalled Gertrudes as being "very accepting." He continued, "She said that one of her passions is to connect with African Americans and tell them about their history in Africa and to let them know that, as she always says, 'we are one.' [She believes that] there is a disconnect between African Americans and Africans, and she's trying to bridge the gap. One of her missions is to connect with more African Americans [and] teach them about Africa.'"

Gertrudes subsequently invited Marvin to attend a celebration of the thirtieth anniversary of Angola's independence from Portugal, hosted by the voluntary association for immigrants from the African country that she helms. Here Marvin, along with a cousin who attended the party with him, felt accepted by the larger Angolan expatriate community as well. "Once we told everyone there that our family came from Angola, they all said, 'Welcome home. You're home now.' They even made me and my cousin get up on the dance floor. You know, they do a ring dance? . . . They told us, 'You gotta come dance. Dance for your homeland!'"

In turn, Gertrudes would attend Marvin's family reunion some months later. "Her presence was powerful," Marvin recollected. "[She talked] about the importance of us coming together as a group of Africans. She expressed that we are all Africans and that Europeans try to divide us but now we must come together. And she also told our family some very interesting facts about the Mbundu people. And that was awesome, just for the family to hear about the people we descend from . . . directly from an Mbundu person. It was very powerful. She had the full attention of the whole family. Everybody was just sitting there in awe of her presence. . . . It was uplifting and powerful just to hear her tell us something about our African roots."

The social exchange carried out between Marvin and Gertrudes points to how genetic genealogy testing circulates as a "diasporic resource." As anthropologist Jacqueline Nassy Brown explains, diasporic resources can include "cultural productions such as music, but also people and places . . . [and the] iconography, ideas, and ideologies" of one black community that are employed by another as formative schema for political consciousness, collective empowerment, and identity formation.[27] In Brown's work, the concept describes, for example, how knowledge of a historic event such as the civil rights movement of the mid-twentieth-century United States circulated globally via the media, popular culture, and social networks to become an important touchstone of self-determination for blacks in Liverpool, England in the 1990s.[28] In the context of genetic genealogy testing, the concept of diasporic resources elucidates how genetic information occasions "biosociality" between African communities and their diasporas, even in the absence of evidence of specific kinship ties.[29] An imprecise pedigree connects Marvin and Gertrudes as "genetic kin" and "Africans." The diasporic relatedness resulting from ethnic lineage testing is genetic inference inspired by genealogical aspiration and enacted through social interaction.

In recent years there has been increased scholarly interest in the study of "deterritorialized" or diasporic communities.[30] Rogers Brubaker recently described this ideational proliferation as a "'diaspora' diaspora": "a dispersion of the meanings of the term in semantic, conceptual, and disciplinary space."[31] While efforts to refine the concept of diaspora persist, many scholars are in agreement that its hallmarks include dispersal from long-held geographic homes; the constitution of a collective identity or consciousness in response to the experience of dispersal; connection to a place of geographic origin forged through practices such as communication, travel/tourism, philanthropy, and political engagement; and the circulation of collective memories, myths, or imaginaries about the homeland. Diverse diasporas, born of distinct historical, political, and economic push-and-pull factors, share these general contours.

Some theorists suggest that the African diaspora that began in the sixteenth century is "exceptional" among human dispersals of the past and present because it was a forced migration set in motion by the demand for slave labor. Futhermore, it spurred the process of ethnogenesis—the substitution of specific African identities for more general collectivities, such as Pan-African, African American, and Afro-Caribbean.[32] As William Safran maintains, a *"specific* homeland cannot be restored" to slave descendants. Because an African homeland cannot be restored, it has been imagined or "rememoried."[33]

How "Africa" has been envisioned by its slave-descended diaspora is a topic of debate among theorists. At issue is the *ethics* of imagining Africa and diasporic connection: What is the substance of diaspora? Who in the diaspora gets to imagine "home"? How is it imagined and to what ends? While some scholars maintain that the conceptions of Africa that underlie diasporic consciousness may have many foundational bases, including political ideology, cultural production, desire, common experiences of oppression or redemption, and communication practices, others contend that diasporic claims to and about Africa—particularly those of African Americans—can be essentialist, homogenizing, and instrumental.[34]

Paul Gilroy, arguably the most influential critic of originary imaginings of Africa, argues in *The Black Atlantic* that "Africa" has been inaccurately conceived as a transhistorical umbilicus linking blacks globally to a re-gal, prelapsarian past. Indeed, a principal theme of the theorist's body of work is antiessentialism, in particular, the contention that notions of black transnationalism should not be based upon the "the stern discipline of primordial kinship and rooted belonging." Gilroy's discomfort with the idealization of roots stems from insights gained from his valuable inqui-ries into "raciology"—the constellation of discourses, many drawn from the biological sciences, that sustain and justify epistemologies of race and racism and, in turn, social inequality. As an antidote to racial essentialism, Gilroy alternately advances an understanding of diaspora as network, in-terchange, and circulation. "Primordial kinship" and the search for roots are thus contrasted with an ethicocultural conception of diaspora.[35]

Notions of diaspora rooted in technologies of kinship may be better conceptualized as "cultures of relatedness" in which biological facts are not the necessary conditions of possibility for social ones. In Carol Stack's classic 1974 ethnography, *All Our Kin*, for example, kinship among urban blacks in "The Flats" of inner-city Chicago is based on the exchange of economic resources and caring labor between residents. As Stack shows, kinship terms such as *aunt* and *brother* are used by members of the com-munity, but these categories do not connote nature or blood; rather, these terms are engaged despite lack of demonstrable biogenetic links. Simi-larly, Judith Butler offers "the social organization of need" as one example of kinship based on "consensual affiliation" rather than "blood ties."[36] Re-cent scholarship on new reproductive technologies has shown that "biol-ogy" and "family" can be decoupled through egg donation, surrogacy, and adoption.[37]

Kinship can thus have many bases. Viewed through the prism of this recent scholarship, the discourses and practices of kinship facilitated by genetic genealogy testing can be understood to scale up to diaspora with-out necessarily scaling down to human biological essences. Indeed, the forms of sociality fostered by genealogy testing—both the aspirations for affiliation that inspire its use and the relationships it may occasion—are conduits through which the networked conception of diaspora that Gilroy advocates may take shape. Affiliations that incorporate biogenetic facts may nonetheless be the "families we choose."[38]

I have advanced the concept of the factness of diaspora to describe how phenomena seemingly extrinsic to genetic genealogy testing like that of-fered by African Ancestry facilitate its legitimacy. The legitimacy of genetic genealogy testing is built on cultural scaffolding including the "authentic expertise" of scientist-entrepreneur Rick Kittles, the process of affiliative self-fashioning embarked upon following the receipt of test results, and the diasporic relatedness that this information may support. Mistrust of scientific authority and concerns about privacy have a nonunique but significant history in black communities. A shared background between a scientist and consumers, then, becomes crucial to making the facts of genetic genealogy testing efficacious and meaningful. As Henry T. Greely points out, the forms of association on offer through genetic genealogy testing, while tracing lines of matrilineage and patrilineage, do not and cannot establish direct lines of descent and thus in practice are necessarily flexible and "fictive." As a consequence, root seekers also become root makers, taking up those elements of the testing that facilitate associations that are important to them.[39] The factness of diaspora provides a window on how diasporic resources are put to the purpose of constructing individual and collective identity and helps us to understand the processes by which root seekers come to selectively invest in genetic genealogy testing.

Notes

1. This chapter is revised from Alondra Nelson, "The Factness of Diaspora: The Social Sources of Genetic Genealogy," in Barbara A. Koenig, Sandra Soo-Jin Lee, and Sarah S. Richardson, eds., *Revisiting Race in a Genomic Age*, 253–270 (Newark, NJ: Rutgers University Press, 2008).

2. Alex Haley, *Roots: The Saga of an American Family* (New York: Doubleday, 1976).

3. Matthew Frye Jacobson, *Roots Too: White Ethic Revival in Post–Civil Rights America* (Cambridge: Havard University Press, 2006).

4. L. Luca Cavalli-Sforza, Paolo Menozzi, and Alberti Piazza, *The History and Geography of Human Genes* (Princeton: Princeton University Press, 1994); Duana Fullwiley, "The Molecularization of Race: U.S. Health Institutions, Pharmacogenetics Practice, and Public Science after the Genome," in *Revisiting Race in a Genomic Age*, 149–171; Michael F. Hammer, "A Recent Common Ancestry for Human Y Chromosomes," *Nature* 378 (November 23, 1995): 376–378; Mark A. Jobling and Chris Tyler-Smith, "Fathers and Sons: The Y Chromosome and Human Evolution," *Trends in Genetics* 11, no. 11 (November 1995): 449–456; Mark D. Shriver and Rick A. Kittles, "Genetic Ancestry and the Search for Personalized Genetic Histories," *Nature Reviews Genetics* 5 (August 2004): 611–618.

5. Rick A. Kittles, personal communication, February 4, 2006. The new company received much media attention; typical newspaper articles included: A. J. Hostetler, "Who's Your Daddy? Genealogists Look Inside Their Cells for Clues

to Their Ancestors," *Richmond Times-Dispatch* (Va.), April 24, 2003; Stephen Magagnini, "DNA Helps Unscramble the Puzzles of Ancestry," *Sacramento Bee* (Calif.), August 3, 2003; Steve Sailer, "African Ancestry, Inc. Traces DNA Roots," *Washington Times,* April 28, 2003; Frank D. Roylance, "Reclaiming Heritage Lost to Slavery," *Baltimore Sun,* April 17, 2003.

6. The company sells two forms of genetic analysis with the brand names MatriClan and PatriClan that trace matrilineage and patrilineage, respectively. MatriClan analyzes genetic information linked to mitochondrial DNA that is inherited by both male and female children from their mothers. The PatriClan test examines the genetic sequence of the Y-chromosome to trace lineage from son to father, to father's father, to father's father's father, and so on. The company's extensive Web site, http://africanancestry.com, details the testing procedures and results.

7. African Ancestry reports that approximately 25 to 30 percent of male root seekers using its PatriClan (Y-chromosome) test will not match any of the paternal lines in the African Lineage Database (ALD). In such instances, the customer may be advised to have his sample matched against a "European database." See Greg Langley, "Genealogy and Genomes: DNA Technology Helping People Learn More About Who They Are and Where They Come From," *Baton Rouge Advocate,* July 20, 2003. A page about the PatriClan (Y-chromosome) test on African Ancestry's Web site states: "We find African ancestry for approximately 65% of the paternal lineages we test. The remaining 35% of the lineages we test typically indicate European ancestry. If our tests indicate that you are not of African descent, we will identify your continent of origin." "Discover the Paternal Roots of Your Family Tree," http://africanancestry.com/patriclan.html (accessed July 1, 2010). Because the ALD (African Lineage Database) is extensive but not exhaustive, however, there is some chance that matching "African" genetic markers are not yet included.

8. Nadia Abu El-Haj, "The Genetic Reinscription of Race," *Annual Review of Anthropology* 36 (2007): 284. See also Troy Duster, *Backdoor to Eugenics,* 2d ed. (New York: Routledge, 2003). On black experiences, see Paul Gilroy, *The Black Atlantic: Modernity and Double Consciousness* (Cambridge: Harvard University Press, 1993).

9. I described this ethnographic research in more detail previously. See Alondra Nelson, "Bio Science: Genetic Genealogy Testing and the Pursuit of African Ancestry," *Social Studies of Science* 38, no. 5 (2008): 759–783. On coproduction, see Sheila Jasanoff, *States of Knowledge: The Co-Production of Science and the Social Order* (New York: Routledge, 2004); Jenny Reardon, *Race to the Finish: Identity and Governance in an Age of Genomics* (Princeton: Princeton University Press, 2005).

10. I distinguish "the factness of diaspora" from Bruno Latour's "factish" (fact and fetish). See Latour, *Pandora's Hope: Essays on the Reality of Science Studies* (Cambridge: Harvard University Press, 1999), chapter 9. While both concepts are concerned with and reflect the dual constitution of scientific and cultural knowledge, the combination of the artifacts of reason with a field of value, with

the factness of diaspora, I am specifically concerned with the historical experience of displacement and oppression and the subsequent aspirations for reconciliation that animate a particular orientation to the cultures of science. Latour asks whether an idea is "constructed well enough to become an autonomous fact?" (ibid., 274). Here, I am interested in the values that shape the adjudication and interpretation of facts, such that we must understand them as "factness."

11. For the concept of "biogenetic" facts, see David M. Schneider, *American Kinship: A Cultural Account* (Englewood Cliffs, NJ: Prentice-Hall, 1968), 24.

12. Thomas Jefferson Foundation, "Report of the Research Committee on Thomas Jefferson and Sally Hemings" (January 2000), http://www.monticello .org/plantation/hemingscontro/hemings_report.html. See also Mia Bay, "In Search of Sally Hemings in the Post-DNA Era," *Reviews in American History* 34, no. 4 (December 2006): 407–426.

13. Daughters of the American Revolution (DAR) is a genealogy- and membership-based organization for women who can trace their lineage to an individual who aided in the cause of the United States' independence from England. The DAR has a checkered history with regard to race relations. In 1939 it prohibited renowned African American singer Marian Anderson from performing at the DAR-owned venue Constitution Hall in Washington, D.C., that only allowed whites on its stage. As recently as 1984, a woman who fulfilled all DAR membership requirements was not initially allowed to join the group because she was African American. Ronald Kessler, "Black Unable to Join Local DAR: Race is a Stumbling Block," *Washington Post*, March 12, 1984.

14. Coproduced, written, and hosted by Harvard University Professor Henry Louis Gates Jr., this PBS genetic genealogy documentary franchise also includes *African American Lives 2* (2008), on which Kittles was a collaborator, and *Faces of America* (2010).

15. Shriver and Kittles, "Genetic Ancestry."

16. On Rick Kittles's educational and professional background, see http:// africanancestry.com/management.html and http://genemed.bsd.uchicago.edu/ ~kittleslab/.

17. Nikolas S. Rose, *The Politics of Life Itself: Biomedicine, Power, and Subjectivity in the Twenty-First Century* (Princeton: Princeton University Press, 2007), 82.

18. In order to protect the privacy of my informants, all names used here are pseudonyms unless otherwise indicated. The actual names of the purveyors of African Ancestry are used because they are public figures. I interviewed subjects who attempted to trace their family genealogy by conventional means prior to purchasing genetic genealogy testing services as well as subjects whose first foray into genealogy was the purchase of a test kit.

19. Carolyn J. Rosenthal, "Kinkeeping in the Familial Division of Labor," *Journal of Marriage and the Family* 47, no. 4 (November 1985): 965–974.

20. Nelson, "Bio Science," 759–783.

21. Ibid., 771.

22. Joseph Dumit, "Is It Me or My Brain? Depression and Neuroscientific Facts," *Journal of Medical Humanities* 24, nos. 1–2 (June 2003): 39.

23. Deborah A. Bolnick et al., "The Business and Science of Ancestry Testing," *Science* 318 (October 19, 2007): 399–400.

24. Catherine Nash, "Genetic Kinship," *Cultural Studies* 18, no. 1 (January 2004): 1–33.

25. Schneider, *American Kinship*. As I address further on, this is the common usage of these kinship terms, but not their exclusive meaning. See also contributions by Janet L. Dolgin, Susan McKinnon, Rayna Rapp, and Kath Weston in Sylvia Yanagisako and Carol Delaney, eds., *Naturalizing Power: Essays in Feminist Cultural Analysis* (New York: Routledge, 1995).

26. Janet Carsten, ed., *Cultures of Relatedness: New Approaches to the Study of Kinship* (Cambridge: Cambridge University Press, 2000).

27. Jacqueline Nassy Brown, "Black Liverpool, Black America, and the Gendering of Diasporic Space," *Cultural Anthropology* 13, no. 3 (August 1998): 298, and *Dropping Anchor, Setting Sail: Geographies of Race in Black Liverpool* (Princeton: Princeton University Press, 2005), 53.

28. Brown, *Dropping Anchor*, chapter 2.

29. For the concept of "biosociality," see Paul Rabinow, *Essays on the Anthropology of Reason*. (Princeton: Princeton University Press, 1996), 102–103.

30. Arjun Appadurai, *Modernity at Large: Cultural Dimensions of Globalization* (Minneapolis: University of Minnesota Press, 1996).

31. Rogers Brubaker, "The 'Diaspora' Diaspora," *Ethnic and Racial Studies* 28, no. 1 (January 2005): 1.

32. "Exceptional" is Khachig Tölölyan's term in "Rethinking Diaspora(s): Stateless Power in the Transnational Moment," *Diaspora* 5, no. 1 (Spring 1996): 13. For the process of ethnogenesis, see Michael Angelo Gomez, *Exchanging Our Country Marks: The Transformation of African Identities in the Colonial and Antebellum South* (Chapel Hill: University of North Carolina Press, 1998); and Tiffany Ruby Patterson and Robin D. G. Kelley, "Unfinished Migrations: Reflections on the African Diaspora and the Making of the Modern World," *African Studies Review* 43, no. 1 (April 2000): 11–45. There are, of course, many African diasporas, including twentieth-century and present-day movements spurred by globalization. This chapter is concerned primarily with the older migrations that were spurred by the slave trade and dispersed Africans to the Americas, although its insights are, hopefully, more broadly applicable.

33. William Safran, "Diasporas in Modern Societies: Myths of Homeland and Return." *Diaspora* 1, no. 1 (Spring 1991): 90. As developed in Toni Morrison's *Beloved*, "rememory" is the continuous existence in the present of something lost or forgotten in the past. Morrison, *Beloved: A Novel* (New York: Plume, 1988).

34. Authors arguing for a multicausal foundation of diasporic consciousness include Appadurai, *Modernity at Large*; James Clifford, "Diasporas," *Cultural Anthropology* 9, no. 3 (August 1994): 304–305; Brent Hayes Edwards, *The Practice of Diaspora: Literature, Translation, and the Rise of Black Internationalism* (Cambridge: Harvard University Press, 2003); Patterson and Kelley, "Unfinished Migrations," 13–15; Safran, "Diasporas in Modern Societies," 83–84; and Rinaldo Walcott, "Outside in Black Studies: Reading from a Queer Place in the Diaspora,"

in E. Patrick Johnson and Mae G. Henderson, eds., *Black Queer Studies: A Critical Anthology* (Durham: Duke University Press, 2005), 90–105. For the essentialist camp, see Gilroy, *Black Atlantic*; Anthony Appiah, *In My Father's House: Africa in the Philosophy of Culture* (New York: Oxford University Press, 1992); Kamari Maxine Clark, *Mapping Yorùbá Networks: Power and Agency in the Making of Transnational Communities* (Durham: Duke University Press, 2004); and E. Frances White, "Africa on My Mind: Gender, Counter Discourse, and African-American Nationalism," *Journal of Women's History* 2, no. 1 (Spring 1990): 73–97.

35. Gilroy, *Black Atlantic*, 123.

36. Carsten, *Cultures of Relatedness*; Carol B. Stack, *All Our Kin: Strategies for Survival in a Black Community* (New York: Harper and Row, 1974), chapter 4.; Judith Butler, *Antigone's Claim: Kinship Between Life and Death* (New York: Columbia University Press, 2002), 74.

37. See, for instance, Carsten, *Cultures of Relatedness*; Sarah Franklin and Susan McKinnon, "New Directions in Kinship Study: A Core Concept Revisited," *Current Anthropology* 41, no. 2 (April 2000): 275–279; Deborah R. Grayson, "Mediating Intimacy: Black Surrogate Mothers and the Law," *Critical Inquiry* 24, no. 2 (Winter 1998): 525–546; and Corinne P. Hayden, "Gender, Genetics, and Generation: Reformulating Biology in Lesbian Kinship," *Cultural Anthropology* 10, no. 1 (February 1995): 41–63.

38. Kath Weston, *Families We Choose: Lesbians, Gays, Kinship* (New York: Columbia University Press, 1997).

39. Henry T. Greely, "Genetic Genealogy: Genetics Meets the Marketplace," in Koenig, Lee, and Richardson, *Revisiting Race in a Genomic Age*, 215–234.

2 Jews—Lost and Found

Genetic History and the Evidentiary Terrain of Recognition

NADIA ABU EL-HAJ

Most commonly associated with the network of disciplines, institutions, and practices that make up the world of biomedicine, the new genetics has also facilitated the study of the origins and kinship of contemporary population groups. In this essay I consider one genetic historical research project: the search for historical links between the Lemba of southern Africa, who believe themselves to be descendants of the ancient lost tribes of Israel, and contemporary Jews. I demonstrate the ways in which genetic historical studies of their origins—more specifically, genetic studies of patrilineal descent—are becoming an evidentiary ground on which historical claims are made *plausible* (or implausible), cultural, religious, and political practices are made possible, and disputes are adjudicated. I focus on the work of a U.S.-based Jewish organization best described as a missionary group engaged in a multicultural project to "recognize" nonwhite (would-be) Jews.[1] In so doing, Kulanu, as the group is named, seeks to expand the known Jewish world beyond the boundaries of a white world.

More broadly, I lay out the contours of a distinctive politics of recognition, while focusing on the significance of recognition *for the recognizer's* practices of self-fashioning. As argued by Patchen Markell, in the early 1990s prominent theorists of recognition proposed "that many contemporary social and political controversies can be understood . . . as attempts to secure forms of respect and esteem that are grounded in, and expressive of, the accurate knowledge of the particular identities borne by people and social groups."[2] According to Charles Taylor, as individuals we are all rooted in a moral space that grounds our ability to evaluate and determine "the good life" (for oneself). That moral space or "the good life" is articulated within culture—the "unique, authentic identity of a distinctive 'people' or Volk."[3] To fail to recognize cultural *difference* then, which is a constitutive failure of the liberal (settler) nation-state, is to perpetrate a fundamental injury. It is to deny what it means to be human—that we are all, irreducibly, always already part of a linguistic community, of a culture.[4]

By way of contrast, the grammar of Kulanu's politics of recognition goes something like this: Your cultural/religious difference matters, and yet it doesn't matter. We want to reveal a common genealogical identity on the basis of which you can, following a suitable religious education, be formally reintegrated into the Jewish world. *Judaism* and recognizing individuals from lost tribes *as fellow Jews* demands religious education and formal conversion before a rabbinic court. It requires that communities abandon significant elements of their religious and cultural difference. The common horizon in this politics of recognition is not a humanity characterized by the fact of cultural diversity that must be recognized and preserved. It is a Jewish identity defined on the basis of genealogical descent and (for, the most part, normative) religious practice. And the historical injury to be redressed is perhaps best understood as one about the self: if we cannot, as white American Jews, incorporate racial diversity into our Jewish world, what do *we* become?[5] This is a multicultural project configured through the lens of an identity politics that grounds itself in a genealogical identity. That genealogical community is produced as antiracist by the call to recognize nonwhite *Jews* as Jewish kin.

Through this consideration of the cultural and political practices that have emerged out of research on lost tribes, I want to comment more broadly on a constitutive logic of the genetic historical subject. If, as Elizabeth Povinelli has demonstrated, the politics of recognition presupposes an archive, the genetic historical archive may prove to be (or, in Derrida's articulation, may prove *to have been*) essential to the "hope" of self-described lost tribes to be recognized by the mainstream of the Jewish world and by the Israeli state as (potential) Jews.[6] Not, however, in any simple causal or deterministic sense. As will become clear in the discussion that follows, ambivalence reigns regarding the significance of genetic evidence to matters of (Jewish) identity: it matters, it doesn't matter; it matters, it shouldn't matter; it matters; it doesn't *make* the Lemba (or anyone else) Jews.

This ambivalence stands at the heart of the genetic historical subject, albeit in different ways vis-à-vis different communities of Jews and would-be Jews. This is a biological archive, I argue, but it is not the determining biological archive of race: one is not (considered) a Jew *because one shares a particular biology.* A logic of choice, culture and agency is built into the historical and cultural imagination of genetic historical quests. In this instance, "religion" mediates the distinction between biology and identity: religion is understood to be a matter of *belief.* It involves for Lemba the *choice* to learn "proper" Judaism and to convert, to be recognized as Jews by a rabbinic court. Nevertheless, such choices are made possible against the background of genetic historical facts that make claims to Judaic origins plausible. Collective and individual practices of self-making embrace the production of cultural truths out of bodily matter and simultaneously assert the *distance* between biology and agency, genes and culture. The genetic historical subject is borne within that zone of (in)distinction between biology on the one hand and agency—framed as a matter of "choice," in this instance—on the other.

The play between biology (as male ancestry) and agency (as religious choice) defines the path for "returning" to Judaism open to members of self-declared lost tribes. For the Lemba's belief in being descendants of a lost tribe to be credible, genetic historical facts are needed to verify the oral tradition of Judaic men having traveled to Southern Africa and founded the Lemba community. For Lemba individuals to be recognized as (returning) Jews, individuals must choose to study and practice proper Judaism. And, as the genetic historical archive provides a background of intelligibility in relation to which that "choice" is encouraged and facilitated by the Jewish mainstream, not only does the persistent biological-genealogical definition of Jewishness become clear. So too does the centrality of the Jewish state as final arbiter in deciding "Who is a Jew," even for those committed to living in and maintaining the diaspora.

The Archive of Possibility

In January 1997 the journal *Nature* published a report on a study of descendants of the male priestly line who are known in Jewish tradition as the Cohanim. If the Cohen lineage has been passed from father to son originating with the biblical figure of Aaron, as the Bible tells the story, it should be possible to confirm the biblical account through Y-chromosome analysis.[7]

Researchers collected DNA samples from 188 Israeli, British, and North American Jewish men.[8] They compared the Y-chromosomes of Jewish men who self-identified as Cohanim with men who self-identified as either Levites (a second priestly line) or as "lay-Jews," Israelites.[9] If the biblical and oral traditions of priestly origins and descent are historically accurate, "observable" differences should exist between the Y-chromosome haplotypes of "Jewish priests and their lay-counterparts." The 1997 *Nature* paper announced an observable difference "confirm[ing] a distinct paternal genealogy for Jewish priests." Those results were tested in a subsequent study that concluded that "a single haplotype ([named] *the Cohen Modal Haplotype [CMH]*) is strikingly frequent in both Ashkenazi and Sephardi Cohanim," suggesting a common origin for communities that have been separated for most of the past 500 years. The 1998 paper went further than a claim to common Cohen origins, however.[10] The authors suggested that the CMH *"could be* a signature of the ancient Hebrew population."[11] That *possibility* emerged as the evidentiary basis for genetic historical studies of Lemba origins.

Identification

Tudor Parfitt, a scholar at the School of Oriental and African Studies in London, decided that he might be able to use the results of the Cohanim study in order to solve what he considered the "riddle" of the Lemba. Together with colleagues at University College London's Center for Genetic Anthropology, Parfitt helped to organize a Y-chromosome study of Lemba origins. Parfitt and his colleagues hypothesized: "The combination of the presence of the CMH at high frequency in the Lemba and its absence in neighboring Bantu populations would be supportive of Lemba claims of a paternal Judaic ancestry, especially if its frequency is relatively low in other Semitic groups."[12] Relying on various studies that note the CMH's "absence" or "low frequency" in a few other populations ("Yakut, Mongolians, Nepalese, Armenians, Greeks, and Cypriots and, interestingly, in Palestinian Arabs"), the CMH is argued to be not just "Semitic" in origin but more specifically Judaic. If the CMH could be found in a similar percentage of the Lemba as it was in the general Jewish population (among "Israelites," at about 9 or 10 percent), the Lemba's assertion of Jewish ancestry might be plausible. An apt illustration and extension of Bruno Latour's argument about the production of scientific facts—that their circulation and citation in scientific papers moves laboratory objects and claims from the domain of controversy into the domain of fact (the "black box")—using the CMH as the normative measure of Hebrew origins in the design of the Lemba study helped to establish it as evidence of Hebrew ancestry.[13]

The researchers concluded they had plausible if inconclusive evidence of a link between the Lemba and (ancient) Jews. "Clearly, there has been a Semitic genetic contribution," they write, but whether or not the gene flow came from an Arab source (Yemenis) or a Jewish one is difficult to disentangle, at least vis-à-vis most of the sampled Lemba Y-chromosome haplotypes. But the presence of the CMH is another matter: "The CMH *has been suggested as* a signature haplotype for the ancient Hebrew population, *and it may be performing that function in this study.* . . . However, it is possible that the Lemba CMH Y chromosomes are a consequence of a relatively recent event that, in Lemba oral tradition, has acquired a patina of antiquity."[14] While in general "there is no need to present an Arab versus a Judaic contribution to that gene pool, since contributions from both are likely to have occurred," they conclude, "the CMH present in the Lemba could . . . have an exclusively Judaic origin."[15]

Recognition

The relationship between genealogy and Jewishness has long been the subject of discussion. The question of whether Jewishness is a racial, a national, and/or a religious identity was rigorously debated in the nineteenth and early twentieth centuries. And while the early Zionists—and especially Labor Zionists as they gained prominence in Mandatory Palestine and later in the Israeli state—sought to produce a distinctly *national* Jewish identity, one that would be secular and separated from its religious "roots," genealogical descent, national identity, and religious identity have remained entangled. Scholars who study the genetic history of modern Jews have argued they may be in a position to resolve the long-standing debate regarding what makes one a Jew—"shared culture or common descent."[16] The public debates over the Lemba's possible Jewishness that emerged in the wake of genetic historical evidence, however, make clear that culture (religion) and common descent are not alternatives to be decided between.

In presenting their work publicly, researchers insist that genetic genealogy adjudicates neither the question of whether or not a man is a Cohen nor the question of whether or not an individual or a community is Jewish. For example, following the "discovery" of the CMH, researchers argued that the presence or absence of the haplotype on an individual's Y-chromosome has no bearing on whether or not a particular man is a Cohen, although many a self-identified Cohen has contacted these researchers in order to take the test.[17] In the words of Vivian Moses of University College London's Center for Genetic Anthropology: "There is a significantly greater frequency of this genetic pattern in the Cohanim than there is among the others. . . . People keep asking us, let me give you a bit of my DNA and you tell me whether I am a Cohen. It doesn't work like that. There isn't a Cohen gene. It is a statistical phenomenon that among the Cohanim you find this pattern. Whether it is indicative of Cohenism is another matter. If someone has this pattern, but doesn't think he's a Cohen does it mean he really is? That is a thing one can debate about."[18]

Such discoveries confirm the veracity of an oral tradition *in general*. As a statistical fact, a specific modal haplotype is found at a relatively high frequency in a population—an aggregate of individuals—self-identified as members of the male priestly lineage. (Modal haplotypes are measures of *relative* frequency: the CMH can be modal at 50 percent as it is among the Cohanim because it is found at a higher rate than among Israelites who are the comparison group; the CMH is also "modal" at 10 percent for Israelites because it is found at a lower frequency in non-Jewish populations.) The CMH is not found on the Y-chromosome of every self-identified Cohen. About 50 percent of self-identified Cohanim do not carry it. Moreover, the CMH is found on the Y-chromosomes of Jewish men who do not believe they are Cohanim as well as on the Y-chromosomes of non-Jewish men. The CMH cannot test whether or not a particular man is a Cohen any more than it can test whether or not a particular Lemba man is a Jew. For that matter, it cannot determine whether or not the Lemba, *as a group,* are Jewish. Genomic facts of generational connection and halachic traditions of both priestly status and Jewishness remain and should remain distinct, researchers insist. And, as researchers have repeatedly

argued , the Y-chromosome—as a marker of male descent—has no bearing on a religious community and identity premised on descent down the
maternal line.[19]

But let us keep in mind the entangled origins of religion and race—an
entanglement especially knotted in nineteenth-century thought on Sem-
ites in general and on Jews in particular.[20] And let us keep in mind the
inability to separate biology (as race, as population), religion, and nation
that persisted well into the twentieth century in Zionist thought and Israeli nation-state building. What then, in the wake of genetic historical
evidence, is the relationship between genealogical and religious answers
to the question of who *might be* a Jew?

Assuming for the sake of argument that scientists have resolved that
the CMH is the modal haplotype of the ancient Hebrew population,[21]
does the presence of the CMH in the Lemba population (at the "right"
frequency) make the Lemba Jewish? "Being Jewish is a spiritual, metaphysical state and DNA is a physical characteristic, like nose size," Karl
Skorecki, one of the principal researchers, has argued, "But we wouldn't
dare go around saying we're going to determine who is Jewish by the
length of their nose. Similarly we're not going to determine who is Jewish
by the sequence of their DNA."[22] Or, as argued by Shaye Cohen, a professor of Jewish studies at Harvard University, "As a historian, I find the
whole enterprise rather silly. Are the Lemba descendants of the lost tribes
who disappeared from the face of the earth? The answer, of course, is no."
They might well be, however, "a kind of modern lost tribe"—"a group
of people unbeknownst to us and to themselves carrying Jewish genetic
material." According to Cohen, the Lemba will "be accepted as Jews 'if
the Jewish people want them to become Jews. And that's the way it's been
since Moses and Aaron.'"[23]

The *Proceedings of the National Academy of Sciences* study did not transform the Lemba community into (recognized) Jews, either in the eyes of
the Lemba (for whom it might have confirmed a long-standing belief in
their Jewish origins, however the meaning of that ancestry is configured)
or in the eyes of Jewish individuals or groups whose own claims to being
Jewish are unlikely to be called into question regardless of the results
of genetic historical work.[24] Nevertheless, this research has far-reaching
implications for the question of recognition. On the basis of what cri-
teria might "the Jewish people want them to become Jews," to return to
Shaye Cohen's words? What might the evidentiary terrain of recognition
be(come)?

Epistemology and the (Scientific) Grid of Intelligibility

In a letter published in Kulanu's *Newsletter*, its president, Jack Zeller, questions the need to prove one's Jewishness.

It is demeaning for one Jew to have to prove his Jewishness to another Jew. . . . Kulanu bases identity on oral traditions and practices as if they are one's "notarized signature" . . .

Recently, the Lemba, regarded by anthropologists and some Jewish *mavens* of numerous stripes as "non-Jewish," have turned the tables with the active help of Tudor Parfitt, a London-based anthropologist and "honorary Lemba," who was himself helped by a group of eminent geneticists, most of whom are Jewish. (The Lemba have been found to have an anomaly on their Y chromosome that depicts their Middle Eastern heritage and, in fact, marks their priestly clan as closely related to the *Cohanim*.) Exciting, but also tragic. DNA sequences are interesting, but we have to hide our shame for needing to wait for this scientific evidence to convince us of their Jewishness.[25]

Most Jews (and others), however, do not regard oral traditions as "notarized signatures." For nonbelievers in the biblical tradition of lost tribes, persons for whom neither oral histories nor the presence of rituals that "resemble" Jewish ones function as evidence of (possible) ancient Hebrew descent, genetic evidence might provide a "background of intelligibility" against which the authenticity of oral traditions can be considered, evaluated, and debated.[26] After all, it was on the basis of the *PNAS* study that PBS filmed and aired a NOVA video on the Lemba that investigated the question of whether or not they really are a lost tribe. The *New York Times* and *Haaretz*, the two most respected newspapers in the U.S. and in Israel, reported on the finding and suggested that the Lemba may well be of ancient Hebrew descent. And the American Museum of Natural History in New York screened the NOVA episode and held a public discussion about its findings as part of their special exhibit on genomics in 2001. Moreover, Kulanu arranged a speaking tour by Tudor Parfitt to synagogues and Jewish community centers around the U.S. in which he discussed his ongoing research on the Lemba as well as the more recent genetic findings. The belief that the Lemba may be descendants of one of Israel's so-called

lost tribes, in other words, is no longer as quickly dismissed as the obsession of a "possibly kooky" group, as Kulanu was once described to me by
someone who works at a Jewish cultural institution in New York. (That
same institution later sponsored a talk by Tudor Parfitt on the Lemba;
Kulanu organized the talk.)

The epistemological power of genetic history might best be thought
of in terms of the demands of the archive: There are particular "rules of
formation" within which certain kinds of statements—historical claims,
in this instance—(can) appear as truth statements.[27] And these kinds of
statements must come in particular forms. The document—collected,
classified, and stored in official archives—has been essential to the historical profession since its establishment as a scientific project in the
nineteenth century.[28] By way of contrast, oral traditions and other kinds
of memorial practices or testimonies have not been considered reliable
("objective") sources of historical evidence. Genomic databases conform
to the demand for objectivity. The practices of genetic history generate
novel historical archives credible within our "documentary culture," ones
that can be invoked in struggles to constitute a recognizable public (in
this instance, the Lemba as Jews) even as they transform what counts as
a document and shift the forms of evidence to which groups can turn in
their demands for recognition.[29]

During the discussion that followed the screening of the NOVA documentary *The Lost Tribes of Israel* at the American Museum of Natural
History in Manhattan,[30] a member of the audience objected to the whole
discussion of the Lemba's possible Jewishness: one "feature of what determines Jewishness is belief in the Bible and the use of certain prayers,"
and the Lemba demonstrate neither. Tudor Parfitt responded: "The fact
is that the Lemba do have a whole range of practices and prayers which,
while not being very similar to those used by mainstream Judaism, nevertheless do appear to be Jewish in some way. They look rather like Old
Testament practices, and they certainly seem to predate the coming of the
Christian missionaries."

In the aftermath of genetic evidence, the question of recognizable
or normative religious belief and practice has become more convoluted
than this interchange suggests, however. Since this work became publicly
known in 1999, Kulanu (which means "all of us" in Hebrew) has dis-
patched visitors (mostly rabbis) and funded Judaic education programs in
Lemba communities designed to prepare Lemba for formal conversion.
And, as one report implied, much needs to be done before conversion is

possible: "I will be speaking for a lengthy time on our education and service plans [before the Lemba Cultural Association] meeting and also providing Jewish prayer to open and close the meeting. Last meeting, much to my surprise, the 'chaplain' called on a Lemba who opened his New Testament and made a prayer from it."[31]

Moreover, contact between Lemba and South African Jewish youth has been encouraged and orchestrated: as reported in Kulanu's newsletter in the summer of 2000, a "mini-camp" for ten Lemba youth and "their counterparts in the white Betar youth movement" was held recently, and there were plans (if sufficient funds could be raised) to have Lemba youth participate in a three-week end-of-year camp. "'We are accepting the Lemba as Lemba who have Jewish ancestry and not because we expect them to return to Judaism. . . . By going away together the [Lemba] youth [who have "had little or no exposure to Judaism"] will have the opportunity to experience first hand a little about Judaism and a Jewish way of life. Once they have an understanding of what Judaism is all about *an informed choice can be made.* This is where socializing and exposing the Lemba to a Jewish environment becomes an important factor."[32] Against the background of their now identifiable (male) Jewish ancestry, the Lemba (more accurately, Lemba *individuals*) may well decide to choose Judaism, if education and contact are properly facilitated.

Whatever the caveats or cautions of the *PNAS* publication, at the popular level its conclusions have been translated into a near certainty. And that "fact" has had particular effects: Jewish groups and communities, however limited they may be, have initiated sustained relationships with Lemba communities—as fellow Jews. Culture and descent are inextricably intertwined: suddenly Judaism becomes *their* religion and Jewishness becomes *their* culture by virtue of their genealogical descent, even if they don't, at present, engage in the doing of "Jewish things."[33] In turn, now recognizable Jews by virtue of their descent, *their* culture (*their* religion) is something that they need to be taught.

Throughout the published papers as well as in public forums and newspaper accounts, researchers involved in this work refer to Judaism as a religion, to Jewish identity as a matter of religious belief and practice, as a matter of choice. Insisting on religion as the appropriate category for understanding what makes a Jew a Jew enables them to separate genealogy from identity, science from politics (and genetic history from race science). Researchers in genetic history present their work as nonpolitical: The CMH does not adjudicate the Jewishness of the Lemba. It simply reveals a potentially interesting and heretofore unknown historical fact. But perhaps phylogenetic evidence is better named prepolitical—that is how it is represented by journalists who report it, activists who invoke it, audiences who seem fascinated by it, and scientists who engage in double-talk on the matter (it matters, it doesn't matter).[34] This kinship "is . . . the sphere that conditions the possibility of politics without entering into it," to borrow Judith Butler's words.[35] As genealogical facts, Y-chromosome haplotypes reveal a history that, if true, makes possible the granting of Jewish "citizenship" to the Lemba, but only following the choice to convert to Judaism, after which Lemba individuals can achieve recognized membership in the Jewish world (which implies all sorts of financial consequences as U.S. based Jewish groups support projects in "developing" Jewish communities) or, more literally, citizenship in the Israeli state. That political rationale for bestowing recognition discloses the dynamic relationship between "biology" and "choice," genetic haplotypes, religious faith, and group membership. In addition, it demonstrates how *in practice* the relationship between "individual" and "group" identification is impossible to disentangle: as a statistical fact, the results of the Lemba study open up the possibility that this group really might be descendants of ancient Jews. In turn, Judaism can be encouraged and taught, and, after a suitable education, individuals who choose to learn and practice normative Judaism will be able to be recognized, in accordance with (Orthodox) rabbinical legal definitions, as ("returning") Jews.

A Return to Jewishness

In a recent article, Steven Kaplan considers the persistent racial underpinnings of modern Jewish identity. Examining the case of Ethiopian Jewry, he argues that claims about whether or not they are Jews point to the ways in which Jews do indeed consider themselves a racial group. "The physical, genetic, and historical characteristics which appear to separate Ethiopian Jews from other Jews, and are the subject of so much attention, are only a problem if one operates under the assumption that these (traditional racial) markers are shared by other Jewish groups." In sum, "Ethiopian Jews are . . . the topic of so much interest and discussion precisely because they challenge existing 'racial' ideas of Who is a Jew."[36]

It was not just in the late nineteenth and early twentieth centuries that scholars arguing about the Jewishness of Ethiopian Jews identified phenotypic characteristics said to distinguish them from other Ethiopians. "Indeed, the massive Ethiopian aliyah of the 1980s produced in its wake a wealth of material claiming to distinguish Jewish Ethiopians from other Ethiopians on the basis of their physical appearance" (80). They are not as black as other Ethiopians, for example (83). Descent, another constitutive component of racial thought, Kaplan argues, also dominates discussions of the Jewishness of Ethiopian Jews. Scholars who have documented that Ethiopian Jews are descendants of fourteenth- to sixteenth-century converts (and not of the biblical patriarchs) have been accused of undermining Ethiopian Jewish claims to Jewishness. Moreover, recent genetic studies reporting that Ethiopian-Jewish Y-chromosome modal haplotypes fall outside the general Jewish Y-chromosome pool have raised political fears: Israeli scientists were reluctant to publish the results, a "recognition of the reality that membership in the Jewish people is commonly (if inaccurately) believed to be based upon racial-genetic ties" (87).

Kaplan makes an important point. Descent is a significant criterion of Jewishness, even more so with the establishment of the Jewish state, which "transformed the 'Who is a Jew?' question from a theoretical or existential question to a practical issue with broad political implications" (89). Nevertheless, I want to take seriously Kulanu's representation of its work as *antiracist*. I do so not because I accept that representation as true. Rather, that self-understanding helps us to think about differences between the political logic of racial versus genetic historical thought.

For Kulanu activists, working to reintegrate lost tribes and lost Jews is born of a commitment to social justice, tolerance, multiculturalism, and antiracism. The newsletter advertises Kulanu's work in promoting "diversity"—whether by announcing the publication of its books (*Jews in Places You Have Never Thought Of*) or organizing lectures, for example, at the 92nd Street Y in Manhattan, designed to teach about "exotic" Jews and Jewish diversity.[37] A self-consciously liberal project, their liberalism belongs to a very particular historical moment. It belongs to a "'post-civil rights' context in which 'most Americans believe themselves and the nation to be opposed to racism and in favor of a multiracial, multiethnic pluralism.'"[38] It is the liberalism of a "multicultural imaginary" that attempts to "address the multiplicity of social identities and traditions constituting and circulating through the contemporary nation," in this instance, a diasporic nation of Jews.[39]

From Kulanu's antiracist perspective, the facts of genetic history have helped them expand world Jewry beyond the boundaries of a "white" (Jewish) world. By going "beneath" racial phenotype, this Y-chromosome research has revealed a kinship between (known) Jews and (these) Africans, between (these) whites and (these) blacks. And that is not a belief of Kulanu activists alone. Take the following exchange between a member of the audience and Tudor Parfitt at the AMNH session on "The Lost Tribes of Israel."

> AUDIENCE MEMBER: I personally feel that the whole concept of the lost tribes is, to me, utterly ridiculous in the sense that . . . tribes are not lost to us, we are lost to them. . . . And myself, being a Jew of color historically with roots in Morocco, I personally do not consider myself to be lost to anyone. My question is, therefore, I personally feel that the genetic research can also be divisively used in a harmful way in some respects. . . . How can it benefit our understanding of the idea of diversity in the Jewish community?
>
> PARFITT: I think . . . [genetic research] . . . has been very useful for the Lemba, and also in a way for their neighbors. After all, for the last one hundred years the Lemba have made attempts to get themselves accepted in the context of South Africa by the white Jews in Johannesburg and elsewhere, and indeed, one or two committees of inquiry were sent to the Lemba villages by the white Jewish community who always declared that they were not Jews. And that was the end of it, and there was no contact between them. The only contact between them was that sometimes Lembas were servants in white Jewish households, and that was the beginning and the end of it. And now, since the genetic work was done I know that there has been a proper symbiosis between at least some aspects of the white Jewish community and the Lemba. . . . So in terms of Jewish diversity, I think it has proved to be extremely useful. The very fact that in North America now, as I said, the Lemba are considered by very many, particularly liberal Jews, to be part of the family of Israel, very largely because of this genetic work, is precisely along the lines of increasing Jewish diversity.

If this is not really the unmaking of race, let alone of racism, it *is* the separation of phenotype from descent in the biological imagination. I once asked a researcher in an anthropological genetics lab working on African American origins whether it really was possible for the police to use Y-chromosome or mtDNA testing to determine the race of a suspect. He answered: of course. Certain Y-chromosomes have a distinctly African origin, for example. He then paused and said: "But that doesn't mean the suspect will actually look black." In this scientific epistemology, the *phenotypic* differences of Ethiopian Jews do not render them non-Jewish, not according to a biology based upon the search for shared origins and continuous descent that uses *noncoding* markers, i.e., genetic markers with no (known) phenotypic effects.[40] At the same time, however, shared descent is not enough to make (nonwhite) groups or individuals Jewish: so too do we need evidence of their willingness to convert, of their own desire to be Jewish. But to complicate matters even further, for some groups and individuals, conversion—the choice of Jewishness—is only socially and politically felicitious against the background of intelligibility that the anthropological genetic archive provides. It then becomes a choice *to return*. As Kaplan points out with respect to the Falash Mura, a group of Ethiopian self-defined Jews who want to immigrate to Israel but whose ancestors had converted to Christianity, descent is *the* legal criterion determining their "right of return" under Israeli law. In the words of one Israeli government decision, only "'members of the Ethiopian community who are defined as the 'seed of Israel' and have *returned* to a Jewish way of life—are entitled to make aliyah."[41] There *is* a biological or behavioral determinism here. But rather than a simple replication of racial logics, it is distinct: once I find out who I have always already been, I can begin to—I am *authorized to*, indeed perhaps I must—engage in cultural and religious practices that *are* who I am *really*.

If looking at groups who challenge the taken-for-granted assumptions about who is a Jew helps us to reveal the persistent power of genealogical-biological definitions of Jewishness, so too does such a view from the margins lend insights into the centrality of the State of Israel for the Jewish diaspora's self-definition. Kulanu's primary commitment is to Jewish life *in the diaspora*: to discovering it, recognizing it, and facilitating it. The activist commitment to finding "lost Jews" is borne in part of an anxiety about the decline of the U.S. Jewish population through intermarriage, which is a phenomenon that was documented, reported on, and discussed by American Jewish organizations and the Jewish press throughout the 1990s, sometimes referred to as a "second holocaust." As one Kulanu board member put it, "Not a week goes by that I do not receive passionate e-mails from emerging Jewish communities all over the developing world. In Africa alone, new native communities in Nigeria, Ghana,

South Africa, Zimbabwe, and other places are literally pleading with us to send them Jewish teachers, books, and religious articles. We Jews do not have a demographic problem, we have an attitude problem. That problem is called racism, and we need to deal with it directly and forthrightly."[42] While committed to life in the diaspora, however, the State of Israel remains paramount: for groups such as Kulanu, a full "return" to Judaism for members of lost tribes requires the imprimatur of the Israeli state. Once someone *can make* aliyah, even if *they choose not to*, then he or she has returned to the Jewish fold. With that as their priority, there is no apparent contradiction for self-fashioned liberal, antiracist Kulanu activists when they join forces with Israeli right-wing nationalist-settler groups to demand that the Israeli state recognize the Bnei Menashe (a self-declared lost tribe in India) as Jews and to return them not just to the religion of Israel but to the state. And to the Occupied Territories they have gone.[43] This multicultural project, insofar as it is framed through the lens of an identity politics concerned solely with the self, cannot concern itself with anyone outside the albeit now expanding Jewish world.

Kulanu's commitment to the diaspora is perhaps best described as a diasporic Zionism. Far from presenting a radical alternative to the nationalist vision, it is a politics that seeks to sustain and nourish the diaspora that is caught in the long shadow of the Israeli state, which is the only authority that can finally determine who is a Jew, even as that resolution is infinitely deferred. The theoretical or existential question of "Who is a Jew?" can no longer be severed fully from the practical, political concerns regarding citizenship in the Jewish state, not even for those committed to the diaspora. The diasporic Jewish self has been fundamentally reconfigured by the nation-statist logic of Israel. And the genetic historical archive may well emerge as a powerful evidentiary (back)ground for both existential *and* practical resolutions to the question of membership for those who wish to "return."

Notes

Anthropological genetics is a discipline that seeks to reconstruct human origins and migration routes out of Africa, to study the genetic diversity of the human species, and to map the origins and phylogenies of particular populations. I refer to research on the origins and phylogenies of specific populations as genetic history, a subfield of the larger anthropological genetic discipline.

1. This is not to imply that there are not "nonwhite" Jewish communities who are recognized members of the Jewish world or citizens of the Jewish state. In Kulanu's rhetoric, however, the Jewish world could be far more multiracial than it is today. As an organization, it works for the integration of (largely) nonwhite "lost Jews" or "lost tribes" and converts into the Jewish world.

2. Patchen Markell, *Bound by Recognition* (Princeton.: Princeton University Press, 2003), 39.

3. Ibid., 154.

4. See Charles Taylor's earlier work, *Sources of the Self: Making of the Modern Identity* (Cambridge: Harvard University Press, 1989), and *The Ethics of Authenticity*, (Cambridge: Harvard University Press, 1992).

5. On the long-standing centrality of liberalism or liberal self-fashioning to American Jewish identity, see Eric L. Goldstein, *The Price of Whiteness: Jews, Race, and American Identity* (Princeton: Princeton University Press, 2006).

6. I am not arguing that genetic historical evidence has any legal standing today. There are, however, a lot of Web-based discussions about whether it does, and evaluating whether it should. There is also at least one court case (if not a successful one) of someone trying to use genetic evidence as the basis for invoking the Law of Return in Israel. There is evidence of the beginnings of a debate about whether or not genetic evidence should have any legal standing with respect to the question of who is a Jew. See Jacques Derrida, *Archive Fever: A Freudian Impression, Religion, and Postmodernism* (Chicago: University of Chicago Press, 1996).

7. The Y-chromosome is passed down from father to son virtually unchanged. By deciphering the sequence of nucleotides, researchers delineate lines of descent presumably archived in the history of genetic polymorphisms (variations/mutations) as they are passed down from fathers to sons. (The nucleotides are the structural components of DNA, containing four different chemical bases—adenine, cytosine, guanine, and thymine. Deciphering nucleotide sequences means determining the order of the chemical components at any stretch of a given chromosome: A, C, G, T or A, G, C, T, and so forth.)

8. K. Skorecki, M. G. Thomas, K. Skorecki, H. Ben-Ami, T. Parfitt, and N. Bradman, "Y Chromosomes of Jewish Priests," *Nature* 385, no. 6611 (1997): 32–32.

9. Like Cohanim, Levites are a paternally defined group of male Jews who had, according to biblical accounts, responsibilities in religious practice. In Second Temple times, they were understood to be secondary (in status) to the Cohanim.

10. The Cohen modal haplotype, the most common haplotype found in Cohen men, is present in approximately 50 percent of Cohanim (0.449 of the Ashkenazi Cohen sample, and 0.561 of the Sephardic Cohen sample).

11. M. G. Thomas, K. Skorecki, H. Ben-Ami, T. Parfitt, N. Bradman, and D. B. Goldstein, "Origins of Old Testament Priests," *Nature* 394, no. 6689 (1998): 138–39 (emphasis added). This paper also estimates "coalescence time" (the date of origin) for the CMH. While dating plays a key role in much of this genetic historical work, and while it is very inaccurate, for the purposes of this paper I leave it aside.

12. M. G. Thomas, K. Skorecki, H. Ben-Ami, T. Parfitt, N. Bradman, and D. B. Goldstein, "Y Chromosomes Traveling South: The Cohen Modal Haplotype and the Origins of the Lemba—the 'Black Jews of Southern Africa,'" *American Journal of Human Genetics* 66, no. 2 (2000): 675. This was not the first genetic study of the Lemba. That study concluded that Lemba men were of Semitic origin. Moreover, given the "cultural evidence" (practices and rituals that "resemble" Jewish ones), the Lemba were most likely of Judaic origin. See A. B. Spurdle and T. Jenkins, "The Origins of the Lemba 'Black Jews' of Southern Africa: Evidence from p12F2 and Other Y-chromosome Markers," *American Journal of Human Genetics* 59, no. 5 (1996): 1126–1133. The PNAS study sought to test and further refine their conclusions, relying on different genetic techniques to see if they could disentangle a Judaic from a more general Semitic origin.

13. Bruno Latour, *Science in Action: How to Follow Scientists and Engineers Through Society* (Cambridge: Harvard University Press, 1987).

14. Thomas, "Y Chromosomes Traveling South," 685 (emphasis added).

15. Ibid. The evidence on the CMH amongst Lemba men is as follows. The CMH appears in the Lemba male population (as sampled) with a similar frequency to that which occurs in the general Jewish male ("Israelite") population (in just under one out of every ten men). In addition, the CMH was found with a far higher frequency (50 percent) in one particular clan, the Buba (n=13 of whom 7 carried the CMH). (Remember that the CMH shows up in approximately 50 percent of Jewish priests in the 1997 and 1998 studies.) See Skorecki, "Y Chromosomes of Jewish Priests"; and Thomas, "Origins of Old Testament Priests."

16. Neil Bradman, Mark G. Thomas, Michael E. Weale, and David B. Goldstein, "Threads to Antiquity: A Genetic Record of Sex-Specific Demographic Histories of Jewish Populations," in M. Jones, ed., *Traces of Ancestry: Studies in Honour of Colin Renfrew* (Cambridge: McDonald Institute, 2004), 50.

17. FamilyTree DNA, a private genetic genealogical testing company, offers a test for the CMH. It was the first U.S.-based commercial genetic genealogical testing company. Michael Hammer is one of their main scientific consultants and the commercial arm of his laboratory at the University of Arizona runs their samples.

18. This quotation is taken from a speech given by Vivian Moses before the Nineteenth Annual International Association of Jewish Genealogical Societies Annual Meeting. The title of the talk was "Are We All Jacob's Children?" The quotation is taken from a tape recording.

19. There are various streams of Judaism today that recognize paternal descent as the criterion for Jewishness, although under Israeli law the religious question of "Who is a Jew?" depends upon either maternal descent or Orthodox conversion.

20. See Tomoko Masuzawa, *The Invention of World Religions; or, How European Universalism Was Preserved in the Language of Pluralism* (Chicago: University of Chicago Press, 2005).

21. Michael Hammer and several colleagues published a paper in 2009 that reassessed the results of the initial *Nature* papers on the Cohanim. The research-

ers reaffirm their initial conclusion that the CMH (now analyzed in an extended version) originated in the Near East before the dispersion of ancient Jewry, but most contemporary self-identified Cohanim descend not from a single lineage but from "a *limited number of* paternal lineages." M. F. Hammer, D. M. Behar, T. M. Karafet, F. L. Mendez, B. Hallmark, T. Erez, L. A. Zhivotovsky, S. Rosset, K. Skorecki, "Extended Y chromosome Haplotypes Resolve Multiple and Unique Lineages of the Jewish Priesthood," *Human Genetics* 126, no. 5 (2009): 719–724. What effect this new discovery will have on the conclusions of the Lemba study remain to be seen. As far as I know, there is no new study being organized to reassess the conclusions of the original study on the basis of the new data.

22. Quoted in Nadine Epstein, "Family Matters: Funny, We Don't Look Jewish," *Hadassah Magazine* 82, no. 5 (2001).

23. Quoted in Eric Greenberg, "Kohens in Unlikely Places" *Jewish Week* (2002).

24. See Tudor Parfitt and Yulia Erogova'swritings for extended discussions of the impact of this research on Lemba and other communities of presumed lost tribes. Tudor Parfitt, "Constructing Black Jews: Genetic Tests and the Lemba, the 'Black Jews' of South Africa," *Developing World Bioethics* 3, no. 2 (2003): 112–118; Tudor Parfitt and Yulia Erogova, *Genetics, Mass Media, and Identity: A Case Study of the Genetic Research on the Lemba and Bene Israel* (New York: Routledge, 2006).

25. Jack Zeller, *From the President: Proving One's Jewishness* (Silver Spring: Kulanu).

26. Taylor, *The Ethics of Authenticity*, 37.

27. Michel Foucault, *The Archaeology of Knowledge* (New York: Pantheon, 1972).

28. Carolyn Steedman, *Dust* (Manchester: Manchester University Press, 2001).

29. Mary J. Carruthers, *The Book of Memory: A Study of Memory in Medieval Culture* (Cambridge: Cambridge University Press, 1990).

30. In June 2001, a session titled "The Lost Tribes of Israel" was held at the American Museum of Natural History as part of public educational programs organized during the genomics exhibition at the museum. After screening the NOVA video, Karl Skorecki and Tudor Parfitt (two of the primary researchers in this field) were on a panel to discuss the film and their work. I moderated the session. All quotations are taken from a tape-recorded transcript.

31. Yaacov Levi, "Journal from Lemba Lands," *Kulanu* 7 (2000): 13.

32. *Kulanu Newsletter* 7, no. 2. (Summer 2000): 8 (emphasis added).

33. Walter Benn Michaels, "Race Into Culture: A Critical Genealogy of Cultural Identity," *Critical Inquiry* 18, no. 4 (1992): 655–685.

34. See, for example, the difference in statements between Thomas, "Y Chromosomes Traveling South" (published in 2000) and several of the same researchers accounts in the "The Lost Tribes of Israel" documentary.

35. Judith Butler, *Antigone's Claim: Kinship Between Life and Death* (New York: Columbia University Press, 2000).

36. Steven Kaplan, "If There Are No Races, How Can Jews Be a 'Race'?" *Journal of Modern Jewish Studies* 2, no. 1 (2003):79–96.

37. *Kulanu Newsletter* 7, no. 3 (Autumn 2000): 9.

38. Elizabeth A. Povinelli, *The Cunning of Recognition: Indigenous Alterities and the Making of Australian Multiculturalism* (Durham: Duke University Press, 2002), 26–27.

39. Ibid., 26.

40. See Nadia Abu El-Haj, "Rethinking Genetic Genealogy: A Response to Stephan Palmié," *American Ethnologist* 34, no. 2 (2007): 223–26.

41. Quoted in Kaplan, "If There Are No Races," 88–89. Falash Mura had to prove either that they had familial ties to Ethiopian Jews already in Israel or that their family was historically Jewish. As Kaplan points out, "the religious allegiance of the petitioner during the years prior to his or her *aliyah*" was not the determining criterion.

42. *Kulanu Newsletter,* 10, no. 1 (Spring 2003): 5.

43. For a sustained discussion of the Bnei Menashe and Kulanu's cooperation with right-wing messianic settler activists, see Nadia Abu El-Haj, *The Genealogical Science: Genetic History, Jewish Origins, and the Politics of Epistemology* (Chicago: University of Chicago Press, 2012), chapter 6.

3   The Web and the Reunion

http://czernowitz.ehpes.com/

MARIANNE HIRSCH AND LEO SPITZER

"We often visited my mother's exceptionally close and German-speaking family," wrote David Glynn from London in his "personal introduction" to subscribers to the Internet mailing list known as "Czernowitz-L."[1] "To me Czernowitz has always been a familiar concept," he continued, "but I knew absolutely nothing about it. And I could find out nothing about it, since no books in England seemed to make any reference to the Bukowina at all. It was only with the advent of the Internet that Czernowitz began to take a concrete shape in my mind, and I have been amazed by the flood of information to be found there. I am looking forward to the reunion, my first visit to Czernowitz, as an opportunity to understand more of the context from which my family came."[2]

David Glynn's observation about the role of the Internet in concretizing his ancestors' city of origin, and his eager anticipation of a visit to its present-day site as part of a group affiliated with Czernowitz-L, was shared by many on that same mailing list. Indeed, like other such journeys to lost homelands that are also sites of past suffering and persecution, the "return" trip that Czernowitz-L subscribers in 2005 voted on-line to call the "Czernowitz Reunion" emerged from the phenomenally increased availability of the Internet on a worldwide basis over the course of the last decade and its greatly expanded use as a source of information and vehicle of communication.

But can online interaction oriented toward a shared past foster the kind of community—whether virtual, imagined, or embodied—that might legitimately think of participating in a "reunion?" A feminist analysis of the mediations of the Internet sensitive to power structures and their dynamics of inclusion and exclusion is useful for parsing the stakes that a "return" journey to a site of a nostalgic and traumatic past holds for its participants living divergent lives in the present. It can reveal the divisions and inequities that inevitably ensue. We offer the "Czernowitz Reunion" in Ukrainian Chernivtsi (in which we also participated) as a suggestive case study.

The Idea of Czernowitz

In actual fact, of course, the city of Czernowitz can no longer be found in any contemporary atlas. Yet Czernowitz as place and idea has remained very much alive, carried in the memory and imagination of its few surviving Jewish émigrés and their many descendants—of persons like David Glynn and others now scattered throughout the world.[3] The World Wide Web has played a significant role in this. Initially, it was an interest in genealogy and a search for roots relating to the Jewish community of Czernowitz and the nearby Hasidic center, Sadagora, that led to the formation of an informal Internet mailing list in 1997. In 2002 that mailing list was formalized into a moderated listserv, Czernowitz-L. We joined the list at this point, having visited Ukrainian Chernivtsi with Marianne's parents, Carl and Lotte Hirsch, in 1998. As their daughter and son-in-law, and as scholars who had begun work on a book about the afterlife of Czernowitz in Jewish memory, we were particularly interested in the Internet as a site of memory and transmission. Carl and Lotte, already in their eighties but no strangers to e-mail, signed up as well. By 2003, as interest in Czernowitz-L further increased and individual membership subscriptions to it grew, one of its Canadian members, Jerome Schatten, created a Web site for the group (http://czernowitz.ehpes.com) and list members began sending him a variety of materials for upload.

In the years since its formation, list membership has come to include many (perhaps a majority) whose connection to Czernowitz derives only through parents or grandparents. Initially, a few active members still belonged to a generation born in Czernowitz before 1918, Carl Hirsch among them, while a larger contingent, like Lotte Hirsch, had been born in Cernăuți, as the city was renamed after the Bukowina's annexation by Romania in the aftermath of World War I and the dissolution of the Austro-Hungarian Empire. These two native-born groups were largely composed of people who were products of an emancipated and assimilated German-Jewish Eastern European culture that had flourished from the mid-nineteenth century until its shattering and dispersal in the era of World War II. For both, the whole-hearted embrace of the German language, its literature, and the social and cultural standards of the Austro-Germanic world remained core constituents of their identity even during the interwar Romanian years.

But Czernowitz/Cernăuți was also the site where Jews suffered anti-Semitism, internment by fascist Romanians in a ghetto, deportations to Transnistria during World War II, and Soviet annexation. Of the more than sixty thousand Jews who inhabited the city at the start of World War II, only about one-third survived its conclusion. When the bulk of these survivors moved away after the war from the, by then, Soviet-ruled Chernovtsy, they thought it was forever.

With the new availability of the Web, however, opportunities for remembrance, community, and the virtual reconstitution of place came to be unprecedented in scope. Indeed, thanks to the list subscribers, the Czernowitz Web site quickly developed into an invaluable collective digital archive, a repository for memoirs, articles, postcards, maps, family histories, documents, and bibliographic materials—all made easily accessible on a worldwide basis to anyone with access to a computer, an Internet connection, and a Web browser. It became a dynamic, "living," and steadily growing virtual repository. Available to any user at any hour, it permitted casual surfers as well as more systematic researchers public entrée into an immensely rich trove of visual, testimonial, and documentary resources—to a broad range of uploaded informative materials that had been amassed over the years in previously unknown or hard-to-access private holdings and family collections. Documents in German, Yiddish, Russian, or Romanian—in their original languages but, increasingly, also translated into the Web's lingua franca, English—have become broadly accessible for the first time.

Within the site, the reference tools are multiple and easily managed. In addition to a lengthy, albeit critically incomplete and eclectic, reading list, they include a table of "Notable Czernowitzers," a "Family Finder," and an

"Address Finder," listing ancestors of listserv subscribers, their relationship, and their last known residence address in the city—a street address
most often known to them by its German name but also findable (using
the included "Czernowitz Street Name Translator") in its Romanian, Russian, or Ukrainian revisions. Through its "Czernowitz Jewish Cemetery"
link, the Web site also accesses a searchable database that makes graves
findable by name, death date, location, and digital photographic image. It
additionally enables the viewing, downloading, and printing of detailed
maps of the city and region and of a sizable collection of low- and high-
resolution postcards from the Austrian, Romanian, Soviet, and Ukrainian eras.

It is, however, through the many hundreds of photos of people and
places in Czernowitz/Cernăuți from the pre-1945 years, submitted to the
Web site from family albums and private collections, that one gains the
fullest sense of how a notion of Czernowitz, the city and its people, is
shaped in virtual space. Browsing through these, and connecting what
they seem to show with other available information, we can understand
how Czernowitz persists as image and idea in the mind of its present-day
surviving emigrants and their offspring. Picture after picture of persons
and locations within the city reinforce, enhance, and detail a notion of
Czernowitz transmitted visually across time.

Of course, given that many, if not most, of the contributors and subscribers to the Czernowitz-L discussion group and Web site are Jews, it is
largely Jewish Czernowitz—and, to a significant extent, bourgeois Jewish
Czernowitz—that survives in this manner, although many photographs
also include working-class Jews as well as non-Jewish friends, school-
mates, neighbors and coworkers. The predominantly English-language
http://czernowitz.ehpes.com, moreover, also provides links to other regularly maintained Web sites in several other languages and locations—in
Germany, Switzerland, Israel, and the Ukraine—and these, in turn, provide portals to additional resources. Altogether, the various portals and
Web pages establish a digital network, an informational matrix: a series
of chronologically, spatially, and linguistically interconnected and linked
digital pathways that convey a tremendous amount of cultural and historical data about Czernowitz and its subsequent political iterations.

Even so, however, while the ubiquity, numerical abundance, and vast
informative range and quality of items posted to this seemingly ever en-
larging cyberarchive enable richer and more detailed landscapes of memory, the Web page resources exist and remain within the realm of the digi-

tal (even when downloaded and printed), with qualities immanent to that medium. Digital materials, often compressed, cropped, and attenuated, are no more than simulacra. They lack the smells, scale, and tactile physicality of the "real," certainly, but also of the analog originals from which most of them were generated. They are neither objects from the past like their analog sources, nor do they carry traces of human physical touch from the moment when the analog was produced and the intervening years when it was viewed and used. Generally, moreover, they are missing the context in which the analog originals were first collected and displayed in family albums and in private and communal archives.

Despite all of the favorable attributes, therefore, and perhaps because of their extensive availability and ease of use, we would argue that digital images on the Web associated with a lost ancestral home, places like Czernowitz, stimulate a desire for touch. Their very multiplicity and accessibility generate a craving for the haptic—for a connection to the physical world, a longing for the materiality and embodiment of the actual.[4]

As many postings on http://czernowitz.ehpes.com and the Czernowitz-L Internet mailing list illustrate so well, moreover, the use of these sites also tends to foster and facilitate a sense of community and a feeling of shared purpose. In large part, this is due to the fact that list subscribers, no matter where they may actually reside, do share a common interest in the central topic of the list/Web page—in this case, in Czernowitz. Many also have a stake in one or more subtopics: in genealogy, or in historical/cultural details, or in the preservation or renovation of certain sites, the Jewish cemetery, for example. Those shared interests lead users to address each other informally—as "Czernowitzers" on this list—or familiarly, as though they were closely connected or well acquainted. As media critic Andrew Galloway argues, moreover, the digital network itself depends on a structure of "interactivity," a collective "micro-labor performed by the network's user-base . . . a work activity" that consists in clicking, creating files and folders, uploading them, searching for them, sharing them, and, as with Czernowitz-L, discussing them on the listserv.[5] This "interactive . . . work activity," generally unacknowledged, reinforces the participants' sense of belonging to an Internet community—to a social network of acquaintances or "friends."

In actuality, however, these Internet communities are virtual and disembodied sites whose individual subscribing "members" know little, if anything, about each other's past or present lives. And, in the many instances where subscribers do not post photos of themselves (as was true with Czernowitz-L in the 1990s and early 2000s), they remain faceless as well. What happens, therefore, to the notion of community established in digital space when many of its members decide to meet together in actuality? What surfaces in such a gathering? What is transmitted?

The Reunion

In all likelihood, it was the illusion of community fashioned on the Internet, in combination with a yearning for the tactility and materiality of the "actual," that led a number of Czernowitz-L subscribers like David Glynn to propose the organization in 2005 of "a reunion": an "embodied and not virtual," get-together "on the streets where our ancestors lived" (as one list member put it)—in the "wonderful place [that] for decades was . . . lost to us, Czernowitz."[6] Many list members responded enthusiastically to this idea, indicating that, yes, they would be interested in participating in such a gathering and that they would indeed like to "return" to "Czernowitz" in a group journey rather than by themselves or in the company of their families.

After a good deal of online "discussion," participating list members agreed on May 18–25, 2006, as the date of the "reunion." They then elected an organizing committee online and began to address the practicalities of group tourism in Ukraine. Throughout these preparatory stages, all final decisions were negotiated through an elaborate system of online votes. In this respect, the event itself became an online negotiated group project based on a limited knowledge of the personalities and qualifications of members nominated or self-nominated for leadership. But it also took on characteristics of a group pilgrimage—a journey addressing assumedly shared secular and spiritual desires. Through the committee, would-be participants planned for an exploration of key urban sites and monuments associated with Czernowitz's Jewish history, a prayer service at the Chernivtsi Jewish cemetery in the company of the small Jewish community now residing in the city, and a series of meetings, discussions, and memorial events in which the entire group would participate to share reminiscences, honor the past, and assess its persistence in the present. Indeed, in promising participants that their Czernowitz trip would enable them to feel elation from the fact that they would experience—"in the flesh"—physical and cultural sites that a few had remembered from their youth and the rest had only imagined or envisioned, planning for the Czernowitz/Chernivtsi sojourn, as for all pilgrimages, strongly appealed to the senses. It served the need, as Jack Kugelmass has indicated, "to peer behind surface representations to re-experience culture as fully three-dimensional, as real."[7] The divergences between the culture that was remembered or desired by returnees, however, and the city's present reality were not taken seriously into account.

In the course of the organization for this gathering, a number of fundamental questions did not arise. What were participants actually expecting to find on-site? What of the past did they expect to be preserved and reflected in the present-day city? How did they expect to negotiate the divergences between their nostalgic memories of a past "home" and the traumatic recollections of the suffering they or their relatives had endured in the city? And, finally, what did the terminology list subscribers had agreed upon by vote—*to hold a reunion*—actually mean?

Given the generational, geographical, national, linguistic, political, and even religious differences between subscribers and users of Czernowitz-L and the Web site, who (or what community or group) was, in effect, "reuniting"? While none of the participants had actually been alive in pre-World War I Habsburg Czernowitz, a number of them had been born in Cernăuţi in the interwar years and had left the city or region as children or young teenagers after surviving the war. Conceivably, persons belonging to this group might wish to reunite. But the majority of other list members were only indirectly connected to the city—through their parents, relatives, or research interests—and for them the implications of the notion of reunion were much less clear and, in fact, turned out to be problematic.

Sixty-eight participants from nearly a dozen countries in Europe, the Americas, and the Middle East, including the two of us, convened in Chernivtsi representing at least three principal and, in some ways irreconcilable, agendas motivating interest in the gathering:

For the half-dozen or so participants of the "older" generation—persons born in the 1920s or early 1930s in Romanian Cernăuţi—it provided a late-life opportunity for a return-visit-to-place, either by themselves or with their spouses and/or children and grandchildren. In essence, these returnees sought to retrace, revisit, and touch places they associated with their past residence in the city and to transmit accounts of that past, on-site, not only to their offspring but also to other reunion participants. When they did so, we observed, their language of transmission was generally Hebrew or English—the primary spoken languages in the countries where they now resided. But, as we also noted unsurprisingly, everyone in this group could still easily switch into what one of them referred to as "the home language of our youth"—German.

German came less easily to the much larger component within the Reunion group that belonged to what Susan Suleiman has termed the "1.5 generation" who were born in Romanian-ruled Cernăuți or in surrounding villages in the late 1930s or early 1940s. [8] These participants had spent only a few years in the city as very young children before they were deported to Transnistria with their families or, if more fortunate, before they emigrated to new sanctuaries in Europe, Palestine, or the Americas. For individuals in this cohort, the Chernivtsi gathering enabled a material search for roots. Some had lost one or both parents during the war and had come back to look for gravestones or markers in the cemeteries of Czernowitz or Transnistria. The visit provided them with an opportunity for the rediscovery of vaguely remembered or subsequently learned-about childhood sites—family residences, neighborhoods, streets, schools, classrooms, parks, and playgrounds. And it enabled them to search for and reclaim personal documents that had been lost or never formally acquired—birth certificates, certificates of marriage of parents or grandparents, residential or property records. In so doing, it allowed them to certify, in concrete and material fashion, both to themselves and to others, an identity that had been severed from its foundation through expropriation and displacement. The retrieval of documents and addresses, the visit to sites, seemed to compensate momentarily for the vagueness or insufficiency of memory. It seemed to help authenticate, confirm, and detail a past that had haunted them, and for some of them it held out the hope of some form of repair. This promised to be especially true in the context of a group gathering in which memories could be augmented through collective discussion and shared experiences exchanged even among those who did not know each other in their childhood or youth.

Lastly, for the sizable contingent of second- and third-generation participants—the children and grandchildren or nieces and nephews of "Czernowitzers"—born after the war and after their parents or grandparents had emigrated from the city—the gathering provided a related yet different opportunity. Those in this group also viewed the Chernivtsi trip as a chance to "return," but to a world they had never actually known personally. It is this second-generation group within which the two of us also identified. Like those in the "1.5 generation," we too were interested in the discovery and recovery of documents and testaments from archives and official holdings. Yet we also seemed fundamentally driven by a desire to concretize, through direct experience with the city, narratives and images that had been conveyed to us by our parents, parents-in-law, and grandparents over the course of our lives with them. Through this journey, a largely mythic but also profoundly absorbing dimension of a personal identity we had connected to the place and idea of Czernowitz could now become tangible. And we were moved by another desire as well—to bring our parents and grandparents back with us, if not in actuality, then through their words and stories, through the objects they had bequeathed us and the scenes they had so often evoked. Movingly, several second-generation participants brought messages from relatives who were too old to accompany them—excerpts from memoirs they were eager to read aloud to the group, thus conjuring forth their parents and including them within the solidarity of the group.

Return to place for the memorial generation, and coming to place for the postmemorial one among Czernowitz–L users, did thus permit resolution of long-existing material and psychic quests—the yearning to turn virtual Czernowitz, built and detailed from a seemingly limitless digital archive, into a three-dimensional, tactile entity. Returning to and strolling about the city on the Herrengasse, the Ringplatz, Theaterplatz, in the Volksgarten, Jüdisches Haus, the Gymnasia, and university—in places we only knew by their German names—we could situate these in actual physical space, in proper scale, concretely and in color, textured by smells and surrounding sounds.

But even though the return/reunion did enable all this, it was much less successful in evoking the sense of community many had come there to find. Pretrip e-mails had already begun to reveal troubling fissures. Some, for example, had wanted to limit participation only to "Jewish Czernowitzers and their descendants." Spouses of the latter were to be included as well, even if not Jewish, but when a non-Jewish Romanian researcher writing a book about Jewish Czernowitz asked to join the trip, one of the organizers vociferously defended denying access to "outsiders." We were not "objects of study," she insisted, nor would we want onlookers when we might be "moved to tears" at the experience of our "common" past.

Despite the controversy generated in these e-mails, however, the Romanian researcher did come along, joining friends among the participants. But, to the distress of many of us who were deeply disturbed by these exclusions and who initially failed to understand the impulses behind them, the divisive, nasty, exclusionary conflict around her presence continued. The young researcher, we soon saw, became a scapegoat for the objectors, a representative of Romanian anti-Semitism that some participants and most of our ancestors had to suffer, a catalyst for the expression of the very divergent interests and investments in the trip. Arguably, the conflict around her participation became a symptom of the tenuousness of our connection with one another and of our anxiety about our identity as "real Czernowitzers." This unease and sense of competition revolving around identity and authenticity accompanied us through the trip and haunts list-serv communications to this very day: who knows more about Czernowitz and its history, who remembers more accurately, who has more interesting stories to share?

Current inhabitants of Chernivtsi, both Jewish and non-Jewish, presented a different occasion for anxiety and unease. Beyond collecting donations for a Jewish communal and medical organization, most participants in our trip showed little interest in the life ways and situation of Jews now living in the city, almost all of whom were postwar immigrants (or their offspring) from elsewhere in the ex-Soviet Union and thus clearly not "real Czernowitzers." The distance and estrangement was even more intense from the city's current Ukrainian majority. We caught ourselves, and members of our group, relegating these Chernivtsi inhabitants to the background—into a kind of invisibility. Present-day city residents imparted services—in the hotel and restaurants, in shops, as taxi/bus drivers, occasional tour guides and informants, and as providers of access to documentation and other archival resources. But, as Sergij Osatschuk, a Ukrainian Fellow in the Bukowina Research Institute in Chernivtsi, noted about "returnee" visitors to the city: in privileging "Mythos Czernowitz"— an idea of a no longer (and most probably never) existing city—many in our group also tended to regard Chernivtsi's current inhabitants as interlopers in the urban space. Strolling through the center of Chernivtsi, using our old German-language street maps, with old photos overlaying contemporary ones, ordering coffee and apple strudel with *Schlag* in the renovated Café Vienna, we visitors exclaimed positively at the survival of so many Habsburg-era buildings and public spaces. Yet beneath this awe lurked a consistent critique of the present. Osatschuk identifies it well: "the stage set remains, but the actors are no longer present."[9]

Indeed, some in our group even regarded non-Jewish residents in the city with a mixture of apprehension and unease. Because of personal experiences in a few cases, or a more general acquaintance with stories about

pogroms, intense anti-Semitism, and the wartime displacement and murder of Jews with the acquiescence or participation of locals in the population, Ukrainians and the Ukraine still bore a reputation as potentially dangerous. In a couple of instances, participants who held resentments against
Ukrainians expressed a long-internalized anger in denunciatory outbursts
during our group sessions or tours. These aggrieved feelings highlight the
fact that, beside the quest aspect involved in the journey, some persons
might have come to the Ukraine motivated by deep wishes to settle old
scores. Together with the divisions and exclusions and the arguments over
authenticity that marked the trip, they are symptoms of the irreconcilably
divided and contradictory recollections a "return" visit to a site like Czernowitz activates. Trauma and nostalgia, longing and revulsion, sadness
and elation: all these and more are activated by the encounter with a place
that had so far been no more than a memory and an idea generated in virtual space. And, no doubt, they were activated quite differently for different
participants, explaining perhaps the surprising flare-ups in the group.

Imagined Communities

"You must never undertake the search for time lost in the spirit
of nostalgic tourism," Czernowitz's best known non-Jewish German
writer, Gregor von Rezzori, wrote of his own return journey there.[10]
Clearly, given the complicated and fraught relationship of the participants
to "Czernowitz," the "reunion" was more than an instance of nostalgic
tourism. But what, in fact, did it accomplish for those attending the 2006
Reunion and for the reunion group? How did it inflect the memory of
Czernowitz they carry? And how did it connect that memory with life in
present-day Chernivtsi?

The trip did produce many more photos and stories to be posted on the
Web site, more memories and topics to be discussed on the listserv, more
videos to be shared, and more reunions to be planned. While frustration
with the immateriality of the Internet did stimulate the desire for return,
the journey also succeeded in enhancing interest in the Czernowitz Web
site, in expanding its online archive, and in further consolidating the communal connections among the tenuously constructed listserv group.

Even if the actual encounter with the city did not significantly alter
the mythic ideas about Czernowitz that most reunion participants had
brought along with them and that the Internet had helped to enhance and

circulate, the trip did in some ways respond to realities on the ground. In concrete terms, it revealed to participants how much needs to be done to preserve Jewish sites in the city and helped to energize further online discussions among returnees and other list members about how this might be accomplished. Reunion members thus took the lead in raising funds and convincing city authorities to allow the installation of a memorial plaque honoring Traian Popovici, a Romanian mayor who saved almost twenty thousand of the city's Jews from deportation to Transnistria in 1941 and who remains virtually unknown in this Ukrainian city. Many also attempted to bring about the restoration of the shockingly neglected Jewish cemetery: they raised funds, engaged international volunteer clean-up groups, and hired local workers for this daunting job. The return, moreover, gave participants a renewed interest in the city—an involvement, for example, in contemporary events such as the Chernivtsi six hundredth anniversary celebrations that were held in fall 2008. In this regard, much of their energy was concentrated in efforts to gain acknowledgment and recognition for the rich cultural and material impact that Jews had on this city's identity over the course of its past two centuries.

These acts of engagement continue. But they have not yet succeeded in producing a fuller connection between "returnee Czernowitzers" and present-day inhabitants of the city. Communities forged in virtual space through identification with an idea of a past that is remembered both nostalgically and traumatically remain tenuously constituted. Group feeling may be especially precious and thus also fragile, in need of being reinforced through repeated performances of belonging that depend on exclusions and boundaries—boundaries based on common memories, legacies, and experiences. In the case of "Czernowitz," where populations shifted and the identities of perpetrators, bystanders, and rescuers are multiple and contested, "returnees" may have special difficulties trusting the city's inhabitants, acknowledging their lives, and including them as fellow "Czernowitzers." Sadly, therefore, although we all have stakes and responsibilities toward the very same urban space, there is, for now, still more that divides than unites us.

Notes

1. An earlier version of this essay appeared as part of a chapter in Marianne Hirsch and Leo Spitzer, *Ghosts of Home: The Afterlife of Czernowitz in Jewish*

Memory, (Berkeley: University of California Press, 2010). For another account of the reunion trip see Florence Heymann, "Tourisme des mémoires blessées. Traces de Transnistrie," *L'Horreur oubliée: La Shoah roumaine. Revue de d'histoire de la Shoah* 194 (January/June 2011), 319–342.

2. David Glynn, "Postings from 2006: Introductions," http://czernowitz .ehpes.com.

3. For accounts of the history of Czernowitz, see Hirsch and Spitzer, *Ghosts of Home*; Hugo Gold, ed., *Geschichte der Juden in der Bukowina.* 2 vols (Tel Aviv: Oleamenu, 1962); Florence Heymann, *Le Crépuscule des lieux: Identités juives de Czernowitz* (Paris: Seuil, 2002).

4. For a detailed discussion of the term *haptic* in art history and media theory, see Laura U. Marks, *Touch: Sensuous Theory and Multisensory Media* (Minneapolis: University of Minnesota Press, 2002), esp. "Introduction" and chapter 1.

5. Alexander R. Galloway, "Three Middles," unpublished paper, presented to the Columbia University Faculty Seminar on the Theory and History of Media, November 2009.

6. See correspondence regarding reunion trip in Cz-L Archives, comments posted March-December 2005, http://czernowitz.ehpes.com.

7. Jack Kugelmass, "The Rites of the Tribe: American Jewish Tourism in Poland," in Ivan Karp, Christine Mullen Kreamer, Steven D. Lavine, eds., *Museums and Communities: The Politics of Public Culture* (Washington, DC: Smithsonian Institution Press, 1992), 401–403.

8. On the "1.5 generation" see Susan Suleiman, *Crises of Memory and the Second World War* (Cambridge: Harvard University Press, 2006).

9. Sergij Osatschuk, "Czernowitz heute und der Umgang mit dem gemeinsamen kulturellen Erbe," http://www.czernowitz.de/index.php?page=seiten& seite=55.

10. Gregor von Rezzori, *The Snows of Yesteryear: Portraits for an Autobiography* (New York: Vintage International, 1989), 290.

4   Queering Roots, Queering Diaspora

JARROD HAYES

This essay tells the story of a number of returns: returns, like Alex Haley's *Roots*, to the origins of diasporic identities, returns that mess up or queer the paradigm Haley establishes, and a return to the queer roots of deconstruction as an allegory for the very roots narrative it deconstructs.[1] By reading Jacques Derrida as an Algerian writer whose Jewish roots keep returning in his more autobiographical writings, it is possible to understand deconstruction as, in part, an allegory for diasporic identity. By reading his works alongside those of other French-language Sephardic writers like Albert Memmi, one can also return to the Jewish African roots of deconstruction. As a part of Africa, the Maghreb has its own diaspora, part of which is Jewish; the Maghreb thus has a unique contribution to make to the field of diaspora studies. In the Maghreb, Jewish and African diasporas intersect and overlap, and the Maghrebian Jewish diaspora is just as African as it is Jewish. Through a more extended engagement with the Maghreb, specifically, and Francophone studies more generally, diaspora studies can not only return to its own roots but also queer them. Indeed, even the queer subfield of diaspora studies that has emerged since the late nineties can be further queered through such a return to the Jewish Maghreb.

If Haley's *Roots* can be read as a paradigm for understanding roots narratives, such narratives are nonetheless characterized by several interrelated paradoxes. The first paradox is political: whereas a return to roots attempts to remedy the alienation resulting from a historical uprooting, an assertion of roots can as easily justify oppression by excluding those considered not to share them. The second is narrative: whereas roots narratives claim merely to discover an origin that preexists the search for and so-called discovery of roots, the telling of the story effectively creates the origins and the identity rooted in them. The third is sexual: whereas roots narratives frequently rely on a patrilineal family tree structured by heterosexual marriage and reproduction and would therefore seem to exclude queerness, African and Caribbean writers, among others, frequently find a diversity of sexual practices and identifications upon returning to roots. While the writers examined herein are *not* homosexual, their return narratives queer the relation between diasporic identity and its roots by acknowledging their own fictionality. They simultaneously challenge the heterosexuality of the family tree that typically structures return narratives and propose alternative, multiple roots that ground an identity based on not only sexual diversity, but also diversity in general. Queer roots, in these accounts, thereby challenge the patrilineal lines of descent implied by roots by disrupting the linear process of storytelling that constitutes identity.

Maryse Condé's novel *Crossing the Mangrove* (*Traversée de la mangrove*), though set in the Caribbean and not the Maghreb, offers a helpful point of departure in that it illustrates these three paradoxes along with their interconnectedness.[2] This novel begins in a Guadeloupean village with the discovery of a body, that of its central character Francis Sancher, whose story is told by different villagers. Indeed, the jumble of competing versions of Francis's life parallels the jumble of roots in a mangrove swamp, which offer an alternative image to the single, unitary root promoted by Afrocentric understandings of Caribbean identity and thereby highlight its multiple origins. In addition, Condé gives the mangrove a queer twist in the rumors spread by other characters about a homosexual relationship between Francis and a Haitian buddy. Finally, that *makoumè*, the Creole word for "sissy faggot" that Condé uses to describe this rumored relationship, is also the word for a "gossiping woman" and links questions of sexuality to the novel's gossiplike structure where there is no beginning or end to the story of Francis's life, no cause-and-effect explanations that could fit into and be strengthened by such a chronological order. *Crossing the Mangrove* thus also serves as an example of how queer roots can disrupt the linear process of storytelling that constitutes identity and thereby disrupts the *structure* of the roots narrative as well.[3]

Through Condé, we can go back and reread Haley, too, as mangrovelike.[4] Indeed, Haley's novel actually consists of two parallel narratives, both of which take the form of trajectories or journeys. The first begins in an Africa of the past, ends in present-day America, and is the story of Kunta Kinte and his descendants. Its trajectory is that of the middle passage, of an uprooting. The second narrative proceeds in the opposite direction, both geographically and temporally. It begins in America and is the story of *retracing* the family tree and of *telling* Kunta Kinte's story; it is the story of a quest for, then discovery of, roots, of a rerooting through the *writing* of a narrative. In this second narrative, origins are an end not a beginning; they are the result of the search (or the story of the search), not its starting point or cause. In a subtle way, therefore, *Roots* thus actually suggests the writtenness of roots, and, in its bidirectional structure, it is as much about diaspora as about African origins. Originally used to describe Jewish (or Greek or Armenian) dispersal, the notion of diaspora was adopted by descendents of African slaves imported to the new world to position themselves in relation to their roots. The African American spiritual "Go Down Moses (Let My People Go)," about the captivity of the Israelites in Egypt, is but one classic example of an African American identification with the Jewish diaspora. In this earlier career, *diaspora* was used to stress connections between African Americans and their African roots in a Pan-African approach to African American studies.

In contrast, it has become fashionable of late to cast roots and diaspora as polar opposites. Yogita Goyal has articulated this distinction between earlier and more recent approaches to diaspora particularly clearly: "Theorists in cultural studies routinely invoke diaspora as a syncretized configuration of cultural identity: shifting, flexible, and invariably anti-essentialist. This notion pointedly revises an earlier definition of diaspora structured by a teleology of origin, scattering, and return. While these older conceptions of diaspora posited an organic link to Africa and imagined both symbolic and actual returns to the homeland, the new one focuses on displacement itself, maintaining that the lack of mooring in national or racial certitudes generates anti-essentialist identities."[5] Yet, so stark a contrast would be misleading if one tried to use it to characterize the revision of the concept of diaspora in black British cultural studies during the late eighties. From Paul Gilroy to Kobena Mercer to Stuart Hall, roots would remain important to theorizations of diaspora, even when these very theorizations of diaspora also challenged notions of rooted identity.[6] Paul Gilroy's *Black Atlantic* (1993), for example, one of the most frequently cited texts in diaspora studies, stresses the importance of both roots and routes—of African origins and the crisscrossing of the Atlantic—in defining black identity.

Since the beginning of the nineties, uses of the term *diaspora* have exploded.[7] As early as 1997, however, David L. Eng considered potential tensions between queer studies and the increasing popularity of the concept of diaspora in Asian American studies by listing reasons why the home or roots upon which diaspora relies as a concept might be inhospitable to queers so that "queer entitlements to home and a nation-state remain doubtful."[8] In an even earlier and often-cited work in diaspora studies, Stefan Helmreich (1992) offered an explanation as to why such a inhospitality might define the very structure of diaspora, because the term *diaspora* carries the sexual implications "of scattered seeds . . . metaphorical for the male 'substance' that is traced in genealogical histories. . . . The word 'sperm' is etymologically connected to diaspora . . . [which] thus refers us to a system of kinship reckoned through men and suggests the questions of legitimacy in paternity that patriarchy generates."[9] James Clifford's assertion that "diasporic experiences are always gendered" is thus quite an understatement.[10] In other words, the very concept of diaspora implies a heterosexual, masculinist, and patrilineal definition of the relation between a diasporic community and its roots, so that, to refer back to the sexual paradox described at the beginning of this essay, in its heterosexuality, the concept of diaspora may not differ that much from roots.

Nonetheless, very quickly after Eng's critique, the concept of diaspora became a productive one for an emerging body of work at the intersection of queer theory, on the one hand, and, on the other, postcolonial studies as well as what some have called "queer of color critique."[11] The term *queer diaspora* quickly followed.[12] Drawing on Helmreich's work, for example, Gayatri Gopinath proposes the concept of queer diaspora to "challenge postcolonial diasporic narratives that imagine diaspora and nation through the tropes of home, family, and community that are invariably organized around heteronormative, patriarchal authority" and to enable "a simultaneous critique of heterosexuality and the nation form while exploding the binary oppositions between nation and diaspora, heterosexuality and homosexuality, original and copy."[13] Gopinath therefore goes beyond the presence of same-sex desires and sexual practices in diasporic cultures not only to queer diaspora as a concept but also to diasporize, so to speak, as a mode of queering the nation.

In the introduction to their collection *Queer Diasporas* (2000), Cindy Patton and Benigno Sánchez-Eppler also offer a number of reflections that helped to define some key concepts of the then emerging subfield by rooting an account of queer diaspora in one of the earliest narrations of dispersals, that of Adam and Eve from Eden, by reading Genesis as a foundation myth for heterosexuality: "The simultaneity of the expulsion from Eden and the installation of heterosexuality suggest that Western sexual and diasporal discourses are fundamentally, if anxiously, related."[14] It is perhaps through a slip that Patton and Sánchez-Eppler conflate pre-lapsarian paradise with the promised land as the site of prediasporic origins, but this confusion might nonetheless serve as a productive reminder that "the biblical story is not one of autochthony but one of always already coming from somewhere else."[15] That is, there is not a before the dispersal except in a mythical origin that is always already marked as unobtainable, unreconstitutable. The Boyarins make this point in their jointly authored "Diaspora: Generation and the Ground of Jewish Identity," in which they propose an alternative, biblically based "genealogy" of Jewish identity that uses diaspora to counter Zionism and sees diaspora and connection with a homeland as totally compatible.[16] The convergence of their argument with Patton and Sánchez-Eppler's underscores the affinity between what James Clifford calls their "*diasporist* anti-Zionism"[17] and Daniel Boyarin's own contribution to queer diaspora studies.[18]

A single scene from a 1953 Jewish Tunisian novel is especially useful for highlighting the queer potential of diaspora to disrupt Zionism. The narrative of Albert Memmi's *Pillar of Salt* (*La statue de sel*) is framed as the childhood memories that its narrator Alexandre Mordekhaï Benillouche remembers while taking an exam.[19] A particular chapter, entitled "At the Kouttab School" ("Au Kouttab," referring to Hebrew school), offers a mise en abyme of this retrospective structure when Alexandre, after witnessing a peculiar scene in a Tunis streetcar as a high school student, looks back on an earlier childhood episode within the overall analepsis of the novel (which, after all, takes its title from the consequences Lot's wife suffers upon *looking back* on a burning Sodom). In the streetcar episode, a grocer from the island of Djerba (known for its historically large Jewish population) singles out a two-year-old Muslim boy for teasing after inquiring whether he is circumcised. When the boy's father says no, the grocer attempts to "purchase" the boy's penis at higher and higher prices and thereby separate it from him. After a series of more and more adamant refusals, he reaches into the boy's pants and pretends to snatch his penis without paying. In this lesson of defending his penis against the threat of castration, the little boy learns to fight for the male privileges that his penis signifies by fighting off the castrating aggressor.

In the streetcar, Alexandre identifies with the boy across ethno-confessional lines to such an extent that he experiences a physical sensation of both pain and pleasure in his penis, which he assumes to be the same as what the little boy is feeling. This sensation, like that evoked by the Proustian *madeleine*, revives an identical feeling from his much earlier past, thereby bringing an entire scene into the present. One day at the *kouttab*, after the rabbi leaves the room, a class of boys decides to stage a circumcision ceremony. They choose the smallest among them to be circumcised, and, yet again, a younger Alexandre identifies with the frightened victim so totally that he experiences the very same fear. He again experiences this identification as a physical sensation at the site of his own penis, which tingles with excitement. This scene ends climactically, and quite literally so, since the older Alexandre describes his own reaction as an explosion of *jouissance*.

Initially, I focused on the implications for *Tunisian* nationalism of the interconfessional identifications and homoeroticism this scene brings into play.[20] I argued that the Jewish jouissance (what Daniel Boyarin calls "Jewissance"), revived in *The Pillar of Salt* through this return to roots in memory, can contest a politics of purity that would define the Maghrebian nation as solely Arab and Muslim.[21] Now I have come to see the implications of the same scene in relation to *Israeli* as opposed to Tunisian nationalism in order to contest Memmi's later, explicitly pro-Zionist essays in support of a Jewish right of return to Israel as a Jewish state.[22] In particular, the pleasure that Alexandre takes in reviving physical pleasure experienced at a moment of fear, the fear of castration, recalls a centuries-old Jewish reaction to the anti-Semitic feminization of Jewish men.[23] Rather than attempting to conform to Gentile masculinity, this reaction often consisted in a rejection of it, until, that is, the emergence of Zionism in the nineteenth century.[24] It is precisely this rejection of masculinity, this pleasure in emasculation, that Zionism has sought to counter in the impulse exemplified by Max Nordau's figure of the "Muscle-Jew." For inasmuch as the Zionism that led to the Israeli state claims to return the nation of Israel to the promised land, it is not merely a return to roots; it is also a narrative of progress, of gendered progress, which requires the masculinization of its men in relation to European nations.

Whereas Memmi advocates a physical return to Palestine in his political writings, in his novels he returns to queer roots planted in a predominantly Arab nation, roots both Jewish *and* Arab, which are just as intertwined as those of Condé's mangrove. Such a queering of the roots of diaspora thus distinguishes Memmi's novels from his Zionist essays. For, no matter how many Zionist essays Memmi pens, the emasculated "Oriental" penis of his first novel (*Oriental* being Memmi's word) will always come back to haunt the gendered politics of Zionism as described by critics like Daniel Boyarin and resisted by both Daniel and Jonathan Boyarin in their more explicitly political writings.[25] This penis also queers diasporist anti-Zionism, of which the Boyarins and Ammiel Alcalay serve as prime examples for Clifford in their assertion of the diasporic nature of Jewish identity as a basis for a critique of Israeli nationalism, especially in relation to the Palestinian question.[26]

Memmi's peculiar relation to the roots of diaspora also constitutes a useful point of comparison with the models of queer diaspora that have been proposed to date. For Gopinath, retrieving a queer South Asian diaspora leads directly to queering the nation because of the compatibility of nationalism and diaspora in the hegemonic models of diasporism she critiques, in which "queerness is to heterosexuality as the diaspora is to the nation." In other words, Gopinath argues, within the nationalist discourses of the South Asian diaspora elite, "if within heteronormative logic the queer is seen as the debased and inadequate copy of the heterosexual, so too is diaspora within nationalist logic positioned as the queer Other of the nation, its inauthentic imitation."[27] Yet, because of what Ella Shohat calls "the Zionist rejection of the Diaspora,"[28] in Zionist discourses diaspora may haunt the nation differently than in other contexts. In Israel certain secular contexts (the military, for example) can be relatively hospitable to lesbians and gays in a way that is entirely compatible with Zionist logic. Here gay roots are neither queer nor do they necessarily alter the relation between roots and diaspora. Likewise, in spite of a Zionist desire to eradicate the diaspora, not all forms of Jewish diasporism are as anti-Zionist as Shohat's, Alcalay's, or the Boyarins'; in fact, Israel's Zionist policies receive crucial support from some parts of the diaspora. Yet, the specific example of Memmi allows us to understand how it is not only the case that queerness can be found within the Jewish diaspora but also that diaspora can be understood as having, in some instances, an antagonistic relation with the Israeli nation. Rather than simply queering the Israeli state, therefore, Memmi's novelistic queering of the Jewish diaspora challenges the territorial claims made by Zionist roots narratives.

This comparison, therefore, between Memmi's diasporic fiction and the queer South Asian diaspora that Gopinath theorizes, already highlights a certain instability with regard to the relation *of* roots and diaspora. Some diasporic discourses presume stable roots that can ground a stable identity. Others promote diaspora as a destabilization of any roots that might ground identity in a homogenized community whose purity could thereby be policed. It is because of differences like these that a number of scholars in diaspora studies have advocated a comparative approach to the field.[29] Since, as a part of "overlapping diasporas" (i.e., both an African and a Jewish one), Jewish Maghrebian literature in French is doubly diasporic,[30] it offers an ideal site for bringing diasporas into comparison while nonetheless retaining careful attention to the specificities of individual diasporic cultures. In carrying out such a comparatist practice, one is better positioned to seek answers to a number of questions that might be considered fundamental to any attempt to define the field of queer diaspora studies: Where is the queer in queer diaspora or roots? Does one have to queer roots in order to queer diaspora? or vice versa? Does the one necessarily lead to the other? Will queering diaspora entail queering roots in every diasporic context? Is either diaspora or roots inherently queer in relation to the other?

If there can be no roots without diaspora, and, likewise, no diaspora without roots, queering roots or diaspora must occur somewhere in the dialogic relation between the two.[31] More specifically, this critical move is related to a structural peculiarity of the narrative moves necessary to connect a diaspora to its roots, a peculiarity that is in fact precisely what I have called the narrative paradox: roots narratives narrate a "return" to a prior "origin" that is actually *not* prior since it is an *effect* of the narration, not its cause and thus not actually an origin. The narrative itself can therefore only be considered a return if the notion of return is complicated, along with the notions of priorness, origins, and roots. Queer roots, in other words, are origins that are not original; queer diasporas exist through "returns" to these origins-that-are-not-origins. This defining aporia at the heart of roots narratives can also be likened to the deconstruction of origins most succinctly articulated by Jacques Derrida in *Of Grammatology*: "The trace is not only the disappearance of origin . . . it means that the origin did not even disappear, that it was never constituted except reciprocally by a nonorigin, the trace, which thus becomes the origin of the origin."[32]

In *Writing and Difference*, Derrida would explain this aporia only slightly differently: "The writing of the origin, the writing that retraces the origin, tracking down the signs of its disappearance, the lost writing of the origin. . . . But what disposes it in this way, we now know, is not the origin, but that which takes its place; which is not, moreover, the opposite of an origin. It is not absence instead of presence, but a trace which replaces a presence which has never been present, an origin by means of which nothing has begun."[33] It might then seem that, from this perspective, roots narratives would be impossible or, at the least, acts of bad faith. Indeed, in the more recent *Monolinguisme de l'autre*, Derrida asserts that any autobiographical act relies on a return to roots whose deconstruction means that it necessarily involves the writing of a fiction:

> In its common concept, autobiographical anamnesis presupposes *identification*. And precisely not identity. No, an identity is never given, received, or attained; only the interminable and indefinitely phantasmatic process of identification endures. Whatever the story of a return to oneself or to *one's home* [*chez-soi*], into the "hut" ["*case*"] of one's home (*chez* is the *casa*), no matter what an odyssey or bildungsroman it might be, in whatever manner one invents the story of a construction of the *self*, the *autos*, or the *ipse*, it is always *imagined* that the one who writes should know how to say *I*.[34]

Nonetheless, in spite of the fact that return narratives create their origins retrospectively, *Monolingualism* carries out exactly what it claims is impossible. For, in this very text, Derrida returns to his own Algerian Jewish roots through an autobiographical account of his relation to the French language. In spite of Derrida's deconstruction of origins, therefore, origins keep coming back whenever the autobiographical appears in his writing.

Furthermore, the passage just quoted from *Writing and Difference*, itself remarkably similar to the passage from *Of Grammatology*, appears as part of Derrida's analysis of the work of another North African Jew, Edmond Jabès, whose intersecting diasporas he shares to a certain extent. Is it a coincidence that Jabès's *Book of Questions* preceded Derrida in questioning rootedness as signified by a site of origins?[35] This shared critique extends into the realm of political discourse in Jabès's diasporist understanding of the expression *people of the Book,* by which "the Book" becomes both the homeland of the diaspora and the promised land to which return narratives can make "territorial" claims. If such a roots narrative can be characterized as Zionist, in its acknowledgment of the narrative paradox, it is indeed a queer Zionism. Derrida would echo this queering of Zionism in his reading of Jabès, in which he also writes, "The return . . . does not retake possession of something. It does not reappropriate the origin."[36] I suggest that this sentence be read as rejecting Zionist territorial claims.

One of the reasons why Derrida and Jabès—like Memmi, and Condé—can be said to queer both roots and diaspora is that they all bring the narrative paradox out of the closet. Yet, if this were the only reason, *queer* here would only be queer in a rather abstract way, far too removed from the critique of sexual normativity that has proved to be the strength of queering as an analytical move. Like Condé and Memmi, however, in queering roots and diaspora, Derrida outs not only the narrative paradox but also the sexual one, both of which are just as intertwined in Derrida's writing as in Condé's mangrove. *Jacques Derrida,* for example, which Derrida jointly authored with Geoffrey Bennington and includes another of Derrida's Algerian roots narratives ("Circumfessions"), contains a photograph alluding to the eponymous image of *The Post Card,* which Derrida claims depicts Plato and Socrates engaging in intercrural intercourse.[37] The photograph in *Jacques Derrida* replaces Socrates with Derrida, who is sitting in front of Bennington (in Plato's place), which implies that Derrida is taking it in the behind from Bennington, who becomes his sexual top.[38] These "positions" parallel those of the two men's texts on the pages of *Jacques Derrida*: Derrida's at the bottom beneath Bennington's on top.

Furthermore, as with Memmi, "Circumfessions" returns Derrida to the moment of his circumcision, with the result that his circumcised penis becomes a figure for his Jewish Algerian roots. Unlike the numerous representations of circumcision in Franco-Maghrebian fiction that return to circumcision in memory only to bring it back as trauma, Derrida's discussion evokes a jouissance that parallels Memmi's. Reading Derrida's penis through the model provided by Memmi, then, allows us to understand that, when Derrida's penis enters his writing, it stands as a site for his emasculation consistent not with the erection of phallogocentrism but with its deconstruction. A similar emasculation occurs when he lavishes so much attention on Jean Genet's penis in *Glas,* which also contains an important reference to a synagogue from Derrida's childhood.[39] In general, *Glas* consists of two simultaneous readings, one of Genet, on the right, another of Hegel, on the left. As the reader turns each page, Genet's literal penises rub up against Hegel's erections (Derrida's understanding of the *Aufhebung* or raising up or synthesis of the dialectic), thereby making Memmi's "Jewissance" seem tame in comparison. Yet erections are not only turned inside out (invaginated) but also cut short through castration.[40] Given Derrida's propensity for playing with penises, how could one not associate the homoerotic elements with the critique of phallogocentrism in his earlier, more conventionally philosophical writing? Since this critique cannot eliminate the phallus, it literalizes it in a move that is both homoerotic and emasculating.[41] In Lacanian terms, if the phallus must be veiled to function as such, Derrida unveils it.

With so many penises on the pages of Derrida's writing, one might wonder whether, instead of deconstructing phallogocentrism as I have suggested, these penises reinforce a phallic order from which they cannot be dissociated.[42] Indeed, in psychoanalytic discourses especially, castration might be considered that which *founds* masculinity, not that which undoes it. While my comments on Derrida's penises might seem at first glance to contradict feminist critiques of such understandings of castration, it is my hope that they will instead contribute to a response to second-wave feminist Germaine Greer's call, first made about forty years ago but arguably still relevant today: "Women must humanize the penis, take the steel out of it and make it flesh again."[43] I also hope that my comments here might contribute to feminist writing about the penis[44] as well as to the already rich engagement with Derrida on the part of a number of feminists.[45]

If Helmreich understands diaspora as an *in*semination whose root is the penis qua phallus, Derrida might be said to offer an alternative understanding best characterized as a *dissemination*, another key term within Derrida's understanding of writing: "Numerical multiplicity . . . serves as a pathbreaker for 'the' seed, which therefore produces (itself) and advances only in the plural. It is a singular plural, which no single origin will ever have preceded. Germination, dissemination. There is no first insemination. The semen is already swarming. The 'primal' insemination is dissemination. A trace, a graft whose traces have been lost."[46] Derrida thus scatters his seeds not in service of the reproduction of heteronormative models of homeland, diaspora, and the relation between the two, but to sow a diasporic model of identity through a queer return to roots in writing. Along with the death knell of phallogocentrism that tolls in

Glas (which, although not translated in the English version, means death knell),[47] the key concept of dissemination in Derrida's writing might be read as a queerer model of diaspora than what Helmreich offers. When read alongside Derrida's treatment of his body in its more material manifestations, the penis that has been instituted as a kind of root for diaspora—that which disseminates it—turns out to be a cultural artifact that can be written in multiple ways, some of which consist of cutting into the very "thing" that is written. Commonly considered to be the origin or root of masculinity, its writing/cutting can also sever the very link it is usually considered to institute.

If Derrida's earliest writings carry out a deconstruction of origins, his more recent autobiographical writing literalizes those origins as his own Jewish Algerian roots. If de Man characterizes every narrative as an allegory of reading that is also an allegory of its own deconstruction, Derrida has instead inverted the de Manian hierarchy by retrospectively providing the more literal autobiographical narratives that allegorize his earlier, more abstract deconstruction of origins.[48] Derrida's queer roots thus appear as having already been deconstructed; they disseminate impossible origins and can be planted only in diaspora. Derrida's own rites of return thus take us back not only to his Jewish Algerian roots but also to the Jewish roots of diaspora as a concept. These roots help us to queer diaspora in part by understanding it as a deconstructivist dissemination that is both theoretical and literally sexual. Yet the heteromasculinist associations behind the literal image that figures diaspora as a sowing of seeds are nonetheless resisted in a manner consistent with the diasporic tradition of the emasculated Jewish man, described by Boyarin and Eilberg-Schwartz, in which Jewish, queer, and diasporic are as inextricably linked as the roots of a mangrove.

Notes

1. Alex Haley, *Roots: The Saga of an American Family* (New York: Bantam, 1976).

2. Maryse Condé, *Traversée de la mangrove* (Paris: Mercure de France, 1989), trans. As *Crossing the Mangrove* by Richard Philcox (New York: Doubleday, 1995).

3. For more developed versions of this reading of Condé, see Jarrod Hayes, "Looking for Roots Among the Mangroves: *Errances enracinées* and Migratory Identities," *Centennial Review* 42, no. 3 (1998): 459–474, and "Créolité's Queer

Mangrove," in Timothy J. Reiss, ed., *Music, Writing and Cultural Unity in the Caribbean* (Trenton, NJ: Africa World Press, 2005), 307–332.

4. In "Routes: Alex Haley's *Roots* and the Rhetoric of Genealogy," *Transition* 64 (1994): 21, David Chioni Moore teases the mangroves out of *Roots*.

5. Yogita Goyal, "Theorizing Africa in Black Diaspora Studies: Caryl Phillips' *Crossing the River*," *Diaspora* 12, no. 1 (2003): 5.

6. Paul Gilroy, *There Ain't No Black in the Union Jack: The Cultural Politics of Race and Nation* (Chicago: University of Chicago Press, 1987); Kobena Mercer, "Diaspora Culture and the Dialogic Imagination: The Aesthetics of Black Independent Film in Britain" (1988), in Jana Evans Braziel and Anita Mannur, eds., *Theorizing Diaspora: A Reader* (Oxford: Blackwell, 2003), 247–260, and "Black Art and the Burden of Representation," *Third Text* 10 (1990): 61–78; Stuart Hall, "Cultural Identity and Diaspora" (1990), in Nicholas Mirzoeff, ed., *Diaspora and Visual Culture: Presenting Africans and Jews* (London: Routledge, 2000), 21–33; and Gilroy, *The Black Atlantic: Modernity and Double Consciousness* (Cambridge: Harvard University Press, 1993).

7. For an overview of the field of diaspora studies, see Braziel and Mannur, *Theorizing Diaspora*. See also James Clifford, "Diasporas," *Cultural Anthropology* 9, no. 3 (1994): 302–338; and Brent Hayes Edwards, "The Uses of *Diaspora*," *Social Text* 19, no. 1 (2001): 45–73.

8. David L. Eng, "Out Here and Over There: Queerness and Diaspora in Asian American Studies," *Social Text* 52/53 (1997): 32.

9. Stefan Helmreich, "Kinship, Nation, and Paul Gilroy's Concept of Diaspora," *Diaspora* 2, no. 2 (1992): 245.

10. Clifford, "Diasporas," 313.

11. See, especially, Roderick A. Ferguson, *Aberrations in Black: Toward a Queer of Color Critique* (Minneapolis: University of Minnesota Press, 2003).

12. The first use of this term, as far as I can tell, appears in Gayatri Gopinath's 1998 dissertation, "Queer Diasporas: Gender, Sexuality, and Migration in Contemporary South Asian Literature and Cultural Production" (Columbia University, 1998), of which a revised version was published in 2005 as *Impossible Desires: Queer Diasporas and South Asian Public Cultures* (Durham: Duke University Press, 2005). A year after Gopinath's dissertation, Lawrence M. La Fountain-Stokes also used the term *queer diaspora* in his dissertation, "Culture, Representation, and the Puerto Rican Queer Diaspora" (Columbia University, 1999), published as *Queer Ricans: Cultures and Sexualities in the Diaspora* (Minneapolis: University of Minnesota Press, 2009). Since then, several other queer single-diaspora studies have joined the book versions of Gopinath's and La Fountain-Stokes's dissertations to round out queer diaspora studies as a vibrant subfield: Martin F. Manalansan IV, *Global Divas: Filipino Gay Men in the Diaspora* (Durham: Duke University Press, 2003); and Jana Evans Braziel, *Artists, Performers, and Black Masculinity in the Haitian Diaspora* (Bloomington: Indiana University Press, 2008).

13. Gopinath, *Impossible Desires*, 68, 11.

14. Cindy Patton and Benigno Sánchez-Eppler, eds., *Queer Diasporas* (Durham: Duke University Press, 2000), 2.

15. Daniel Boyarin and Jonathan Boyarin, "Diaspora: Generation and the Ground of Jewish Identity," *Critical Inquiry* 19, no. 4 (1993): 715.

16. For the purposes of this essay, I would like to leave the definition of *anti-Zionism* as open as possible. Discursively, I take this term to mean at the least a critique of any roots narrative that would justify the establishment of the state of Israel as a *return* to territory to which Jewish immigrants would have an a priori or God-given right. Politically, I hope this term would allow for a variety of positions, not all of which necessarily involve the denial of Israel's "right" to continue to exist as a post-Zionist state. (I nonetheless must add that I find pronouncements that such a state already exists to be extremely premature.)

17. Clifford, "Diasporas," 326.

18. See Daniel Boyarin, "Outing Freud's Zionism, or the Bitextuality of the Diaspora Jew," in Patton and Sánchez-Eppler, *Queer Diasporas*, 71–104.

19. Albert Memmi, *La statue de sel*, 1953 (Paris: Gallimard, 1966), trans. as *The Pillar of Salt* by Edouard Roditi (New York: Criterion, 1955).

20. See Jarrod Hayes, *Queer Nations: Marginal Sexualities in the Maghreb* (Chicago: University of Chicago Press, 2000), 243–255, 277–286.

21. Daniel Boyarin, *Unheroic Conduct: The Rise of Heterosexuality and the Invention of the Jewish Man* (Berkeley: University of California Press, 1997), xxiii.

22. For this second reading, see Hayes, "Circumcising Zionism, Queering Diaspora: Reviving Albert Memmi's Penis," *Wasafiri* 22, no. 1 (2007): 6–11. For Memmi's Zionist writings, see especially *La libération du Juif* (Paris: Gallimard, 1966) and *Juifs et Arabes* (Paris: Gallimard, 1974).

23. See Sander Gilman, *The Jew's Body* (New York: Routledge, 1991).

24. See Howard Eilberg-Schwartz, *God's Phallus and Other Problems for Men and Monotheism* (Boston: Beacon, 1994); and Boyarin, *Unheroic Conduct*.

25. E.g., Boyarin and Boyarin, "Diaspora."

26. Clifford, "Diasporas," 325–26. See Boyarin and Boyarin, "Diaspora"; and Ammiel Alcalay, *After Jews and Arabs: Remaking Levantine Culture* (Minneapolis: University of Minnesota Press, 1993).

27. Gopinath, *Impossible Desires*, 11.

28. Ella Shohat, *Israeli Cinema: East/West and the Politics of Representation* (Austin: University of Texas Press, 1989), 272–273. On this point, see also Alcalay, *After*, 221.

29. For example, see Kim D. Butler, "Defining Diaspora, Refining a Discourse," *Diaspora* 10, no. 2 (2001): 189–219. Safran's "Diasporas in Modern Societies" contains a section entitled "Diasporas in Comparison" (84–90). And the conclusion to Robin Cohen's *Global Diasporas: An Introduction* (Seattle: University of Washington Press, 1997) has a section entitled "Comparing Diasporas" (180ff).

30. Earl Lewis introduced the concept of "overlapping diasporas" in "To Turn as on a Pivot: Writing African Americans Into a History of Overlapping Diaspo-

ras," in Darlene Clark Hine and Jacqueline McLeod, eds., *Crossing Boundaries: Comparative History of Black People in Diaspora* (Bloomington: Indiana University Press, 1999), 3–32.

31. Mercer uses the term *dialogic* to define diaspora in "Diaspora Culture."

32. Jacques Derrida, *De la grammatologie* (Paris: Minuit, 1967), 90; translated as *Of Grammatology* by Gayatri Chakravorty Spivak (Baltimore: Johns Hopkins University Press, 1997), 61. The expression Spivak translates as "reciprocally"—*en retour*—might also be translated as "in retrospect."

33. Jacques Derrida, "Ellipsis," in *Writing and Difference* (Chicago: University of Chicago Press, 1978), 295.

34. Jacques Derrida, *The Monolingualism of the Other; or, The Prosthesis of Origin*, trans. Patrick Mensah (Stanford: Stanford University Press, 1998), 29.

35. Edmond Jabès, *Le livre des questions*, 7 vols. (Paris: Gallimard, 1963–73). See also Derrida, "Edmond Jabès and the Question of the Book," in *Writing and Difference*, 64–78.

36. Derrida, "Ellipsis," 295.

37. Jacques Derrida, *The Post Card: From Socrates to Freud and Beyond*, ed. and trans. Alan Bass (Chicago: University of Chicago Press, 1987), 18.

38. Geoffrey Bennington and Jacques Derrida, *Jacques Derrida* (Chicago: University of Chicago Press, 1993), 11.

39. Jacques Derrida, *Glas*, trans. John P. Leavey Jr. and Richard Rand (Lincoln: University of Nebraska Press, 1986).

40. On turning the erection inside out, consider the following passage on Genet: "The golden fleece surrounds the neck, the cunt, the verge [*la verge* or the penis], the apparition or the appearance of a hole in erection, of a hole and an erection at once, of an erection in the hole or a hole in the erection" (66). On castration, consider the following passage on Genet: "It (Ça) bands erect, castration. [*Ça bande, la castration.*] Infirmity itself bandages itself [*se panse*] by banding erect" (138). Only the last bracketed insertion is the translator's. For the French originals, see Jacques Derrida, *Glas*, 2 vols. (Paris: Denoël/Gonthier, 1981), 93, 193. Compare also the parallels in "Circumfessions" between the blood of Derrida's circumcised penis and his mother's menstrual fluids.

41. I expand on Derrida's penis and his queer roots at more length in "Derrida's Queer Root(s)," in Michael O'Rourke, ed., *Derrida and Queer Theory* (London: Palgrave, forthcoming).

42. See Jane Gallop, "Phallus/Penis: Same Difference," *Thinking Through the Body* (New York: Columbia University Press, 1988), 124–132.

43. *The Female Eunuch* (New York: McGraw-Hill, 1971), 315. Hélène Cixous would make a similar call, echoed by Alice Jardine in the late eighties: "Men still have everything to say about their sexuality." Alice Jardine, "Men in Feminism: Odor di Uomo or Compagnons de Route?" in Alice Jardine and Paul Smith, eds., *Men in Feminism* (New York: Routledge, 1987), 60. In *Portrait de Jacques Derrida en Jeune Saint Juif* (Paris: Galilée, 1991), Cixous literally writes on "Circumfessions" by reproducing entire passages of it onto which she writes commentary by hand. Figuratively, therefore, she is writing on his penis.

44. For other feminist writing on the penis, see Nancy K. Miller, "My Father's Penis," in *Getting Personal: Feminist Occasions and Other Autobiographical Acts* (New York: Routledge, 1991): 143–148; and, although more about the phallus than the penis, Judith Butler, "The Lesbian Phallus and the Morphological Imaginary," *differences* 4, no. 1 (1992): 133–171.

45. See especially Gayatri Chakravorty Spivak, "Displacement and the Discourse of Woman," in Mark Krupnick, ed., *Displacement: Derrida and After* (Bloomington: Indiana University Press, 1983), 169–195. A number of the essays in Jardine and Smith's *Men in Feminism* also take up this engagement.

46. Jacques Derrida, *Dissemination,* ed. and trans. Barbara Johnson (Chicago: University of Chicago Press, 1981), 304.

47. *Glas,* 315: "Glas du phallogocentrisme."

48. Paul de Man, *Allegories of Reading: Figural Language in Rousseau, Nietzsche, Rilke, and Proust* (New Haven: Yale University Press, 1979), 76–77.

5 Indigenous Australian Arts of Return

Mediating Perverse Archives

ROSANNE KENNEDY

For many Australians of Indigenous descent, going home to Aboriginal family and country has become an emotionally freighted possibility in the wake of a National Inquiry into what is known in Australia as "the Stolen Generations." In 1996 the Human Rights and Equal Opportunity Commission, at the request of the federal government, conducted a National Inquiry into the policies, practices, and effects of separating children of mixed descent from their families and communities over the twentieth century. Commissioners heard testimonies from over five hundred survivors of child removal, many of whom articulated feelings of isolation and disconnection—accepted neither in white nor Aboriginal culture. The testimonies described childhoods scarred by physical, sexual and emotional abuse and adulthoods marred by unstable relationships and violence. The National Inquiry's landmark report, *Bringing Them Home,* found that children of mixed descent were removed not because they were regarded as "white children" but "because their Aboriginality was 'a problem.'"[1] It controversially found that the policy of removing children, with the aim of eradicating Aboriginal culture, identity and family bonds, constituted genocide.[2] *Bringing Them Home* conceptualized "going home" as "fundamental to healing the effects of separation," and it recommended financial and psychological support for genealogical re-

search and family reunions.[3] In practice, however, many Stolen Generations oral histories and memoirs document the compromises and painful
challenges of return: families are dispersed, parents have passed away or
have new families, or reunions fail to produce the anticipated emotional
connections.

Both before and after the National Inquiry, Aboriginal women used
personal forms such as autobiography, testimony, and oral history to perform and commemorate defiant acts of return to Aboriginal culture and
identity. For example, in *My Place* (1987), a roots narrative that became
an Australian classic, Sally Morgan describes her efforts to recover her
Aboriginal heritage, which her mother had denied for fear her children
would be taken by authorities.[4] Fifteen years later, Hollywood director
Philip Noyce brought the Stolen Generations to international attention
through his popular film, *Rabbit Proof Fence* (2002). The film adapts Doris
Pilkington Garimara's narrative of her mother Molly's capture, institutionalization, and long walk home, as a fourteen year old, to her mother and
country. In a shocking twist, however, the film documents the traumatic
repetition of removal: ten years after Molly returned home, she was again
taken to a native settlement, this time with her two young daughters.[5]
Again she walked home, carrying the infant and leaving the other child.
Tragically, authorities later took the infant, and Molly never saw her again.
Ironically, this exceptional story of escape and return, rather than the far
more common story of institutionalization and assimilation, has become
the iconic Stolen Generations narrative. Indeed, it is the untold stories of
those who *never* return that most forcefully register the magnitude and
cultural losses caused by child removal.

Developing a nuanced cultural memory of Indigenous child removal,
compulsory assimilation, and return—especially in a global context in
which "genocide" conjures images of mass killing—presents several challenges. The first is to articulate the particular methods of dispossession
of land, family, and identity to which Indigenous people were and still are
subjected. Historian Patrick Wolfe contends that framing the destruction
of Indigenous culture as "cultural genocide" invites comparison with the
Holocaust, which inadvertently "devalue[s] Indigenous attritions," as they
pale in comparison to the extreme violence of the death camps.[6] Rather
than posit analogies, he identifies a particular form of violence that pre-
vails in settler colonial societies such as Australia. Settler colonialism,
Wolfe argues, is a "specific social formation" characterized by a "logic of
elimination" that is motivated by the need to secure territory rather than

by race.[7] Settlers seek to destroy and disperse Indigenous tribes so that their lands, owned collectively, can be secured. The native is allowed to survive when "disguised" as white and no longer associated with a tribe.[8] While critics of *Bringing Them Home* have disputed its claim that between 10 and 30 percent of mixed-descent children were removed, almost all Indigenous Australians were affected by the brutal methods settlers developed to extinguish Aboriginality as a living culture.[9] Understanding this form of annihilation, which permits physical survival while destroying culture, is crucial for grasping obstacles to return.

The Indigenous trauma of broken family bonds and compulsory assimilation also presents archival challenges. Ann Cvetkovich observes that trauma that occurs in the private realm tends to slip out of visibility. Private trauma, she argues, calls into question "common understandings of what constitutes an archive. Because [sexual] trauma can be unspeakable and unrepresentable . . . it often seems to leave behind no records at all."[10] Child removal and institutionalization, which often included sexual and physical abuse, long went unnoticed as trauma because these acts were carried out in private, and were normalized as rescue and benevolence. Often, the only records of an individual's removal and fate are those preserved by government bureaucrats who perpetrated elimination. The challenge is to use such records—what I am calling *perverse* archives—to create an Indigenous cultural memory of dehumanization and survival.[11]

Artists and writers, often motivated by their own family histories, have turned to state archives to explore this history. Kim Scott's novel, *Benang: from the heart*, and Judy Watson's artist's books, *A Preponderance of Aboriginal Blood* and *Under the Act*, incorporate documents and language from Aboriginal Protection Board archives, bringing into visibility governance regimes designed to destroy Indigenous identities, cultures, and genealogies.[12] Produced in the wake of *Bringing Them Home*, these works share features of roots narratives, but they are not primarily auto/biographical accounts of a search for identity or a return home. Rather, they are powerful aesthetic works that use Indigenous knowledges, languages, and materials imaginatively to resignify, while also documenting, violent settler practices of dispersal and erasure. Scott and Watson's mediations of these archives reveal the intimate workings of state policy on individual lives, thereby providing both historical and subjective insights into processes used to expunge Aboriginal culture. Whereas Wolfe identifies elimination as a structural feature of settler colonialism, their works dramatically reveal its gendered operations at a personal level. Both show how efforts to "eliminate the native" particularly affected Indigenous women, who were sexually targeted by white men but often lost their children. Scott and Watson demonstrate that even perpetrator archives, however surprisingly, may function as sites of attachment and affective investment, especially in an oral culture in which written records are scarce. Their works reveal, in rich detail, the material processes through which Indigenous people were estranged from Aboriginal family and culture, while performing, through the creative process, subversive acts of witness, commemoration, and return.

Reading Through Blood: Judy Watson's Artist's Books

Judy Watson, of mixed Scottish, English, and Aboriginal descent, is one of Australian's leading contemporary artists, and one of eight Indigenous Australian artists commissioned to create work for the Musée du Quai Branly, Paris. Her oeuvre exemplifies an Indigenous feminist visual arts practice grounded in a return to cultural and familial roots. In 1990, at the age of thirty, she traveled to the country of her maternal grandmother, Grace Issacson, of the Waanyi people in northwestern Queensland. Like many people of mixed descent, Grace's life was deeply affected by Aboriginal protection policies. Her mother, fearful that Grace would be forcibly taken, relinquished her to a white family to be trained as a domestic and was denied access to her. Grace also lost contact with a brother. Watson's reconnection with her grandmother provides "a primary inspiration" for her artwork: "Spending time with her, I absorbed her memories, gained an insight into her life and the ways she saw the land, was shown bush foods and sites." Reconnection with Grace has enabled Watson to affirm her "identity, ancestral links and connection to Country" and forms the basis for artworks that exemplify an imaginative investment in her grandmother's experiences.[13] Watson views herself as both Aboriginal and non-Aboriginal and is interested in "how two histories, black and white, are parallel with slippage and overlay through contact and cohabitation."[14] Her artworks are complex cultural translations that address Indigenous and non-Indigenous audiences.

In the 1990s Watson visited European museums, seeking out Aboriginal remains, especially those proximate to her grandmother's country. Her realization that "some of the works may have been made with the hair of her ancestors was a revelatory moment."[15] She sketched these objects, giving them titles such as *our skin in your collections* and *our hair in your collections,* thereby drawing attention to the curatorial practice of collecting, transporting, and archiving Indigenous objects and body parts. These titles, in their direct address, resonate with the powerful postmodern feminist interventions of American artist Barbara Kruger, known for public art installations that hailed the viewer. Perhaps this cultural echo is not surprising, as Watson, like Kruger, is concerned with the objectification and surveillance of female bodies. Watson's dual interests—in family genealogy and in institutional holdings of Aboriginal artifacts and remains—come together in two recent artist's books.

Produced in 2005, *a preponderance of aboriginal blood* was commissioned by the State Library of Queensland to commemorate the 1967 referendum, a watershed in the modern Aboriginal rights movement, and to commemorate one hundred years of voting rights for women. It consists of sixteen etchings that mediate archival documents relating to the Aboriginal Protection Act in the state of Queensland in the 1930s and 1940s, when Watson's grandmother came under the act. Documents include personal letters from individuals inquiring about eligibility to vote, applications for exemption from the act, and permission for Aboriginal children to attend the school for white children. An application seeking exemption asks: "Does applicant (or his family) habitually associate with aboriginals? Is he (or she) thrifty? Does he (or she) understand the value of money?"(figure 5.1).[16] Watson transforms these artifacts into materials for an Indigenous cultural memory by remediating them through the use of blood marks—an example of her characteristic "blood language."[17] She creates these blood marks by stamping an etching dipped in a semi-transparent ochre wash—ochre is a preferred material in Indigenous painting—onto copies of archival documents. To the eye, it looks as if blood has been spilled over the documents, pooling and spreading unevenly so some areas are exposed. While it is possible to read the documents through the blood wash, the words are not immediately legible and require the viewer to pause. Watson's blood language captures the irony of "protection" from an Indigenous perspective. The "blood-stained" documents visually register the violent effects of the Aboriginal protection regime while simultaneously revealing the discourses that controlled and disenfranchised Aboriginals. The blood marks invite viewers to reflect on the Indigenous blood spilled since colonization and the racist bureaucratic obsession with classifying Indigenous people according to bloodlines. They also convey the significance of "country": the ochre reds

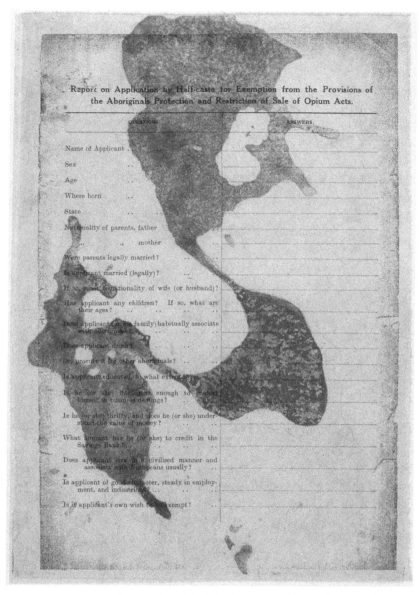

FIGURE 5.1 *a preponderance of aboriginal blood* (2005); etching with chine collé; page 3 from artist book, edition of five plus artist proofs. Printers: Suzanne Danaher and Tricia Hatcher (numero uno publications/grahame galleries + editions). *Image courtesy Judy Watson and grahame galleries + editions*

evoke the Australian desert, and some marks visually resemble a topographic map.

In 2007 Watson produced a second artist's book, *under the act*, dedicated to her grandmother Grace Isaacson and originally exhibited in the Cultural Warriors Indigenous Art Triennial exhibition at the National Gallery of Australia.[18] This book, like the earlier one, uses the technique of blood marks printed on archival documents to transmit her grandmother's experience of separation and assimilation. In *under the act*, however, Watson juxtaposes impersonal bureaucratic language with a family portrait. The opening page displays a sepia photograph of a dark-skinned Aboriginal woman and a lighter-skinned toddler on her lap—presumably Grace and her child (figure 5.2).[19] The image's austere formality is conveyed through stiff poses and immaculate European dress and hairstyles. The white of the woman's collar and cuffs and the child's dress is strangely illuminated, while the woman's features merge with the background. Woman and child look solemnly at the camera, expressions blank. The outline of a blood mark is superimposed on the photograph, and the title, "under the act," is typed at the top. On the next pages, Watson creates a palimpsest, layering the now transparent image over documents, mediating and partially obscuring both layers with blood marks. The layering of image, blood mark, and title economically reminds viewers that Aboriginal mothers and their children were subjected to the Aboriginal Act but enjoyed no civil rights under it.

The genesis of the portrait of mother and child—who took it, under what conditions, and for what purpose—is not revealed to the viewer. Reading the photograph in the context of other archival documents in *under the act*, however, the governance structures of the protection regime and the power of portrait photography in anchoring the ideology of assimilation become visible and new readings emerge. The image may have functioned as visible evidence confirming the pseudo-science of "absorption," for the child is lighter-skinned than the mother. It may have assured contemporary viewers that this particular Aboriginal woman and her child had assimilated to the standards of the white family. The portrait implies that the mixed-race family was socially acceptable, with outward signs of assimilation, such as dress and self-presentation, apparently signifying a seamless transition from Aboriginal to white norms. Yet, the white father is absent: it is as if this child is the product of an immaculate conception rather than an act of interracial intimacy that cannot be acknowledged publicly through the father's image. If the father were, in fact, absent,

FIGURE 5.2 *under the act* (2007); etching with chine collé; page 1 from artist book, edition of twenty; Printers: Basil Hall Editions (numero uno/grahame galleries + editions). *Image courtesy Judy Watson and grahame galleries + editions*

To The Sgt
Camooweal

Dear Sir

    I just heard Alf Isaacson
has been into Camooweal and asked your
permission if he could marry Gracie Camp
Well Sargent he is a fool, as I have not heard
from you about it I thought I would drop
you a line. I have had her just about
five years and I dont think there is another
woman living would have put up with
her nonsense really I dont, I looked after
her just the same I would my own
daughter & I did not think you would
take her from me without letting me
know, I think it is a insult Alf Isaacson
marrying when he has a respectable family
because she has told me she did not
like when he first asked her to marry
& she said no but, she might think
he cant live without her & she wanted

Mt Isa
June 8th 1934.

FIGURE 5.3 *under the act* (2007); etching with chine collé; page 5 from artist book, edition of twenty; Printers: Basil Hall Editions (numero uno/grahame galleries + editions). *Image courtesy Judy Watson and grahame galleries + editions*

his abandonment would be grounds for removing the child. The ideology naturalized in the portrait—the primal bond of mother and child—masks the reality that children of mixed descent, like the child in the photo, were at constant risk of being removed. The image gains poignancy because viewers know, after *Bringing Them Home*, that many Aboriginal mothers, regarded as expendable by authorities, had their children callously taken and never recovered from that loss.

Other documents from the file include poignant but disturbing letters from the mistress of May Downs, the pastoral station where Grace had been a domestic since childhood, to the director of Native Affairs. The white woman's letter reveals the tangled and contradictory nature of intimate interracial relations in an era when racism was common sense. She is "discusted" by Grace's proposed marriage to a white man, but simultaneously reveals her own deep attachment to Grace: "I looked after her just the same as I would my own daughter and I did not think you would take her from me without letting me know" (figure 5.3). Positioning Grace as both a beloved daughter and an object, the woman's language seamlessly combines the intimate and the bureaucratic, masking and naturalizing the assumption that Grace is less than fully human. In her expression of grief at the unexpected loss of Grace, the white woman obscures the reality that it is Grace's mother who has in fact lost her daughter. Watson's resignification of these documents through blood marks exemplifies a feminist method grounded in a politics of bringing the personal into the public sphere. Through her technique, Watson invites viewers to reflect on the affective and legal contradictions to which these documents bear witness while simultaneously reclaiming them for an Indigenous cultural memory.

Narrating "Genealogical Bewilderment": Kim Scott's *Benang*

Whereas Watson directly mediates archival documents, Kim Scott incorporates language from the era of absorption into a novel that aims to convey the subjective experience of coming of age without knowledge of one's genealogy or heritage. Scott, born in 1957, descends from the Nyoongar people in the southwest of Western Australia, the setting for *Benang*. The novel returns to and reframes, from an Indigenous perspective, writings by Arthur O. Neville, the notorious chief protector of Aborigines in Western Australia from 1915 to 1940. Neville controversially proposed to solve the "half-caste problem"—the rapidly expanding population of mixed-descent people—through miscegenation and absorption. At a national conference in 1937, he argued that the fate of mixed-descent people was "ultimate absorption" into the white population. Contemporary critics countered that "absorption [is] little more than a euphemism for extinction."[20] In testimony at the National Inquiry, survivors described feelings of isolation and loneliness that resulted from being separated from their families as babies and toddlers. One witness commented: "It's like you're the first human being . . . you've just come out of nowhere."[21] Scott's novel, *Benang: from the heart*, weaves a narrative from such testimony. He undertakes the challenge of telling a story that conveys to the reader, who may be unfamiliar with this history, both the settler's methods for eradicating Indigenous culture and the "genealogical bewilderment" that ensues when children are routinely separated from their Aboriginal mothers and kin.[22]

Benang tells the story of a young man who imagines himself to be "the first white man born" in accord with the policy of absorption.[23] Harley, who narrates the tale, believes that his grandfather, Ern, a Scottish immigrant who arrives in a forsaken town in Western Australia in the 1920s, has engineered his birth to prove the theory of absorption. Ern habitually takes young women of mixed descent as domestics and wives, casting them off when they are no longer of use. Harley is the offspring of one such woman, Ellen, and Ern's son, Tommy. Ellen "disappears" shortly after Harley's birth—presumably captured by authorities and placed in a mission. Ern later "rescues" Harley from his father, and sends him to an elite boarding school. When Harley meets his father Tommy for only the second time since childhood, he demands to know why he relinquished him to Ern. Agitated, Harley "murders his father" in a car accident, the displaced expression of a wish to murder his white grandfather. After the accident, in a hallucinogenic state, Harley's recalls or imagines—it isn't clear which—Ern sexually abusing him. At the funeral, he feels lonely, as if "I myself represented the final killing off; the genocide thing" (446). In its inscription of "killing the father," *Benang* indigenizes the Oedipus myth. Like Oedipus, Harley does not know his mother and runs the risk that he may unwittingly sleep with her, a sister or a cousin—an anxiety expressed in Stolen Generations testimonies. In *Benang*, however, killing the white patriarch is motivated not simply by an unconscious sexual desire; it is necessary for racial survival.

In the novel the archive is a trope that symbolizes the settler's obsession with the Aborigine. Searching through his grandfather's study, Harley discovers that Ern has amassed an archive—"certificates of birth, death, marriage; newspaper clippings police reports; letters"—which documents the intimate lives of Aboriginal women and their mixed-descent children. The archive uses quasi-zoological terms—*full blood, half-caste,* and *octoroon*—to classify its subjects according to the rules of absorption (25). A cache of photographs is aligned to demonstrate how the "color" fades from one generation to the next: "There were portraits arranged in pairs . . . families grouped according to skin colour. And, sudden enough to startle me, my own image" (26). His discovery of his grandfather's keen interest in the "science" of eugenics—and the carefully planned subject position for *him,* within a racially engineered family—enrages him. He scorns his white identity, achieved through the sexual coercion and disposability of Indigenous women: "My grandfather's success. Absorbed, barely alive" (35). What, he wonders, does "success" mean when it is the end of a culture, a people, rather than a beginning?

A good deal of the novel is concerned with imagining the effects of policies of absorption and dispersal on the lives of Indigenous women and their children. Although Harley attempts to establish his family genealogy, the lines of descent, especially for women, break off abruptly. Trying to find out what happened to Kathleen, the first of Ern's wives, Harley follows "a trail of old Aborigines Department papers" through a mission, domestic service, and the removal of several of her children. Like all the women in his family, including his mother, "Kathleen exits this story too quickly" (139). When he later visits a woman called Ellen—a "maybe-my-mother"—she wonders why, "after all that had happened," he should "want to go scuttling back to blackfellas" (398). *Benang* registers the effects of elimination—the genealogical uncertainty and ruptures in genealogy—at the level of narrative form. The disappearances of women, and the resulting gaps in the family line, frustrate Harley and the reader's attempts to map his genealogy. Who exactly *are* his relations? What has happened to them? Can he legitimately claim an Aboriginal identity? Through imagining the effects of elimination on women as mothers, the novel links gender, genocide, and generation: separating children from their mothers results in the loss of Indigenous culture, language, and traditions in future generations.

Benang is not an easy novel to digest or classify. It has many apparently magic realist moments, such as when Harley finds himself "strangely drifting" above the earth. The absurdity of such scenes should not be read as conforming to the genre of magic realism but rather as Scott's attempt to register the surreal effects of Western ways of thinking on Aboriginal lives. For instance, *uplift,* used as a moral concept typically applied by the English to racial and economic "others," means "to elevate intellectually, morally or spiritually."[24] Neville exemplifies this usage in his assertion that *"biological and social absorption* [of Aboriginals will] *dilute the strain . . .* [and] *uplift a despised race'"* (27). Scott, however, ironically refigures the concept from an Indigenous perspective, using the geological meaning of *uplift*—"to rise or ascend; to be moved or carried upwards [by] . . . a storm, a wind"—to describe Harley's predicament. Like a tree in the wake of an earthquake, for Harley, being "uplifted" means being uprooted from his Aboriginal heritage. He repeatedly narrates scenes in which he finds himself "strangely uplifted" by climatic forces, such as sea currents, and as "hovering" above the earth. By associating "uplift" with aimless drifting, the novel innovatively registers the dislocating effects of cultural dispossession and challenges the benevolent account of absorption as "in the best interests of the child."

Harley determines to become his "grandfather's failure" by claiming his Aboriginal heritage (31). To this end he undertakes a journey with his "uncles" Jack and Will, tracing the family's routes and belonging places. At each site, rich in cultural and family meaning, his uncles tell stories of family and how they struggled to escape the authorities and survive the devastating depression of the 1930s. Ern, confined to a wheelchair and rendered mute by a stroke, is forced to passively witness the narration of a past he sought to shape in his own image. Frequently, Jack and Will disagree about which story should be told, how, and by whom. Harley observes that Will's choice of formulaic genres such as "westerns" and "cowboy novels" fails him "in his attempts at history." He prefers "Uncle Jack's more circumspect tales," handed on by his full-blood grandmother Fanny, which bring into language "the things that cannot easily be said"— massacres that are not spoken of because they are too painful or have been forgotten (192). Harley's reflections on his uncles' choice of genres raises, within the narrative, the vital issue of narrative form: what form is most appropriate for telling a story of cultural annihilation and resulting "genealogical bewilderment" as it impacts on individual and group lives over several generations?

Despite its confronting subject matter, *Benang* is a humorous and ironic work of recovery and return. In its final pages the narrator reflects on his own and the culture's survival: "I am still here, however too-well-disguised [as white]. . . . We are still here, Benang" (494–495). *Benang*, a Nyoongar word, means "tomorrow." The novel envisions forging a family and handing on traditions to children as fundamental to physical and cultural survival. Eventually, in a fantastical but nonredemptive ending, Harley reunites with two nonbiological sisters, one of mixed descent, with whom he has children. The family negotiates a future based on "shared experience" and "shared responsibilities," which enables Harley to hand down stories about place, family, and cultural heritage to their children. This imagined family—two mothers, a father who is "strangely uplifted," and children of uncertain lineage—constitutes a queer response to patriarchal practices of sexual coercion and absorption. In contrast to the heteronormative family in Baz Luhrmann's epic melodrama, *Australia* (2008), framed as a tribute to the Stolen Generations, Harley's relationship with the mothers of his children is "no romance" (450). Nor is it a Western or an adventure story—there is no intact Aboriginal culture to return to, but only thin traditions that can be reinvented in the present. By telling this story of survival beyond the planned end of "ultimate absorption," *Benang* brings Indigenous resistance to the settler logic of eliminating the native into national and transnational memory.

Indigenizing Diaspora?

At a moment when Western nations are expressing fatigue with memory culture, there is a danger that the Indigenous trauma of dispossession will be forgotten before it has been adequately remembered. Scott's novel, like Watson's graphic works, contributes to a transnational project of commemorating Indigenous losses *and* celebrating survival while providing historical insight into the destruction of culture that complicates any act of return. Through their visual and literary arts, they make the archives of assimilation testify publicly to a truth that has remained largely hidden both in Australia and internationally: Australian settlement was secured through a biopolitical regime entailing the surveillance and control of the bodies and intimate lives of Indigenous people as a means of dispossessing them of their lands and rights and eradicating their collective identity as members of a group. As reparative works that grieve for and commemorate the losses of the past, *Under the Act* and *Benang* exemplify the "universally human dilemmas of memory and mourning among survivors of post-colonial trauma."[25]

While these works contribute significantly to a transnational memory of Indigenous dispossession, they also have implications for theories of diaspora and return. To date, most feminist work on diaspora, like diaspora theory more generally, has focused on well-established cases such as the African and South Asian diasporas.[26] Indigenous experiences of removal and resettlement tend to fall outside the parameters of diaspora theory. Whereas theories of diaspora posit a group identity and culture that survives dispossession, settler colonial practices aimed to eradicate Aboriginality as an identity and living culture. Moreover, diaspora has been conceptualized in terms of the forced movement of a population from a home to one or more areas outside the original nation. While Indigenous people were forced off their traditional lands and corralled in reserves, they did not leave Australia and resettle elsewhere. Indeed, the deep attachments Indigenous people have to "country" and its impact on their sense of belonging and well-being makes the idea of mass exile off-shore unthinkable.[27]

The texts that I have considered suggest that feminism needs to develop a more expansive conceptual vocabulary for understanding and engaging with the global and diverse experiences of dispossession and return if some experiences are not to be cast, once again, in the shadows.[28] This project will require attention to the specificity of national policies and their transnational histories as well as an understanding of Indigenous forms of mobility both within and beyond the borders of the nation. It will, as James Clifford suggests, require theorists to think "indigeneity and diaspora together."[29] This is an urgent project not only for developing a more inclusive understanding of dispossession and return but for achieving social justice for Indigenous people as they continue to confront initiatives to dispossess them of land, rights, and self-governance. It also raises crucial questions for the future: for instance, if diaspora were reframed, would it be a useful concept for Aboriginal peoples? Do Indigenous experiences inform other cases of dispossession and return? What support is there, from governments, for Indigenous return to country? In Australia, for instance, federal and state governments have expressed unwillingness to support small Aboriginal clans to return to and live on their remote homelands, due to the cost of infrastructure and transport and lack of jobs and resources. This reluctance places a practical limit on the possibility of return. Addressing these issues may enable feminist scholars to develop a more inclusive and indeed global understanding of the histories, experiences, and challenges of diaspora and return.

Notes

1. Human Rights and Equal Opportunity Commission, *Bringing Them Home: Report of the National Inquiry into the Separation of Aboriginal and Torres Strait Islander Children from Their Families* (Sydney: HREOC, 1997), 272.

2. Ibid., 275. The 1948 UN Convention on the Prevention and Punishment of the Crime of Genocide, informed by Raphael Lemkin's definition of genocide, encompasses "acts committed with intent to destroy, in whole or in part, a national, ethnical, racial or religious group," including "forcibly transferring children of the group to another group" (ibid., 270–271). For excellent analyses, see Ann Curthoys and John Docker, "Defining Genocide," and Robert Van Krieken, "Cultural Genocide in Australia," in Dan Stone, ed., *The Historiography of Genocide* (New York: Palgrave Macmillan, 2008). Since Australian courts did not find "intent to destroy," the concept of "cultural genocide" is legally ineffective in Australia. Indigenous peoples strongly support its use to convey their "heartfelt . . . sense of inflicted violence, pain and suffering" from settler-colonialism (Van Krieken, "Cultural Genocide," 131).

3. Human Rights and Equal Opportunity Commission, *Bringing Them Home*, 233.

4. Sally Morgan, *My Place* (Fremantle, WA: Fremantle Arts Centre Press, 1987).

5. Philip Noyce, *Rabbit-Proof Fence* (Australia, 2002); Doris Pilkington Garimara, *Follow the Rabbit-Proof Fence* (St. Lucia, Qld: University of Queensland Press, 1996). For further analysis of these texts, see Rosanne Kennedy, "Vulnerable Children, Disposable Mothers," *Life Writing* 5, no. 2 (2008): 161–184.

6. Patrick Wolfe, "Settler Colonialism and the Elimination of the Native," *Journal of Genocide Research* 8, no. 4 (2006): 401–402.

7. Ibid., 388.

8. Ibid., 402.

9. On this controversy, see Robert Manne, *In Denial: Stolen Generations and the Right* (Melbourne: Black Ink, 2001).

10. Ann Cvetkovich, *An Archive of Feelings* (Durham: Duke Univ. Press, 2003), 7.

11. My use of "perverse" is suggested by Kim Scott's comment that A. O. Neville's writings were "a continual—albeit perverse—source of inspiration." Kim Scott, *Benang: from the heart* (South Fremantle, WA: Fremantle Arts Centre Press, 1999), 497.

12. Judy Watson, *a preponderance of aboriginal blood* (Brisbane: Numero Uno, Grahame Galleries + Editions, 2005); Judy Watson, *under the act: an artist book* (Milton, Qld.: Numero Uno, Grahame Galleries + Editions, 2007).

13. Judy Watson and Louise Martin-Chew, *Judy Watson: blood language* (Carlton, Vic.: Miegunyah, 2009), 153.

14. Ibid., 132.

15. Brenda Croft and Hetti Perkins, "Judy Watson" in *Australian Indigenous Art Commission: Musée du Quai Branly* (Paddington, NSW: Art and Australia, 2006), 43.

16. Watson, *A Preponderance of Aboriginal Blood.*

17. See Watson and Martin-Chew, *Judy Watson.*

18. See Brenda Croft, ed., *Culture Warriors: National Indigenous Art Triennial* (Canberra, ACT: National Gallery of Australia, 2007). This show exhibited in 2009 at the Katzen Arts Centre Museum, American University. See also http://www.american.edu/americantoday/campus-news/20091006-Indigenous-Art.cfm.

19. Watson, *Under the Act.*

20. Russell McGregor, *Imagined Destinies* (Carlton, Vic: Melbourne University Press, 1997), 179.

21. Human Rights and Equal Opportunity Commission, *Bringing Them Home*, 13.

22. Ibid., 233.

23. Scott, *Benang*, 13.

24. See *Oxford English Dictionary Online* for both meanings of *uplift*. *Oxford English Dictionary Online* (Oxford: Oxford University Press, 2010).

25. Kobena Mercer, "Art as a Dialogue in Social Space," *Rethinking Nordic Colonialism*, http://www.rethinking-nordic-colonialism.org/files/index.htm.

26. See Tina Campt and Deborah Thomas, eds., "Gendering Diaspora," special issue, *Feminist Review* 90, no.1 (2008).

27. For a feminist and Indigenous account of the affective and practical significance of homelands, see Deborah Bird Rose, Sharon D'Amico et al., *Country of the Heart: An Indigenous Australian Homeland* (Canberra: Aboriginal Studies Press, 2002).

28. For feminist approaches to home and migration not framed in terms of diaspora, see Sara Ahmed et al., ed., *Uprootings/Regroundings* (New York: Berg, 2003).

29. James Clifford, "Indigenous Articulations," *Contemporary Pacific* 13, no. 2 (2001): 472.

PART II

Genres of Return

6   Memoirs of Return

SAIDIYA HARTMAN, EVA HOFFMAN, AND
DANIEL MENDELSOHN IN CONVERSATION
WITH NANCY K. MILLER

NKM: I will ask you all the same first question, and we'll see what happens from there. What was the impulse to write your book?

EH: Well, the impulse has a bit of a history. I came to the subject in this book quite late. When I started writing my first book, *Lost in Translation*, the immediate problematic which preoccupied me, and which had preoccupied me already quite a long time then, was the displacement which I actually experienced.[1] The displacement of emigration, of coming from Poland to Canada, and being out of a culture, language, etc. and transposing myself into a new one. And I say this partly because I think that memory works from the present, often. So, the narrative, which, in a sense, I was working with then, started with that present, with the present of my actual emigration and the identity which was foregrounded for me then, was the identity of an immigrant, because identity is also not written in stone for any of us, and it can change with different preoccupations, different stages of our lives.

The Holocaust at that point was a given, it was a given with which I had grown up, which was always there as part of my family history and the stories which I heard from childhood on, but it was not until later that I started disentangling it as a particular thread and as a particular aspect of my own history, my generation's history, and a broader legacy as well. And then the present changed. My parents died, for one thing, and I felt I was losing that palpable link to that past, and also the survivors as a generation were passing on, and there was a sense that the wand of knowledge, of understanding, of that legacy was being passed on to the second generation. At the same time, there was a kind of cultural phenomenon as well—the perhaps not sudden but growing and increasing preoccupation with the Holocaust, which, I think, we've all been aware of. And, while this was an improvement, I feel, over the latency period, over the period where the subject of the Holocaust was a taboo, nevertheless, I felt that in this cultural preoccupation there were some dangers of reductiveness and simplification and that, if I wanted to keep the complexity which I'd felt actually in survivors' stories, that I needed to address the subject at the same time—this was a past which was still not a past for me, it still impinged, and I wanted to find out, to think about the ways in which it impinged on me, it impinged perhaps on the broader second generation, the ways in which the knowledge of the Holocaust was passed on, transmitted, how the second generation's knowledge differs from the first generation's. Perhaps I should stop there . . .

NKM: Despite the difference in generations, it seems logical for Daniel Mendelsohn to follow, because of the Holocaust link.

DM: Well, yes, but I would also say, no. I mean only in the sense that we have very different relationships to the event. Indeed, one of the things I'm always foregrounding in my book is precisely that: how remote it is to me. I'm not the child of survivors. I'm not the grandchild of survivors. The entire thing that made my book possible, I think, is the fact that I have a very oblique relationship to the event itself—in the book I'm writing about what happened to my grandfather's brother, a man I never knew—so it was always at an angle to me. And that angle is precisely what the book is about: how do you think about the event, or know about the event, when it is actually becoming more and more remote. I think the primary issue that I struggled with in the book was how do you access something that doesn't belong to you, in fact. It belongs to Eva more than it belongs to me. So that's what I'm interested in in the book: how do you know about something that isn't your "property," so to speak, except in the most abstract possible sense.

I mean, what brought me to write my book wasn't even a strong interest in the Holocaust per se, but rather a very strong, old interest in family history, which I owe to my very interesting grandfather, a great raconteur and storyteller about the old country, about his family's past.[2] And so already as a young child of ten or eleven I was interested in family history—I vividly remember the family tree I was building when I was twelve years old, making charts on pieces of oak tag, that sort of thing. (And, you know, now, of course, you just have to buy the right software and it comes out very nice and pretty from your printer, but in those days it was quite different!) So I was very interested in genealogy, family history, "the old country"—you know, when you're the grandchild of immigrants, as I am, people used to talk all the time about the old country. So, anyway, there I was in my teens, making family charts and index cards and family trees, and what frustrated me from a very early age was that there was this entire limb of this family tree that had obviously been cut off. There were these people you could not know about because they had just sort of disappeared, and it bothered me as a researcher—I would say, indeed, that my mentality as a researcher was offended before my mentality as a family member, as a Jew, as a anything else was. I just couldn't believe that you could not know anything about these people because they had vanished off the face of the earth. But, as we know, nobody just "vanishes off the face of the earth." Every one of those people had a particular fate, we knew that; but about my great-uncle, Shmiel, it was impossible to know anything, and I was sort of possessed by this mystery from a very early age.

There were, it's important to remember, also practical problems at that time to the kind of research I subsequently did in order to write my book. In those days—I mean, the mid-1970s, the early 1980s, when I was furiously working on family history—there was still the Iron Curtain, so you couldn't easily do the kind of research that I subsequently did, research that involved extensive travel in Eastern Europe, in former Soviet territories, and extensive, very open, and direct interviewing of local residents about the war. So it all seemed very impossible to get at, back then—the mystery of "what happened to Uncle Shmiel," as we used to say in my family.

And then, of course, the world changed, the Soviet Union fell, travel was easier—and there was also an explosion of information on the Internet, Jewish genealogy Web sites, and so forth. But why it was, precisely, that at the age of forty, in the year 2000, I suddenly thought, "Oh, now I have to go find Uncle Shmiel," I really couldn't say. I wish I had some lovely story to tell you about what it was that spurred me. Maybe it was turning forty—actually, I sometimes do think that may have something to do with it. You know, at a certain point in your life, you realize that there's more of it behind you than in front of you, and before you go into the part that's left you need to make your peace with the part that came before. So maybe it was that.

NKM: You've provided a perfect segue for Saidiya.

SH: As I listen to Eva and Daniel speak, I am reminded that it is critical to think about these experiences comparatively, while never forgetting the ways in which they are distinct. We can think comparatively about the experience of loss, but we also have to contend with the incommensurability between the histories we're describing. In my case, it was the absence of documentation and the paucity of slavery's archive regarding the experience of the captives that determined the hybrid form of *Lose Your Mother*.[3] Writing the book had everything to do with the form in which the dead returned to me.

In *The Lives of Infamous Men* Foucault notes that the dead, and specifically the infamous, the subaltern, and the exploited, return to us in the very form in which they were driven out of the world.[4] So the dead returned to me as numbers, as ciphers, or with names tossed off as crass insults and jokes. My challenge was how to tell a story about this incredible effacement and disfiguration of personhood. When thinking about the slave trade, its status as "an event" is troublesome; after all, we are talking about an experience of war, and captivity and predation, which lasted for over four hundred years. The paradox of captivity and enslavement is both its remoteness, in that I'm the fifth generation out of slavery, and its proximity, less because of what's transmitted across generations in terms of memory than in the forms of structural violence and dispossession that continue to make that history pertinent to the present. So how can I then write all of this as a narrative? How do I write a story about the long durée of a nonevent about objects, commodities, and cargo? Or reconstruct lives with scraps from the archive? At the same time, I didn't want to write a story that was solely a metadiscourse about history or that settled for invoking the unspeakable as the justification for an aborted narrative. I did not want to make an instrumental connection between the past and the present, but instead to suggest that the Atlantic slave trade was formative of modernity and that slavery is a dimension of the present that we're still living. My journey along the slave route is a device, a vehicle for posing a relation between our age and an age that many of us think of as the past, but which many of us live as the time of the present. The reverberations of slavery can be discerned in contemporary forms of dispossession that are so immediate and unceasing that you can't even begin to think about memorialization, because people are still living the dire effects of the disaster. All of these concerns about time, eventfulness, the life world of the human commodity required a hybrid form, a personal narrative, a historical meditation, and a metadiscourse on history.

It also required me to be the receptacle for foreclosed and prohibited emotions—rage and grief and disappointment. Who wants to carry all that? Who would volunteer for such a task? Novelists, artists, but few scholars. So I had to kind of carry all that rage, grief, and disappointment in order to articulate the relationship between the past and the present. Affect was essential to a critical reading of the archive.

NKM: I guess we might say the book is a journey, but that each of you also made a journey. I'm wondering how you see the difference between the kind of research that you can do now on the Internet, what you can discover in archives and documents, and what happens when you actually go there. Perhaps you can address this decision to return and whether the word *return* is appropriate. How much is fueled by the needs of research? Is there some other kind of drive that takes over from that? How does the actual journey become inscribed in the book?

DM: I was doing an event last year with Leon Wieseltier, and he kept saying, "Why do you keep talking about 'going back'? You were never there before!" Which is clever, but I disagree, because you know, again, when you grow up in an immigrant family, you're always hearing about the country of origin. So it does feel like going *back*. I make no apologies for using this term, which everybody tends to use. Certainly if you're a certain generation of American Jew, people always talk about "going back," even though it's not a place you've been—it's a locution that, if anything, goes to the heart of the strong sentimental role that the country of origin plays in the lives of even distant descendants of immigrants. So I don't see a problem with that, because the sort of imaginary reality of these places is very present to us. I grew up hearing about Bolechow since I was three years old. It felt like a very real place, so I really did feel like I was going back, and in fact—perhaps controversially—when I was in Poland and western Ukraine for the first time, I really did feel like I had come back. It felt familiar—the food was familiar to me, the mannerisms of the people were familiar to me, the way of talking was familiar to me, the things they talked about were familiar. I say "controversially" because that experience of familiarity was not one that I've ever had when I went to Israel, where I never have a feeling of recognition, of connectedness. I've spoken about this very openly, and it's gotten me in hot water every now and then— I remember once, when I was on my book tour for *The Lost* and was doing a talk at a congregation in LA, and a woman stood up and said, "Well, why wasn't your trip to Israel the climax of your book?" She meant the emotional climax, as if getting to Israel, for a person of my background and interests, had to be the be-all and end-all. And so I replied, "Well, because I wasn't *finished* when I was in Israel, I still had to go to three more countries to finish my research," but it was interesting because she persisted and said, "When you wrote about it, you didn't feel like that was where you really *belonged*?" And I said, "Well, no, not really. When I went to Poland, I felt very much at home. I didn't feel so at home in Israel, frankly." So I think that when you make these journeys, you know, you're recuperating all kinds of complicated things—sentimental, emotional, not necessarily rational. But you go back because there's a kind of allure that's exerted by the place of origin. It seems very self-evident to me.

SH: My book was written as an anti-*Roots* narrative, which means that *Roots* was the ur-text. *Lose Your Mother* was both indebted to

Haley's magnum opus and written against it. The path that I was tracing wasn't the road home, it was a slave route. The language of stranger, rather than of kin, framed my journey. The stranger is the most universal definition of the slave, so in that regard such language was suitable. It was terrible to think about all of those people who had been dislocated and deterritorialized even as they were literally on the African continent and making that journey to the coast. These were the ones that I wanted to claim. Like every oppositional narrative, *Lose Your Mother* is haunted by the thing it writes against—the desire for home—and, at the same time, I was acutely aware that I would always be outside home. I was trying to give flesh to a social category—the human commodity, the captive, the slave. In doing so, I had to confront the challenge of personal disclosure, narrating an impossible story, personifying a violence masked by abstraction, and performing affect. Certainly, I was stepping into the path that others had traveled and retracing a route; but what distinguished my journey was stepping into the path of dislocated and disposable persons, so there was no ancestral village or kin group that dictated/directed my search. In this regard, I also wanted to shift the terms of a larger set of discussions about diasporic identity.

NKM: And you also tell other people's stories.

SH: I tell other people's stories. Stories about captives, people I met in Ghana, family stories that embarrassed my mother. There were also dueling temporal frames: the time of slavery and freedom, decolonization and the civil rights movement. Ghana played a crucial role in both frames. My desire to revisit these times had much to do with dreams of undoing the world order engendered by the Atlantic slave trade. This was also the dream of those never able to return home, the dream of the anticolonial struggle, and the civil rights and black power movement. I don't know if that seems like an abstract answer; it didn't feel abstract. I experienced so much pain in the archive and in the course of my journey. I am the progeny of the captive, the slave, the commoner, and it was that particular history, rather than a familial history or an ethnic saga, that I wanted to recount.

NKM: No, not abstract at all. It seems to me that you are talking about the history of a group, rather than your family's individual history, and it's a matter of history, not inherited memory.

EH: We have this discourse of memory, the memory of the Holocaust, but even from my proximity, I didn't actually receive memories of the Holocaust. Memories, more than anything else, are
not genetically transferred from one generation to another. We
did receive something very powerful. We received the emotional
traces of our parents' experiences or our family's experiences
or our collective experiences, but not memories. I'd like to read
briefly from *After Such Knowledge*, in which I describe this impulse actually to go, to make a journey.

That everybody died; that my parents survived by dint of my father's
resourcefulness and my mother's fatalistic fearlessness; that there
were people in whose hands one could place one's life, and others who set vicious dogs on humans: Those were the givens. More
than for our parents, the Holocaust, for us, was the paradoxical
fundament . . .

It was, however, an irony attendant on this that, although we
postwar children were the closest to wartime events in time and in
primal feeling, we were the furthest removed from their grounded,
worldly—that is, political, social, historical meanings. This, I think,
is a crucial distinction: that whereas adults who live through violence
and atrocity can understand what happens to them as actuality—no
matter how awful its terms—the generation after receives its first
knowledge of the terrible events with only childish instruments of
perception, and as a kind of fable . . .

How, then, are we to understand those earliest meanings, the
contents of what was passed on? At first, it was not rational interpretation, or information, or anything like memories; for even if
survivors could recollect their stained spots of time precisely, such
things cannot be passed on like some psychogenetic endowment.
The attic in my imagination, to give only the most concrete example,
probably bore no resemblance to the actual attic in which my parents were hidden.[5]

So, in a sense, you know the impulse for my journey was to
give concrete reality to this imaginary—that really was the main
impulse. Part of the impulse behind this book was to place these
fragments of childhood knowledge and the family knowledge
and a family experience within the broader history.

SH: On that note, I would say that I too had the impulse to translate numbers and ciphers into flesh and blood and to document the existence of those made objects and commodities. But, I had no personal repository of memories to work with.

DM: I mean I think you raise a really interesting issue, which is rather sensitive. But, you know, there has been such a cult of a sort of memory, right? "We must remember," "the moral duty to remember," "never forget," you know—all of it. To which I always respond, "I have news for you. You can't remember what didn't happen to you." Is false remembering better than willed forgetting? I'm sometimes not so sure. So, I think this fetishization of always remembering and never forgetting betrays an artificial and, I think, potentially damaging cultural approach to what memory is really supposed to be about. Obviously, there is value in memorializing events from the past, enshrining them in history, and so forth. The Romans had a very good word for this, which is co-memorate, which is something different from the weird, you-are-there emphasis on mass, shared "memory." I have to say since I wrote my book I've been to a million Yom HaShoah events, and I'm always trying, in an ornery way, I suppose, to make this point. Everybody says "Oh, yes, we're going to remember forever"; but, well, I'm sorry, but you *can't* "remember." There is an important distinction to be made between remembering, which is individual and concrete, and commemoration, which is public and symbolic, and I think it needs to always be made. And I'd say that the very thing that underlies my book and some of the other books we're talking about here—the impulse to go back to give concrete reality to an (as it were) mythic or narrated reality that you grew up hearing about, or some historical event you've learned about in books—derives its significance precisely from the fact we can't, we *don't*, "remember." People who remember don't need to go back. People like me need to go back to Bolechow, my family's town, precisely because I didn't have anything to remember; its reality for me had to be constituted by the journey. Quite often the survivors never go back. They remember enough. They don't need to know what it looks like or sounds like or feels like or smells like or whatever. I think it's very important to remember that memory is individual, you know, you can't remember things that didn't happen to you. And that creates a space, I would say, for the kinds of books, precisely, that we've written, which are about a kind of reclamation which is not a memory because it can't be memory. It's something else. I'm not sure I know what the word for it is, but I think it's something distinct, and the distinction, I think, is important.

NKM: The three of you have used words like *real, concrete, tied to place,* and, Daniel, you gloss the implications for your quest of the word *specific* toward the end of your book. I want to ask you about the moment, Saidiya, when you go to the prison or you're standing on the coast, and when you're there in this tiny town, Eva, in Poland. As readers, we have an almost cinematic experience. Was there a found moment in the book for you, or a found moment in your experience, and is that kind of before and after produced by the going and seeing?

EH: Well, as it happened, there was a lot there, as it happened it was a very full encounter. There was a danger that we would have missed it entirely because we couldn't find Załośce, the place from which my parents came, on the map. We almost went to the wrong town. The day was saved by our driver, who was a soccer coach and therefore had very local maps. But, once we found the right place, we did have a very full encounter, and I won't tell the whole story of it, but part of the fullness was that we found two members of the family which hid my parents, which sheltered my parents, which saved my parents' lives. And so this was a very moving meeting, a very genuine meeting. I think they were as perplexed by our presence there as we were perplexed by, you know, sort of finding Załośce. But, so this was first of all a human encounter and a very active encounter in which there was a chance to give sort of mutual recognition to each other—and I think the question of recognition is very important and I kept thinking about it as I read Saidiya's book: the need for the basic recognition, the basic acknowledgment of something. I think that perhaps we children of survivors don't often think about the other side enough and about the need to recognize them, the life risks that they were taking to rescue those who did survive. As for the place itself, it's a bit complicated, it seems to me, because I do think that there is a need to sort of locate, locate something, locate the past which you have known about, but which you don't know. I'm actually thinking about Freud's formulation of melancholia, a sort of depressive melancholia. He says that mourning in which you knew the object of your mourning can come to an end, but mourning in which you don't know the object which you have lost cannot come to an end. And, in that sense, the second generation was placed in a kind of melancholic position, a kind of placelessness, a kind of nameless, placeless loss. So, you know, I think that locating something does matter a lot. On the other hand, I didn't feel this was a return and I think that, like the word *memory*, return is problematic. One of the reasons it's problematic is because it creates this aporia, it creates this kind of impossible dilemma in one's mind in which you think you can reenter the past and know it completely and touch it. That you can touch it, live it, you know, somehow reenter the past. You cannot—there are real limits to how you can know if not what you can know.

SH: I want to extend Eva's remarks about melancholia by again thinking about the incommensurability of these experiences. For example, there are different forms of melancholia: the melancholia that results from the social foreclosure of certain kinds of grief, that is, the refusal to acknowledge loss. The melancholia produced by the refusal to acknowledge loss or recognize grief has shaped the national discourse on the history of slavery and the slave trade. The slave trade and the centuries-long experience of captivity has actually yet to be remembered, mourned, or redressed. For example, the only people who ever received reparations for slavery were English and French slave owners who received remuneration for the loss of slave property as a result of emancipation in the British colonies and revolution in Haiti. The question of justice remains open in the present, and, because of this, slavery is less the "what happened then" than it is a history that still hurts. This would not be the case had Reconstruction, the first and the second one, been successful. The social order in which we live is shaped by gross inequalities of wealth and human value. In the case of slavery, the issue isn't the incommensurability between the injury and the available forms of redress but the fact that only the slave owners received reparations. All of these concerns determine the kind of stories that we tell about the past and the way we invoke those pasts to make claims in the present. In short, the crime is still unrecognized in the present.

DM: Just because it's not recognized doesn't mean that it's not what it so clearly is, though! Apropos of this, I just spent a week at the American Academy in Berlin and I found myself getting into one of these loony conversations about what you refer to as "incommensurabilities" with the other visiting fellow that week, Senator Tom Daschle, who's from the Dakotas. I was giving a lecture that night about my book, and the two of us were talking to the moderator about genocide, and Tom Daschle started talking about Native Americans and what was done to them; and it was very interesting because the moderator of my talk was resisting very strongly the notion that what happened to the Native Americans in the nineteenth century was a genocide comparable to the genocide of the European Jews during World War II. To my mind, the techniques, the technology of genocide don't have to be identical in order for two cases to be analogous, and I think that quite often the tendency to view European genocides as special and more horrible betray an unpleasant set of preconceptions and prejudices that certainly bear scrutiny if we're claiming to be interested in genocide in the abstract. I mean it seems, at least to me, very clear that what happened to the Native Americans was a very organized genocide on the part of white people for economic reasons that were, more often than not, justified by cultural and racial prejudices. The fact of genocide, that one group is trying to wipe out another group, in its entirety—whether for economic, racial, or cultural reasons—should not be the most salient consideration, to my mind. Anyway, in Berlin, we got into this big, ostensibly friendly argument, but it just seemed to me that what was at issue—Daschle clearly felt *very* strongly about this—was that what happened to the Native Americans be recognized as a genocide. The historical particulars are wildly different in the two cases, obviously—the Native Americans and the Jews of Europe—but genocide is genocide. In both cases, a powerful group of aggressors with strong economic and ideological motivations attempted to exterminate, victimize, relocate, and rob another group of people, as the result of a concerted plan, using the most sophisticated technology at their disposal. And if you think the Holocaust is somehow "worse" because the victims are white Europeans who spoke languages you understand and wore fur coats and read novels and newspapers and were modern, recognizable people, then you need to think hard about your own ideologies, it seems to me. This whole my-genocide-was-worse-than-your-genocide thing seems to me to betray a fundamental lack of moral and historical imagination—an essential failure to understand just why genocide in general is an abomination. The very *idea* that one genocide could be "worse" than another is abominable, as far as I'm concerned.

NKM: I wanted to ask you, Daniel, if you would talk about the end of your book, because when I was reading it I felt intensely curious about how the story would turn out, and I was lucky because I was on a very, very long plane ride.

DM: People always tell me that.

NKM: No, it was great!

DM: I get so many e-mails . . . "I was on a plane . . ."

NKM: Well, I had been to a conference in Budapest about family photographs and many of the subjects that we're discussing today. I had brought your book, but the trip wasn't really long enough. I wanted to save the end for when I wasn't myself at the end of an exhausting trip. I wanted to see how you were going to pull this off, because to take the reader on this journey—the book itself is a journey—the reader has to go through all the finding and the losing, and then there is the final finding. You say you found what you were looking for and yet that something still is going to elude you. There is always a problem of belatedness in autobiography and especially, of course, in all these stories about other people's past. I'm thinking about that moment where you know you're going to finish your book, and you've already finished the journey, and what are you going to end with?

DM: Yes—this goes to the heart of an interesting question about the way that a nonfiction narrative like mine has to be both true and also a good *story*, right? In my case, it's interesting because I thought I'd finished with all my journeying and interviewing and fact-finding, and so had already written the end of the book—and then, quite unexpectedly, I made a big discovery that gave me so many details and specifics that I'd never dreamed of attaining. What I mean is that I had thought I had found out everything I could, and then, during a second trip to Bolechow that I hadn't really planned on making, and which anyway was just going to be a quick trip to take a few more photos for the book, by acci-

dent I found out a lot more, found the details I'd always hoped
for, about my great-uncle's fate. It was one of those serendipitous
things that can happen: I was just in this town for a few hours
and I bumped into someone who bumped into someone, and we
actually, in that moment, found out the solution to the mystery,
which I had thought would be ultimately impossible to solve. So
the end of my book happened *to* me in a funny way. But I wanted
to preserve the sense of the total fortuitousness of what had happened, the unexpectedness with which knowledge can, finally,
come, and so in the book I kept the original ending, the ending
I'd written before I made this great discovery, which I call the
"False Ending." And after that comes the final section which tells
of the great discovery. So, you know, the whole *book,* in some
sense, is about the problem of belatedness, of accidentalness . . .
but that's inevitable when you write about the past, you're always
coming too late because you're interested in the past and it already happened, if you know what I mean. Everything about the
past is already, tragically, "belated." You can't win.

NKM: A Jewish joke, I suppose.

DM: Well, but it's true! You know, so much of my book is about how
I made mistakes about the past: I thought I knew something, and
I didn't, or I thought I knew who somebody was and it turned out
to be someone much more important than I ever thought, and so
on. But that's inevitable to the writing of the history, because we
are not *in* the past. You know, my favorite line from a novel is the
first sentence of *The Go-Between,* "the past is a foreign country;
they do things differently there."[6] And it really *is.* They speak a
different language, the directions to the restroom are different,
everything is different in the past, and I think we need to recognize that. It's just not some transparently available thing, some
place that you could get to and see whole if you only did enough
research, studied hard enough, asked enough questions, and read
enough documents. I think this is a particularly important point
to make because we have a fantasy, particularly in American culture, I would say, particularly *now,* of total recuperability—you
know, every emotion, every experience is transparently available
to anybody who has the price of admission, basically. And, you
know, when you write about these events, events of, let's say,
high and profound trauma to civilization, whether it's in Europe,

whether it's in Africa, you know, ruined civilizations—when you write about this extent of devastation, most of this stuff is lost, right? You know, the whole joke of my book, so to speak, is that I schlepped around for five years all over the world, from Australia to Scandinavia to Israel to Eastern Europe, and in the end there just wasn't that much to find—there wasn't much left. There's this page in my book where I list all the facts that I learned about my great-uncle and the family in all that time, all those years of schlepping, and it's exactly one page long—in a five-hundred-page book. We want to believe we can get it all back, but we can't. So 98 percent is *lost*, and the recognition that most things in life get lost is crucial, I think, particularly now, in the era of total, endless, transparent availability of everyone to everyone else at every given moment of every day. The idea that one can't know something is an intolerable idea right now, and I think it's very important to keep reminding people that most of what happens in the past is unavailable, because it's in the *past*. And only the stuff that's important survives. Or, the stuff that was in the right place survived but most of it's gone. And that's the way it's always going to be.

EH: Well, yes, we are talking about the function of our books, I actually wanted to make the past the past, to separate myself from the past. Which I think is the task for the belated generations. The past lives in us, impinges on us, and for those who had lived through it, there is no separation from it, probably in one lifetime. But for the second generation, for those who come after, it is not our past, and that needs to be understood. Our distance from it needs to be acknowledged. So I wanted to make the past the past, which doesn't mean forgetting it or neglecting it or being indifferent to it. It can, I think, happen only after you process it very fully, after you work through it very fully, but, after a while, I wanted precisely to know that there was a distinction between that catastrophic and horrendous and enormous past and the present.

SH: I would say that I share that desire. I would love for the past to be the past. Reconstruction was one attempt to make the past the past. Social movements are also attempts to create ruptures between pasts and presents. However, my book ends on an expectant note, in which the time of slavery is still open, and the question remains when will this become the past? This is less a question of memory or forgetting than it is one regarding the practice of freedom and the possibilities of transformation. The book concludes with this open question rather than with narrative closure, it ends with the narrator listening for a different kind of song.

DM: But I think what you're saying is both crucial and deeply healthy, in a funny way. And also, I would say, something that a lot of people don't want to think about, because both of these events, in their ways, are still present enough in the lives of living people—are fairly recent, in a weird way. People are always saying to me, "what can we do so that we'll never forget this"? And I look at them and I say, "Nothing. No one can remember everything all the time." I think this is *very* interesting. These things are recent enough to us that we care about them deeply, and we can't bear the thought that one day people will be indifferent to them; but they will. It's inevitable; anything else is a dream. Look, the idea of total memory, total recall of the largeness of the past, is nutty—if you import all of the past into the present, which we increasingly have the technology to do, then you have no room to be in the *present*. That's a fact, right? So it's actually right and healthy for much of the past to slip away, to get streamlined into a form that the present can accommodate. You know, I always say that it's like the Passover story. In the year 2300 BC or whenever it was, believe me, all anyone could talk about was the enslavement in Egypt, because it had *just* happened, and boy was that a big deal! Every one of the tens of thousands of Hebrew slaves who made it out of Egypt had a long spiel to tell everyone he knew the amazing things that happened, who he was with, the name of the horrible overseer who whipped him, blah blah blah. And you know what? Now we talk about it once a year for two hours. But that's a valid model, and that's healthy. That's how cultures move into the present. They commemorate in an organized way. We're not all sitting around saying, "Gosh, was the brick that so-and-so had to schlep up the pyramid heavy!" "Did so-and-so's camel smell bad!" right?

NKM: I think some people are still finding it heavy.

DM: Right, and they're in universities, which is where the people interested in that level of detail belong—the historians, the scholars, the specialists. But the culture in general can't tolerate, has no time for, that degree of specificity. A culture needs a story it can tell once a year to commemorate its history; it doesn't care whose camel smelled and how heavy the brick was.

SH: But, actually, I have a joke about a Passover dinner. I was with friends at an interracial Passover dinner, and, during the remembrance of the bitterness of slavery, a friend joked that for some of us it's the bitterness of freedom that we need to commemorate. Here, again, the question arises as to the distinction between that which is being commemorated and the possibilities which are open or foreclosed in the present. I also think that there is hubris involved in the "need to remember," as if remembering were enough to prevent other crimes.

DM: As it so clearly doesn't.

SH: Yeah, so it's . . .

DM: But what I mean is that, I mean by that joke about, you know, it's the specialists who are interested in the bricks, the camels, but the culture, in order to progress into its own future, cannot remember all the things that happened in all their enormity and detail every minute of every day or else they can't have a *present*.

EH: Can I just quickly say that I'm not suggesting forgetting. I'm suggesting, in a sense, a move from memory to history, a memory with all of its identifications.

DH: Right, but that's what I call commemoration.

EH: To history, to knowledge.

Notes

This conversation took place during the "Rites of Returns" conference, April 2008.

1. Eva Hoffman, *Lost in Translation* (New York: Penguin, 1990).

2. Daniel Mendelsohn, *The Lost: A Search for Six of Six Million* (New York: Harper Collins, 2006).

3. Saidiya Hartman, *Lose Your Mother* (New York: Farrar, Straus and Giroux, 2007).

4. Michel Foucault, "Lives of Infamous Men," *Essential Works of Foucault,* vol. 3: *Power,* James D. Faubion, ed. (New York: New Press, 2000).

5. Eva Hoffman, *After Such Knowledge: Memory, History and the Legacy of the Holocaust* (New York: PublicAffairs, 2005), 15, 16, 34.

6. L. P. Hartley, *The Go-Between* (New York: NYRB Classics, 2002).

7   Return to Half-Ruins

Fathers and Daughters, Memory and History in Palestine

LILA ABU-LUGHOD

'Awda in Arabic means return. For diasporic Palestinians, the charged term evokes nostalgia for the homeland they were forced to flee in 1948 and a reversal of the traumatic dispersion that sundered families, ruined livelihoods, and thrust Palestinians into humiliating refugee camps or individual adventures to rebuild lives armed with little more than birth certificates, keys to the homes left behind, and the stigma of having somehow lost their country to an alien people. The current political insistence on the "right of return" is a demand for righting a moral wrong. It is also a demand that the story of that expulsion not be erased.

Not everyone fled Palestine in 1948, of course. Some Palestinians stayed on the land within the expanding territorial control of the Israeli state declared on May 15, 1948. Hanging on to their own villages or setting up near them, staying on in their cities, they would watch their world transform before their eyes. Dislodged socially and politically, but in place physically, they would learn the language of their colonizers and work among them, often in menial jobs. Those who fled to the towns of the West Bank or to Gaza would only come under direct Israeli military and administrative control twenty years later when Israel occupied, through the 1967 war, those remaining parts of historic Palestine.

The majority of Palestinian refugees, however, found themselves cut off from their homes and their pasts. In Lebanon, Jordan, Syria, Iraq, Kuwait, the U.S., England, and even the countries of South America, they tried to make new lives. Some were successful, financially and culturally; but many, generations later, still live in refugee camps that have become unsettlingly permanent. For those cut off, memories of home were frozen.

Until 1991, my father was one of those exiles who had not been back to see what had happened to his country. From Jordan, where his family had fled, he had taken a boat on borrowed money to the U.S. in search of an education. He had made a life there, working his way through college, marrying my mother, having children, and eventually going to Princeton to get a Ph.D. in Arab history. My father was one of those who refused to go and see his former home even when, quite late, he obtained the American passport that would have entitled him, as a tourist, to enter his homeland, now Israel.

Then something changed. After a sobering illness, he realized that he might die without ever seeing Palestine again. He decided he would go. I remember hearing his excited stories when he returned from his first visit in 1991. His first shock, he said, was arriving at what he knew as Lydda airport to find a huge sign saying "Welcome to Israel." Nevertheless, he was exhilarated. What followed was a decision in 1992 to move "back"—to return. This move, I was to learn when I nervously agreed to visit him in Israel/Palestine five months later, changed his experience of that cataclysmic and defining event known by Palestinians simply as the Nakba, "the catastrophe." He inserted his memories of Palestine directly into the present, into a living history. My father's insertion of memory into the historical present made possible a different knowledge and identification for his children as well. This essay will explore what happened to my father as well as what happened to me as a result of his *'awda*.

Storied Memories

My father was a talker and a storyteller. Because of this, there was no time when we, his children, did not know we were Palestinian. The stories I remember about his boyhood in the 1930s and early 1940s were nostalgic, both comic and bitter. But there were more political stories that began to teach us what it had meant to be Palestinian under the British

Mandate. According to my father, people were barely aware they were on the eve of disastrous events that would make them refugees. They did not realize that the Zionists, not the British, were their real adversaries.

Yet,while I was growing up, I don't recall hearing his stories of 1948, the last months before the fall of his hometown, Jaffa. Were we too young to be told? Did it not mean anything to children who had never seen Jaffa? What happened when my father returned to Palestine was that his memories now became the guide to a living history and a real place. And he told the stories to me and to anyone who would listen.

Jaffa was the heart of my father's Palestine. On the wall of his apartment in Ramallah when I came to stay in 2001 was a large sepia poster: a historic photograph of an Arab man staring wistfully out to sea with a large town in the background. At the top, in Arabic, it said, "Jaffa 1937." On my first visit to Palestine to see him in 1993, I sensed the thrill he felt at having mastered the new situation. The good part was embracing and being embraced by the community he had found, whether in the West Bank or in various other parts of pre-1948 Palestine. The anxiety of being there was betrayed by his dry mouth and the beads of sweat on his forehead as he drove us around, approaching Israeli military checkpoints or getting lost because he couldn't read Hebrew. For me, the landscape was familiar from Lebanon and Jordan, which I had known well growing up. The barren highways and the cities branded by Hebrew sounds and sights were menacing, though, especially when combined with the heavy presence of Israeli soldiers, reservists, and guns.

He was eager to show me and my small family the whole of Palestine, from Jerusalem to Bethlehem, Nablus to Nazareth, Jericho to 'Akka. His tour of Jaffa, the same one, I was a little hurt to discover later, he gave to many others, was about claiming and reclaiming the city in which he had been born, the sea in which he had swum as a boy, and the home he had been forced to flee in 1948. On his own first visit in 1991, he'd asked friends to take him there. Initially he was disoriented. Most of the landmarks weren't there. The neighborhood by the sea where he'd grown up had been razed by then, though twenty years earlier his brother had done what so many Palestinians have done and described: knocked on the door to find out which Jews—Russian, Moroccan, Yemeni, Polish—were now living in their old family homes.[1] Suddenly, my father said he had spotted the Hasan Bek mosque where he had made the call to prayer as a boy. Bit by bit, circling more widely around the mosque, he began to find his way.

It was a former student of his who had made him rethink his refusal to go back. She often traveled to Israel and the Occupied Territories. He recalled that she had told him once, "Ibrahim, Palestine is still there." He was happy, he said, to find this true. There is an image in one of Doris Lessing's *African Stories* (1981) that has never left me. A young girl, a white settler living in southern Africa, looks out over the savanna and acacia trees and sees the large gnarled oak trees of her English fairytales. My father did the opposite. Where I, who never knew anything else, could see only the deep gouges in green hillsides made for Israeli settlements with garish red tile roofs, or miles and miles of highways criss-crossing the rocky landscape and claiming it with modern green signs in Hebrew and English, or non-native evergreen forests to hide razed villages, my father saw beyond, between and behind them to the familiar landscapes of his youth.[2]

He explained that he used to travel as a boy all around Palestine with workers from his father's foundry as they delivered, installed, and repaired water pumps and olive presses. I discovered later that he had also traveled as a politicized high school student trying to organize fellow students, worrying his mother sick, my mother tells me, as he set off by bus. He showed us the orange groves where he might have stolen a fruit or two when young. He pointed out the stubborn cacti still marking the boundaries of Arab fields that no longer exist. Tucked in and among the new structures that dominate the towns and cities, he would point out the arched windows of old Arab houses that had somehow escaped destruction. Half-ruins he built in his imagination, while I strained to make them out amidst the ugly concrete.

My father's tour of Jaffa took us down a boulevard where you passed a majestic colonial post office (where he had tried in vain to get his old postbox, just for the pleasure of being able to receive letters addressed to Jaffa); the law courts where he had dreamed of practicing law, modeling himself on Yusuf Wahbi, a star of Egyptian film whose eloquence could win people over; the spot where there had been an ice cream shop where he and his teenaged friends would go, more to flirt with the European woman who worked there than to eat. These buildings harbored meanings for him that were opaque for me, who saw only the sort of colonial buildings that looked vaguely familiar from other parts of the Middle East—other places the British and French had set themselves up to rule. I had affection for these kinds of buildings in Egypt, just as I felt at home and ease there. Here I was a stranger and my father's memories, perhaps because so caught up in defeat and hostility, were not ones I could easily embrace.

In the book he edited in 1971, *The Transformation of Palestine*, my father would publish an article by Erskine Childers, a distinguished Irish journalist who characterized the Zionist hope from the early part of the twentieth century that the Palestinians would disappear as "the wordless wish." Based on documentary sources including Zionist, British, and Arab radio broadcasts, Childers described what happened in Jaffa in the weeks before it was overrun—a description I had found shocking when I first read it. Again, it was so hard to imagine that this was what my father and his family had lived through—my grandmother had never talked about it to me, her only stories from the past being about her wedding night and other fragments of magic and everyday life in Palestine. The assault, Childers noted, began on April 25, 1948, with units of the underground Irgun followed by units of the official Hagana. Although Jaffa was not part of the Jewish allocation in the UN partition plan, it was bombarded by three-inch mortars, highly inaccurate but devastating psychologically; it was subjected to barrel bombs, described by an Israeli army reserve officer to the U.S. Marine Corps professional magazine as especially designed for Arab towns and consisting of "barrels, casks or metal drums, filled with a mixture of explosives and petrol, and fitted with two old rubber tires containing the detonating fuse," that were rolled down the streets until they crashed into walls and doorways, bursting into flames and multiple explosions;[3] its population was terrorized psychologically by loudspeaker vans with prerecorded "horror sounds" including shrieks, wails and moans of women, sirens, fire alarm bells, and calls, in Arabic, to run for their lives and to remember the massacre at Deir Yassin.[4]

My father, a high school student, had volunteered for the hurriedly formed, city-based National Committee to defend Jaffa. With no training, he, like so many of the small fighting force of fifteen hundred, was issued an old gun unfit for battle. My father's last days and nights "defending" Jaffa at the age of nineteen were spent in various places that were also part of his tour of the city. With no sense of the geography, the streets and buildings meaning nothing to me, I again could not connect my white-haired father in his black beret, his classical music playing on the car radio, with this youth. I struggled to transpose those old black and white photographs of a young man with a dark mustache and bright eyes into this place. But how could I? His trauma in Palestine had lived on in me only as a wounded identification in a hostile U.S. where sympathy for

Palestinians was scarce and aggressive lies about what had happened prevailed. My father recalled that at the end of that fateful April, food was running out, the bakeries had closed, mortar from Tel Aviv was falling on the city. The streets of most neighborhoods were by then empty. The British were escorting convoys of people fleeing. But it was dangerous for young Palestinian men to try to leave the city by land because they were vulnerable to arrest or worse, the British unable or unwilling to protect them. There was only the sea.

On his tour, then, my father pointed to the place where he and his school friend laid down their useless guns when they left. He had lost touch with this brother on another front; the rest of his family was gone. On the morning of May 3, the two joined a throng on a small barge that was transporting people out of the harbor to a ship that was rumored to be the last ship to carry people to safety. Sent by the Red Cross, it was going to Beirut. But then they hesitated, asking themselves what they were doing. They went back ashore. After all, they had been part of the National Committee urging people not to flee, insisting the city was safe, promising that reinforcements were on the way (they weren't). But when they did return, they realized that no one was left. The shooting, my father said, was all coming from the other side. Around three o'clock in the afternoon they saw smoke billowing from the smokestack of the ship. It was about to leave. They put down their guns and ran to catch the last dinghy out. The words of a Belgian sailor who confronted them on board echoed in my father's ears fifty years later: "How could you leave your country?" He was to repeat to himself these words many times, even though he knew there had been no choice.

The tour of Jaffa always ended with the sea. My father ignored the Hebrew being spoken all around him. He refused to go to the Israeli beach café. Instead, he made himself a place on the sand and went in for his swim. All my life I had watched him gaze out to sea—from Alexandria, from Beirut, from Spain, Morocco, New Jersey, and the Caribbean. I had seen him swim out, stretching his long fingers with his wedding band glinting in the sun, his broad shoulders breaking out of the water when he did the butterfly stroke he liked best. He had made us all love the sea. Yet here, in Jaffa, like the man in his sepia poster, he looked out from the place he somehow stubbornly considered home, even though I felt we were vulnerable intruders. His blue American passport allowed him to sit on the beach where he swam as a boy with dolphins and turtles, the beach his mother could see from her window as she drank her coffee. It was his unthreatening white hair and turtleneck shirts that allowed him to pass as a foreigner, not a dangerous or despised Arab "native." The yellow license plates that identified his car as Israeli and thus gave him freedom of movement allowed him to pull up unnoticed alongside the others in the parking lot at the beach. These were the colors of his return to Jaffa.

Memorializing Material Remains

For a daughter, a father's death is always hard. But when he is someone whose life has been tied up with something much larger than family, his death too takes on much more than personal meaning. My father died in Palestine on May 23, 2001, surrounded by family and friends. For me, the first aftermath was intensely personal and fixated on objects. Draped over the back of the black wheelchair with its shiny red wheels were his khaki "bair of bants," as he used to joke, in his self-mocking caricature of an Arab accent. The belt dangled limply. On the bathroom counter was the untouched shaving mug, its water gone cold. Everywhere in his Ramallah apartment were the abandoned signs of his life. His Vivaldi CDs. The oxygen tanks, two big ones by the bed, four small ones lined up in the hall, the one on the trolley with a stenciled Star of David marking it as from "the other side." My father's room held so many small objects that would make a daughter cry: his watch, his glasses, his wallet, his sandals, his dried fruit, his piles of scholarly papers.

We were now to be swept into a more public world. While we, his children with various levels of familiarity with Palestinian society but almost no experience in Palestine, grieved, my father's friends indeed took care of everything. They had to negotiate the complex world of a Palestinian community steeped in the political during an intifada, a world we were hardly prepared for. His death certificate was written; his burial certificate was obtained from the appropriate Israeli ministries. Plans for the funeral in Jaffa were made. Arrangements for the three days of condolence visits in Ramallah were made. Plastic chairs arrived at the apartment and were set up in rows along the walls of the living room, dining room, and terrace. Counters were cleared and bitter coffee made. Posters with his photo on them appeared. Arab coffee, cases of water, and boxes of Kleenex were piled in the kitchen, compliments, I was surprised to learn, of the Palestine National Authority.

The next time we saw my father was on the day of the funeral. He was a frail body lying in a little concrete room with green metal doors set behind Maqasid Islamic Hospital in Jerusalem, ritually prepared for burial. Wrapped in white sheets and bound, he looked small and thin. When I went to look at his face, only a small bit of it uncovered, I had to turn away. He was lifeless—the finality so physical.

But he was at the same time now becoming a symbol for others. Already shrouded as a Muslim, he was also going to be a national hero of sorts. We began the long wait as people gathered for the drive to Jaffa. We were watching tensely for any unusual movement, wondering if "they" were going to prevent us from taking him. A man filmed us with a video camera. It was a relief to find out that he was from Al Jazeera Television, the Arab satellite channel, not then well known outside the Arab world because this was still May, a few months before the events of 9/11 thrust this news station into Western consciousness. The evening before, with the house full of mourners, we had received an unnerving phone call. The man spoke Arabic; he identified himself as from Israeli intelligence, Shin Bet. My legs were weak, and I could only think how glad I was that we were in an area under the Palestinian Authority. All this officer could do was telephone, not come knocking on/down the door. I could never think of Israelis without the sharp black and white images of the French colonial commandos in Pontecorvo's brilliant film *Battle of Algiers* kicking down doors. Had it been a few months later when Israeli tanks reoccupied Ramallah, he would indeed have been able to invade our private grief.

I had quickly passed the phone to my father's friends. I could hear heated discussion in the back bedroom. They were being told that they would not be permitted to bury my father in Jaffa. How had Israeli security known? It was all over Radio Palestine and in the local newspapers: the first Palestinian refugee to be buried back in his hometown. My father's colleagues insisted that we had all the proper documents. But the security officer was insistent. He said he would call back. We were agitated. The men went over possible scenarios, all terrible to me: of being halted as we tried to take the body from the hospital or as we were on the road to Jaffa or as we approached the cemetery. Could we really have a confrontation with the Israeli army while my father's body lay in the hot sun? What should we do? Someone suggested that I should call the U.S. consul general in Jerusalem. When we didn't hear back from the Shin Bet officer that night, we thought it was a good sign.

So it was a relief that nothing was happening that Friday morning be-hind Maqasid Hospital except that people were milling about. More and more people. Eventually it was time to move. An unmarked white van pulled up in front of the morgue, and the coffin was loaded. My sisters and I clung to each other as we peered through the van window at that plain, lonely box. The crowd got into cars and the bus that had come from Ramallah, forming a long cortege. Slowly we drove, looking right and left for Israeli army jeeps or police. But the road was clear.

It was a long drive, on highways and through a back route into the in-dustrial sector that led to the Arab part of Jaffa. In a crowded neighborhood, we parked and got out. Plastered on the walls were bills with newspaper articles about my father and his curriculum vitae. A professor, I realized, is a respected figure in this community. And he was special because of the way he'd come in fresh, breaking through the inertia of strikes, ignoring curfews, refusing all the borders between Palestinians—diasporic, in the occupied territories, and within Israel—and willing communities to take action, as he had done in his years in the U.S.. We were at the center of the Jaffa Arab Association, a place where my father had spoken many times to a community he was exceedingly fond of, these remnants in what had been a Palestinian city. The association was headed by some men who had gone out of their way to help arrange for the burial. For them, my father's support and concern for their activities (squatting in condemned buildings, clearing paths to houses whose access had been blocked by the dumping of garbage for a Tel Aviv landfill, advocacy and social services for the downtrodden Arabs of a rundown neighborhood so different from the gentrified areas where Jews lived) had meant a lot.

The coffin was laid out on a large table in a small room to the left. There were wreaths of flowers. Now draped with the Palestinian flag, the coffin suddenly looked vibrant. My father was no longer the frail mummy we'd seen earlier. His death was being given great meaning. In my grief, I barely heard the long eulogies in Arabic. I was glad they stopped when it was time for the afternoon prayer. Everyone spilled out the doors and followed the coffin. Men carried it down the side streets to the 'Ajami' mosque, jostling to take their turn. In the front of the procession some young men held the Palestinian flag as a banner.

At the mosque, they carried him upstairs. I wondered how long it had been since he had been in a mosque, but this was the way. He was being absorbed into a society and community. All the women stayed outside, but I also noticed that there were many more men waiting outside the mosque than had gone inside. I asked a colleague of his from Birzeit University, "Are all these Christians?" "No," he answered with a smile, "I see a lot of Marxist-Leninists!"

When prayers were over, we began to move. Carried on the shoulders of waves of men, the coffin swayed wildly. Far in front was a Palestinian flag, now defiantly waving. A large procession of people walked together up the hill, holding hands, talking, feeling part of the group. We passed the fish restaurants that my father liked to take people to. Like oranges, fish were for him part of the cherished tastes of home in Jaffa. Stronger tastes than Proust's famed madeleines. Bystanders watched, perplexed. Some children waved, thinking perhaps this was a parade. Many Israelis now live in the Arab neighborhoods of Jaffa, some enjoying tastefully restored houses with Arab tiles and arches, as my aunt would be devastated to discover when we returned to Jaffa a week later. The sea shimmered to our right below, the afternoon sun catching the windsurfers who were out enjoying the gentle breeze. The sense of exhilaration was intense—so many people walking together, following a coffin draped in the flag. Miraculously, it seemed, we were not being prevented from burying him as he wished, in the cemetery overlooking the sea in his hometown of Jaffa. No one failed to mention—at the community center before we headed to the cemetery and several days later at the memorial in Ramallah—that my father had made his 'awda, his return, finally, to Jaffa.

The Past in the Present

For my father, return meant the insertion of honed stories and distant memories into the roughness of history and a genuine confrontation with the present. Surprisingly, he had taken this on with enthusiasm. He who had for so long refused to come began encouraging every Palestinian to return, even if they had to suffer the offensive interrogations of Israeli authorities at the airport and the bridge, the shoes taken off for inspection, the notebooks confiscated, the suitcases emptied, the body searched, even the diaper bags and toiletries opened. When an interviewer on Al Jazeera Television asked him if he wasn't bitter that his dream of return had brought him into a situation where Palestinians were faced with daily problems and herded into zones called A, B, and C, separated by Israeli military checkpoints, he answered, "I do not feel bitterness at all. I feel, rather, that the Israeli presence is a challenge to us. And it is impossible to meet that challenge with bitterness. . . . My coming here, a big part of it, was in order to change this reality. Because I cannot fight far away from the field of struggle."[5]

I saw for myself that confrontation on the ground. I saw the armed riot soldiers facing the young boys throwing stones. But I also saw my father as he approached the Israeli checkpoints steeling himself nervously for the charade and forced smile of this gentleman flashing his American passport to get through. Later I experienced Israel through his illness and death. Through the inability to get anywhere on the West Bank the pain-killers prescribed by the Israeli doctor or the morphine patches his Palestinian doctor wanted for him. And the need to take an ambulance to go to doctors' appointments for fear his oxygen tank would run out while the car overheated at a slow checkpoint. I will never forget the fear on the face of his normally lively friend as we approached the checkpoints; she was an Israeli Palestinian from the north who knew Hebrew and always came along to help him negotiate the hospital. She was not technically allowed to cross into the West Bank with her Israeli identity card, even though that is where she lived with her husband and children.

The physical reality of my father's death was for me inseparable from the details of Israeli domination: from his blue fingertips to the Palestinian medics who rushed him down the stairs to the ambulance but couldn't guarantee that they'd be allowed to pass quickly, from the intrusive phone call of an Israeli officer to the inert flag draped over the coffin in the Jaffa Community Center, from the anxiety about surveillance to the inexpressible generosity of his community, from the fears about the fate of the lecture notes we had to throw into the dumpster as we cleaned out his apartment to the panic we felt the eerie day none of his friends came to visit for fear of a bombing.

I had heard my father's stories all my life, but it is different to walk, orphaned, through a hot dusty checkpoint dragging your suitcases because they won't allow any Palestinian vehicles to cross. It is different to be held up by arrogant soldiers with reflective sunglasses and burnished muscles who willfully delay you. It is different to go to the airport in an Arab taxi. On your way to catch your plane they slowly search the car and disappear for a long time with the driver's identity card, humiliating you with the power to make you sit silent, though you know you are perfectly innocent. Stories of the underground railroad and the smuggling of slaves to freedom, images of displaced refugees from the Second World War trudging with their bundles of possessions—these came to me as I crossed over out of the West Bank to the safety of Jerusalem, then to catch my plane. But they can't capture this particular reality with its growling Hebrew arrogantly proclaiming ownership. With its guns and soldiers everywhere you turn. With its utter separation of Arab and Jew. These experiences, even more than my father's stories, have made me want to write about his expulsion and return. The Palestinian "catastrophe" is not just something of the past. It continues into the present in every house demolished by an Israeli bulldozer, with every firing from an Apache helicopter, with every stillbirth at a military checkpoint, with every village divided from its fields by the "separation" wall, and with every Palestinian who still longs to return to a home that is no more.

Notes

For comments and other help with this essay, I am grateful to my feminist reading group, Janet Abu-Lughod, Lori Allen, Saidiya Hartman, Marianne Hirsch, Timothy Mitchell, Ahmad Sa'di, Julia Seton, and the participants in the workshop on "Al-Nakba in Palestinian Collective Memory" in Montecatini Terme, Italy. I am grateful to Hisham Ahmed-Fararjeh for having shared his interviews with my father and to Roger Heacock for giving me insight into his role at Birzeit University. This is an abridged and slightly edited version of "Return to Half-Ruins: Memory, Postmemory and Living History in Palestine," in Ahmad H. Sa'di and Lila Abu-Lughod, eds., *Nakba: Palestine, 1948, and the Claims of Memory* (New York: Columbia University Press, 2007), reprinted with permission.

1. For descriptions of such visits, see Ghada Karmi, *In Search of Fatima* (New York: Saqi, 2002); Salim Tamari and Rema Hammami, "Virtual Return to Jaffa." *Journal of Palestine Studies* 27, no. 4 (Summer 1998): 65–79; and Omar Al-Qattan, "The Secret Visitations of Memory," in Sa'di and Abu-Lughod, *Nakba*, pp. 191–206. For Edward Said's return to his family home, see the BBC documentary *In Search of Palestine* by Charles Bruce (1998). For an insightful discussion of films about claims to houses and homes in Jerusalem, see Amahl Bishara, "Examining Sentiments About and Claims to Jerusalem and Its Houses," *Social Text* 75, no. 21 (Summer 2003): 141–162; and Ahmad H. Sa'di, "Catastrophe, Memory, and Identity," *Israel Studies* 7, no. 2175–98 (2002).

2. For more on the forests, see Carol Bardenstein, "Trees, Forests, and the Shaping of Palestinian and Israeli Collective Memory," in Mieke L. Bal, Jonathan Crewe, and Leo Spitzer, eds., *Acts of Memory* (Hanover: University Press of New England, 1999), 148–168; and Haim Bresheeth, "The Continuity of Trauma and Struggle," Rochelle Davis, "Mapping the Past: Re-creating the Homeland," and Susan Slyomovics, "The Rape of Qula," in Sa'di and Abu-Lughod, *Nakba*.

3. Erskine Childers, "The Wordless Wish: From Citizens to Refugees," in Ibrahim Abu-Lughod, ed., *The Transformation of Palestine* (Evanston, IL: Northwestern University Press, 1971), 187.

4. Ibid., 188.

5. My father gave me an unlabeled video recording of the interview, which I believe is with Muhammad Khrayshat on the program *Dayf wa Qadiyya* (Guest and Issue), Al Jazeera Television, probably in 1999.

8 Singing with the Taxi Driver

From Bollywood to Babylon

JAY PROSSER

There's a particular kind of music that is a return. A return to the past, to childhood; to where we came from, to what we've lost. Music is structurally return. It moves forward, developing in time, and can't be returned to except in mechanical recordings; but it depends simultaneously on reprise, repetition, patterns heard before. Arising and falling, it is always present. Music only works through memory, our ability to remember themes and notes that have come earlier. And understanding how one listens to music helps one understand how memory works in life. Moving what's been into what's to come, music can work across languages, cultures, and histories. Listening to music has the power to evoke through the ear memories consciously forgotten, emotional, felt in the rhythms of the body.

This key quality common to music and memory is transition, the bridge between past and present, cultures then and there and our world right here and now. Daniel Barenboim, the Israeli-Palestinian conductor—and the only Israeli citizen to hold passports to both nations—has drawn on the transitional character of music to effect culture transitions in history.[1] In 1999 Barenboim set up with Edward Said the West-Eastern Divan Orchestra, joining musicians from Arab countries with Israeli musicians. Their aim was for Israelis to remember and understand Palestinian history and for Palestinians to perform and participate in Western classical culture. Speaking about the enterprise, Barenboim finds in music an ideal for historical reconciliation: "through music we can see an alternative social model, a kind of practical Utopia, from which we might learn about expressing ourselves freely and hearing one another."[2]

In 2006 Barenboim gave the BBC Reith Lectures, in which he spreads wider his practice of deriving lessons for life from music. It is transition that allows Barenboim to correlate music with life: "Transition, let us not forget, is the basis of human existence. In music it is not enough simply to play a statement of a phrase, it is absolutely essential to see how we arrived there, and to prepare it. One plays a statement one way at the beginning of a piece, but when the same statement returns later, in what we call in musical terminology the recapitulation, it is in a completely different psychological state of mind. And therefore the bridge, the transition, determines not only itself but what comes after it."[3] In his first Reith lecture Barenboim makes the connection between music and memory: "The first quality that comes to my mind as to the intelligence of the ear is that the ear helps us tremendously to remember and to recollect . . . and that shows you one of the most important elements of expression in music, one of repetition and accumulation. In any case, the ear has this incredible memory."[4]

In the memoir I am writing of my mother's family, music—against my consciousness at first—has been a way to access the memories of her Baghdadi Jewish and Chinese roots and routes and of my parents' own meeting in Singapore. As together my mother and I go through her archive of different media—stories, documents, objects, and, of course, photographs—music is a recurrent theme and a channel for returning forgotten pasts, and particularly for remembering cross-cultural encounters and the desire for transition. I am finding that even the collaboration with my mother, which is the process of producing the memoir, corresponds to Barenboim's description of music. In the beginning is my mother's "statement"; in writing I "return" to or "recapitulate" it; and this can reshape her present understanding of herself—"what comes after."

For example: recently my parents were inspired to make a cruise from Singapore to Southampton, via various stopping points in India, the Middle East, and Europe, having just read my account in the memoir of their own previous identical journeys. My return in writing to their early lives prompted their actual return to those old sites. From my mother on the boat, I received this further account of capturing memories, adding another layer to what I had already written. She had just visited Bombay, where she spent her childhood, equipped with the maps, directions, names of places, and contacts I had used from my research trip preceding her. But it is music that returns her properly. In the speechless conversation that is e-mail, she writes:

> This is a different world; we are so cocooned here. The ship is OK and the excursions mixed; Phuket was a waste of time, and so was Dubai. But Cochin & Bombay were an amazing experience. Bombay was especially very poignant for me; seeing the coastline at dawn brought tears to my eyes, thinking of my Papa. It was all strange and yet familiar. Your notes and maps were crucial to our visit; we decided to go it alone (because the Jewish ship tour was cancelled) so we went by taxi. During the morning we saw two synagogues (the Magen David & Knesset Eliyahu) and the David Sassoon Library & School. We tried to find the exact spot in Ripon (now Maulana Azad) Rd where we had lived but it was impossible. We had a useless taxi driver who didn't know a thing, so I had to get out & talk to the people (my Hindi came back in a big way!). It was all so crowded there & I have a feeling now that we actually lived along that road which at the time was so quiet I remembered it as a courtyard. There were cloth shops here & there still, but all those dwellings are now shanties occupied by very very poor Indian families as you know. It was sad to see them and yet they went around with smiles on their faces. We treated ourselves to a nice lunch at the Taj Mahal Hotel then took another taxi, a better one, along Chowpatty Beach to Colaba and Malabar Hill, then to the Hanging Gardens and Dhobi Ghat. He then took us back to Byculla to take one or two pictures. He was a nice young man who sang whilst driving; Dad told him I could sing, which the driver made me do, so all the way, we sang in turn then found we were singing the same song together (in Hindustani of course!). It was such an uplifting experience. The driver was amazed I could sing & speak Hindustani! I loved Bombay; not sure if I'll return but it was a very evocative experience and I thought of my Papa who talked so much about the different streets & I found them. I think during the war it was the Jewish mahallah for the poorer Jews![5]

My mother is confronted by the distance in memory from the moment, especially since it's from early childhood, and the fact that the passage of time has changed things visually, externally. It is inevitable and symptomatic of memory's holes that she can't find the actual place—the "exact spot." Where has the past gone? Her return introduces her to a difference. This is so also because the place is not only physically more developed and crowded, but politically and demographically renamed. India, like all of the former British East, has been de-empired, de-Anglicized, and, with the increasing sense of nationalist consciousness, Hinduized. Ripon Road, now Maulana Azad Road, is named no longer after the town in the Yorkshire Moors near to where I now live but after a leading member of the Quit-India movement, a scholar of Arabic descent and the most prominent opponent of a separate Pakistan state and supporter of Hindu-Muslim unity—and most unusually for Bombay, itself now renamed Mumbai after a Hindu goddess, a Muslim.

The whole area of Byculla, where my mother was visiting, is Muslim now, among the poorest in Bombay and one of the most Muslim. But during the Second World War, when my mother lived here, it was where those more impoverished Jewish families came who could escape from Singapore before its fall to the Japanese; Byculla was the Jewish *mahallah,* the Arabic word for "stopping place" that Baghdadi and other Arabic Jews use to describe a Jewish quarter. When I went to Byculla, the caretakers of the synagogues and cemeteries, who were such a help to me, were Muslim. The Jacob Sassoon High School is completely Muslim, still with a Hebrew dedication on its outside wall and still honoring a promise to say on its grounds at least one Hebrew prayer a day. Strange yet familiar indeed. My mother mentions her slap-up lunch at the Taj, right after describing seeing the poor people of Byculla and their shanties, but when she lived here she was a refugee in camp, with no shoes and dependent on donations and rations—in much the same place.

In contrast to the differences the eye notes, vision's characteristics of discernment, distinction, differentiation, music allows the ear to find connections, transitions even, and here it's with an identity precision—the "exactly" that is precisely missing in the visual encounter. The language of Hindi, one of the languages of her childhood even if she grew up multilingual, a language that surrounded her in Bombay as she was coming into language, comes back to my mother almost to her own surprise ("my Hindi came back in a big way!"). I trust that she remembers this language and especially the songs in this language pretty exactly, the sounds still existing in her memory and her body, so different from the changes effected to place. For, separated in age by probably half a century from the young man, she and the taxi driver end up singing the same songs, he knowing, recognizing, and this identity in their music accompanying, probably spurring, his willingness to try to return her to that place. And this shared singing, the identical songs, more than anything seems to make for her "uplifting experience," to make the visit "evocative"—the sound of the voice—calling forth memories and feelings and especially bringing back her father.

What is the power of music to bring back memory? Other media promise better routes and roots (we've figured out we can never separate these) for return. Stories would give us the whole narrative but, often told to us by loved ones, leave things out, family secrets, and are edited unconsciously even when driven by the need to know. Photographs have the lure of reality, the precise moment itself, but may shock us by giving us what we least expect or become fixed themselves and colonize memory. History fills in the gaps of context, we think, giving essential background, but can be hard to integrate into a personal narrative, particularly if this goes against the grain of public events. The qualities of music for Barenboim are really inexpressible, yet correlated to life in part because of this; because "it is really impossible to speak really deeply about music," we can "draw some connection between the inexpressible content of music and, maybe, the inexpressible content of life."[6] Becoming an adult is about becoming visual, discerning, and repressing the ear, our openness to everything and the body and the body's openness to everything. And this openness is perhaps shifted into music to be heard as the inexpressible.

Barenboim lecturing us on how music makes its way into memory speaks about the seven-month advance the ear has over the eye in development in the womb. At the end of one lecture he has a conversation with Antonio Damasio, the neuroscientist of, particularly, human emotion, who confirms through vibration—we might say reverberation—the deep connection of sound to body and emotion. Damasio states that "there are many ways in which music goes very deep because of its closeness to sound, and sound goes very deep because of its closeness to emotion." Barenboim understands Damasio's work as saying "that the auditory system is physically much closer inside the brain to the parts of the brain which regulate life, which means that they are the basis for the sense of pain, pleasure, motivation—in other words basic emotions. And he [Damasio] also says that the physical vibrations which result in sound sensations are a variation on touching, they change our own bodies directly and deeply, more so than the patterns of light that lead to vision, because the patterns of light that lead to vision allow us to see objects sometimes very far away provided there is light. But the sound penetrates our body. There is no penetration, if you want, physical penetration, with the eye, but there is with the ear."[7]

Returning to Bombay, my mother sang Hindustani songs from film music, and as a child she had sung these when her family were repatriated to Singapore after the war. Her father, like most of the returning Singapore Jewish community, which had been halved by the war, found it difficult to get his business, as a spice trader, going again. His daughter, for her singing, would be given some money, ten Singapore dollars—"a lot of money in those days"—by his Indian friends. But she also sang because her father and she enjoyed the songs—the music had penetrated them, if you will. One of our most treasured family possessions is a tape of my grandfather recorded in Singapore when he was eighty, singing his favorite songs—her songs and his songs, his songs becoming hers. My grandfather, a Baghdadi Jew living in Singapore, had been born in Bombay, and my mother in going back there had also been returning to songs her father taught her and to her father's birthplace.

Hindustani music, particularly from old Bollywood films, was my grandfather's favorite kind of music, as it is my mother's—the type they find most emotive—and she says the music where he placed and which shows his great heart. My grandfather also played the harmonium, an instrument that was handheld at first and came to India with the British and that then became a staple of popular Indian music. Jacob Elias identified with all things Indian—food, dress, language, but especially music. And though Jacob was of a Jewish family from Baghdad, he was known as "Jacob Bombai-Wallah"—"Jacob the man from Bombay." One of Jacob's songs on the tape is from *Bombai Ka Babu*, "A Gentleman from Bombay," a 1957 Bollywood film about a man expelled from his native Bombay and trying but failing to find acceptance in a new part of the country.[8] My grandfather's song, "Saathi Na Koi Manzil," sung with Dev Anand's good looks lip-synching over the pining rendition by Mohammed Rafi, the Muslim singer who sang for Hindustani films, is now on YouTube as a song of consolation and despair.[9] The words, "There is [I have?] no destination or companion. There is [I have?] no group of people. This heart has made me walk. Where is it taking me alone? / The roads are of my own country. Even then they are a stranger to me. Who will I call as my own?" are about what's lost, about loss remembered, rootlessness. The song is completely—unutterably in any other form—nostalgic. It is made sadder still when everything, the words and musical theme, is repeated twice. Maybe loss is what many songs, certainly many old Bollywood Hindustani songs, certainly those loved by my mother and her father, catch and hold.

Displacement can produce music, and music can become a way to remember the country left behind. In a coda that reprises and resolves some of the main themes of this family memoir, Maxine Hong Kingston's *The Woman Warrior: Memoirs of a Girlhood Among Ghosts* famously ends with the songs of Ts'ai Yen among the barbarians. Her Chinese language sounds like singsong to her barbarian children, but the poetess reaches for a high note, "an icicle in the desert," which she holds and which sounds like the reed pipe music the barbarians make. Hers are songs that "translated well," and "the barbarians understood their sadness and anger . . . barbarian phrases about forever wandering."[10] Most mobile of forms of memory, most portable, the tunes helping remember longer accounts and simple themes, songs are also a medium of travel. You can imagine song as the progenitor of Walter Benjamin's stories of the first storyteller, the long-distance, long-term traveler.

Israeli Jewish singer Yasmin Levy makes songs about displacement and longing for home. The first song on *La Judería*, "Naci en Álamo," "I have no place / and I have no country / And I have no homeland," is one that shows immediately and perhaps most strongly the characteristic and unmissable catch in her voice.[11] Her father, Yitzhak Levy, was a researcher in Judeo-Spanish culture and the Ladino language, and particularly with her second album, named after the Jewish quarters in Spanish towns, the Ladino correlate of *mahallah,* she is choosing to "follow her father's footsteps and become an ambassador of Ladino."[12] She makes this return to her father by singing in the Ladino language and reviving old musical forms, but much more profoundly by forming or in fact reforming affiliation and connection. The Jews arrived in Spain the same year it was conquered by the Muslims, 711, and both groups leave together under the Spanish Inquisition. "With this album I am proud to combine the two cultures of Ladino and Flamenco, while mixing in Middle Eastern influences. I am embarking on a 500 years old musical journey, taking Ladino to Andalusia, and mixing it with Flamenco, the style that still bears the musical memories of the old Moorish and Jewish-Spanish world, with the sounds of the Arab world. In a way it is a 'musical reconciliation of history,'" as she returns to and remakes music from the time when Muslims lived in harmony with Jews.[13]

If traveling can produce music, this is especially so in crossing cultures, crossing borders, when traditions, forms, and languages can be brought together to make a particular kind of mobile, moving, and emotive music, forming a synthesis from the preexisting into something new. Levy returning to Andalusia goes to one border zone between West and East, North and South, Arab and European. Based in Israel, the Andalus Orchestra goes to the same border zone, according to their Web site playing music "that originated in Andalusia, the southernmost region of Spain, on the Mediterranean coast, overlooking the Moroccan coast. Nearly one thousand years ago, this cultural boundary-zone between North Africa and Europe gave birth to this unique music that intertwines both Arabic and Western Sounds."[14] As an ensemble, they blend Arabic voices and instruments with Western instruments and orchestration. Key to the common practice and goals is the term that Levy uses, "reconciliation." And music's coexistence of voices, human and instrument—the orchestration—allows for reconciliation. In another mode, that of Arabic improvisation and rougher but with a similar open ear, Yair Dalal, of Iraqi Jewish descent, works with other Arabic and Israeli musicians to produce folk music of the Middle East, "songs with which all of the people of the region grew up. Arabs, Jews, Christians, Moslems—people of all nationalities who share the same musical culture"—in particular on his album *Inshalla Shalom*.[15] Such forms of music, such songs, tell of affiliation between Arabs and Jews, Muslims and Jews—what Ella Shohat calls the inextricably "conjunctural" relation between Arabs and Jews in the situation of Jews from the Middle East, the irremovable bridge, really ever present transition, of the hyphen between Arab and Jew in the "Arab-Jew."[16]

From a family of Baghdadi Jews, thus also an Arab Jew, my grandfather was more familiar with Arabic than Hebrew, language of trade and life versus a language of religious worship. Another song he liked to sing and on the tape is a ghazal, a Persian-Arabic expression of both love and the pain of loss, this one translated into Urdu, the language of Muslims of North India and, since the end of the empire, of Pakistan. It is yet another of my grandfather's songs that romanticizes journeying, not settling down. Jacob never lived in an Arab country, and Baghdad is the one place in the family memoir where it's not been possible for any of us to return. My great-grandfather left Baghdad for Bombay probably in the 1880s, just a few years before my grandfather was born, spurred by the opening of the Suez Canal, which was part of the expansion of the British Empire and likely some increasing nationalism in the Ottoman Empire, of which Iraq was then part as a province. As my grandfather (eighty years old) belts out the words to this saddest song on the tape, his voice falters, and, given the contrasting strength of his renditions of other songs, I can't help feeling that this is with grief more than age. What did he know, what do any of us now know, of Baghdad?

Is there a national or, perhaps more truthfully, native sound in music? Rachel Shabi, an Iraqi Jew of my generation, whose parents came straight from Baghdad to England, skipping India and Singapore, recounts realizing, as she listens to an Iraqi Jewish jam session in Israel that there are "Oriental" rhythms. Or—to use her term for Jews from the Middle East in a book which shows their contribution to Israel, as 40 percent of the population (and making up, with Israeli Arabs, the demographic majority, outnumbering Israelis of European descent)—Mizrahi: Eastern.[17] In the most moving chapter, on music, Shabi writes her response to the Arabic Jewish musicians as one of recognition, remembering: "Watching them, I immediately understand that my mother, forever clapping a misfit, irregular beat over evenly syncopated Western tunes during my childhood, was simply marking out a rhythm that I couldn't hear. The alien clapping is normal—appreciated—in this room fully of Iraqi Jews, in Israel." She notes that she had missed and now hears this music because "Oriental quarter-tone melody—music from the Middle East—utilizes notes in between the ones on a Western scale, tones that can sound strange to an unaccustomed ear." These "Middle Eastern Jews came to Israel with ears tuned to the Oriental frequency, set to appreciate the complex half-and quarter-tone arrangements of the East." In Israel, a nation suffering in its conflict with Palestinians in part because of its symptomatic "confusion over cultural capital," Mizrahi music for Shabi "brought the ever present tension to the fore: what to do about these Israelis, essentially so close in culture to the Arab world." There is no way to measure electronically the Arab scale. Not many, particularly Western, musical instruments can play quarter tones, these symbolically laden sounds in between Western notes. But over many centuries quarter tones, tone leading meter, the inverse of Western music, have been the driving element of Arabic music, with its singing arising on different occasions, including of course traveling: "the rousing song of the camel driver, its rhythm corresponding to that of the camel's steps, songs intoned by the young Bedouins riding through the desert on their camels and to the dirges sung by the women."[18]

It's the music of my mother that moves me most, often holding a traveled past. We grew up with her singing those sad songs from Hindustani film music as well as the occasional Chinese (my mother's mother was Chinese and a convert to Judaism) and Arabic/Hebrew song. For a while now I've been consciously consuming this "Eastern" music. While I've never felt English—and this feeling of not being English is stronger than ever now as I write the memoir—Levy, Dalal, Idan Raichel, the music, connects me back to my mother and back past my mother to some genea-logical memory.[19] I don't claim the memory or the music as native, since, from at least two migrant lineages, we were always passing through. But something, via the music, has penetrated.

Not long after I received my mother's e-mail, I attended a concert on Eastern music—Iraqi Jewish songs, Arabic folk songs, Bene Israel Jewish songs, Bollywood: "Rivers of Babylon. An Evening of Eastern Promise: From Baghdad to Bollywood," directed and compered by Sara Manasseh, an Iraqi Jew via India (not Singapore).[20] Jews from all over Asia, and why not non-Jews and from other parts, sang songs, remembering private ones publicly and unashamedly—such as the Indian family sitting in front of me who all knew the words to the Bollywood songs and sang with gusto the one from *Shree 420* ("Mr 420"). In this film, sung by Mukesh and mimed by Raj Kapoor, the memorable song is nationalist, and comic: "Méra Joota Hai Jâpâni." "My shoes are Japanese, these trousers are En-glish, on my head a red Russian hat—still my heart is Indian."[21] The high point the evening held for me was in the *joza* solos by Sohaib Al-Rajab, the world's most famous *joza* player, from Baghdad, descended from a family line of Baghdadi *maqâm* players and virtuosos in the genre of *al-maqâm al 'irâqi*. When Sohaib played his stringed instrument, sad and slow, thin, eerie and difficult, the sounds were so embodied in a shared memory that the audience started less humming in accompaniment than leading his playing with a deep-throated lament or dirge. There seemed to be many people from Iraq there or from places removed from but remembering Iraq. At the end of Sohaib's performance, the band leader was moved to thank the audience for their performance.

The *maqam* is a "technique of improvisation unique to Arabian art mu-sic found throughout the entire Arabian world," which in contrast to Euro-pean genres finds form not in meter, not fixed by time, but in "tone-spatial factor," its melodic passages, phrases, and tone levels producing a strong emotional content.[22] In one version, it can coexist with the Babylonian *piyyutim,* initially liturgical prayers—prayers in song—practiced in every Jewish mahallah, or quarter, but especially in Spain under Islamic rule and in Babylon, Iraq.[23] (Most of the Andalus Orchestra's performances are based on *piyyutim*). In the form of a *piyyut*, I've come across a song by another ancestor, Sliman Ma'tuk, who according to the family tree made the internal migration from Baghdad to the port of Basra in the 1800s. A scholar owning one of the largest libraries in Baghdad—which was until just after my great-grandfather left a culturally Jewish and Muslim city, where many of the musicians were Jewish—Sliman also wrote songs. In the Sassoon Hebrew Collections of the British Library (the Sassoons were also Baghdadi Jews), I've found a manuscript of a lyric Sliman composed. His Hebrew is thoroughly infused with Persian Arabic, as *piyyutim* fused with Arabic poetry and music. "My enemies are surrounding me," his opening quotes the Psalms, then segues into an account of how he is being forced to hide in the Baghdad *hammam*, where he is writing this. It is a moment of persecution under Daoud Pasha, and from there he presumably went on to Basra. But the *hammam*, Arabic for a "public bathhouse," in Baghdad was used by both Muslims and Jews.

There are, of course, clichés about music as the universal language, producing harmony—which have resulted in some pretty bad music. For anthropologist Claude Lévi-Strauss, setting out on his structuralist attempt to collect and explain myths, music verges on being both all language and no language, pure code and opaque materiality. It is "the only language with the contradictory attributes of being at once intelligible and untranslatable."[24] As a professional musician, Barenboim speaks more specifically and more literally about the structure of music as a means to integration, of "the ability of music to integrate, and how it is that a musician is by the sheer nature of his profession in many ways, an integrating figure. If a musician is unable to integrate rhythm, melody, harmony, volume, speed, he cannot make music." In music there are always and only groups, because notes can't have egos, must be in relation, or legato, "linked"—another thing that music teaches us in relation to life. And music, arising from silence and returning to it, has a metaphysical or transcendent quality: "sound proceeds from silence, and evaporates. . . . You can control life and death of the sound, and if you imbue every note with a human quality, when that note dies it is exactly that, it is a feeling of death." Music is finally "a wonderful combination of more knowledge and nothing materially there to show for it."[25]

But music, as especially both Barenboim and Lévi-Strauss know, is mediated, produced in culture. The songs of my grandfather cited here are also a cultural archive. If they bear the trail of my mother's family's migrations as Babylonian Jews via Bombay, it is because the songs are personal and public, emotional and meaningful. Immediate of person, they are also thoroughly mediated by place. And, as well as religious liturgy, film music—even what I think is an American folk song he must have heard on the radio, perhaps revived after the First World War when the radio came to Singapore ("Say, darling, say, when I'm far away / Sometimes you may think of me, dear / The bright sunny days will soon fade away / Remember what I say and be true, dear")—my grandfather sings the second verse of the British national anthem. Who now knows that, who ever knew that—who knows that there even was one? Keeping time and place with the British Empire, moving with its expansion, the Baghdadis were known as the empire's Jews—although my grandfather never forgave the British for abandoning their colony of Singapore to the Japanese, an abandonment that nevertheless forced him to return to one home in Bombay.

The recording we have of him is made in 1970, and the new technology of the audiocassette tape, introduced just six years before, allows the return of my grandfather, to me a long-dead person. But I was there when this recording was made and am also recorded singing on this tape, ringing out the English nursery rhymes that surrounded me in Europe, as I was coming into language and, I suppose, song. In the early magnetic audiocassette tape, before any kind of Dolby noise reduction, I can hear now the sounds of Singapore as I remember them then: from the flat on Short Street, the veranda open to where they used to keep the chickens tied up with string by their necks, the echoes off the concrete floor, as my grandfather sits in his cane chair and sarong. In between songs, my grandfather speaks Malay to his daughter, and her daughter my cousin, who must have just acquired the tape machine and been experimenting. My grandfather spoke many languages: English, Hindi, Arabic, and Malay, an indigenous language of Singapore. Singing is what I remember about my grandfather, not his stories, for which I was neither old nor geographically close enough. I remember him singing as I sat on his knee, on his sarong that I now have. Listening to him singing now is also my return to him.

What kind of return is song? Yair Dalal speaks about a child remembering family and culture through music, child and parent connecting through song. "You teach a child of Mizrahi origin an Iraqi song, and suddenly something in their soul awakes. Afterwards, the child goes home and practices and comes back a week later and says, 'You know, my Dad started to sing the song I was playing.' And that's the connection. That person is back on track."[26] As the thesis of his lectures and the title, later, of his book based on them, Barenboim says something similar about connection, suggesting how musical memory can happen in mind and body—"something in their soul awakes," Dalal says—soulfully: "This is why music in the end is so powerful, because it speaks to all parts of the human being, all sides—the animal, the emotional, the intellectual, and the spiritual. How often in life we think that personal, social and political issues are independent, without influencing each other. From music we see that this cannot occur, it is an objective impossibility, because in music there are no independent elements. Logical thought and intuitive emotions are permanently united. Music teaches us that everything is connected."[27]

Everything is connected. My mother to her father; me to my grandfather; my grandfather to Iraq. When my mother and I listen to the tape of my grandfather's songs, she adds her stories and tells me their meanings. I record her on a second tape for posterity and for accuracy. On this second recording, made now, my mother sings over my grandfather's voice, and it's a duet across another forty years. She is back on track I think—as she was when singing songs with the taxi driver, the young man and the old man and my mother and now myself all knowing the same songs.

Notes

1. Daniel Barenboim, *Everything Is Connected: The Power of Music* (London: Weidenfeld and Nicholson, 2008), 197.

2. Daniel Barenboim, BBC Reith Lectures, 2006, lecture 4, "Meeting in Music," http://www.bbc.co.uk/radio4/reith2006/lecture4.shtml (accessed May 31, 2009).

3. Daniel Barenboim, BBC Reith Lectures, 2006, lecture 5, "The Power of Music," http://www.bbc.co.uk/radio4/reith2006/lecture5.shtml (accessed May 31, 2009).

4. Daniel Barenboim, BBC Reith Lectures, 2006, lecture 2, "The Neglected Sense," http://www.bbc.co.uk/radio4/reith2006/lecture2.shtml (accessed May 31, 2009).

5. May Prosser, e-mail to author, March 30, 2009.

6. Daniel Barenboim, BBC Reith Lectures, 2006, lecture 1, "In the Beginning Was Sound," http://www.bbc.co.uk/radio4/reith2006/lecture1.shtml (accessed May 31, 2009).

7. Barenboim, "The Neglected Sense."

8. *Bombai Ka Babu*, DVD, directed by Raj Kholsa (1957; Shemaroo Entertainment Infinity 2005).

9. "Dev Anand Sathi na Koi Manzil" (Adobe Flashplayer file), YouTube, http://www.youtube.com/watch?v=F1uYlnPQZZI (accessed May 31, 2009).

10. Maxine Hong Kingston, *The Woman Warrior: Memoirs of a Girlhood Among Ghosts* (London: Picador, 1981 [1977]), 186.

11. "Yasmin Levy: Naci En Alamo" (Adobe Flashplayer file), YouTube http://www.youtube.com/watch?v=c4RO9QiwvTM (accessed May 31, 2009).

12. Yasmin Levy, *Romance and Yasmin,* copyright © 2004, Connecting Cultures CC 50016.

13. Yasmin Levy, *La Juderia,* copyright © 2005, Connecting Cultures CC 50024.

14. "Andalus Orchestra," http://www.tom-cohen.com/58251/Andulusic-Orchestra (accessed May 31, 2009).

15. Yair Dalal, *Inshalla Shalom: Yair Dalal and Friends Live in Jerusalem,* copyright © 2005, Najema Music MGDO50.

16. Ella Shohat, *Taboo Memories, Diasporic Voices* (Durham: Duke University Press, 2006), 336.

17. Rachel Shabi, "Everyone Deserves Music," *Not the Enemy: Israel's Jews from Arab Lands* (Bodmin, Cornwall: Yale University Press, 2009), 135–156.

18. Habib Hassan Touma, *The Music of the Arabs,* trans. Laurie Schwarts (Portland: Amadeus, 2003 [1996]), 3.

19. Raichel's "project" works with musicians and singers who come from across the Middle East and Africa to create the sounds that reflect the cultural fusion that *is* Israel. "The Idan Raichel Project," http://www.idanraichelproject.com/en (accessed January 23, 2011).

20. Rivers of Babylon, "An Evening of Eastern Promise: From Baghdad to Bollywood," directed by Sara Manasseh, with guest Sohaib Al-Rajab (*joza*) (Travellers Studio, Harrow Arts Centre, Hatch End, Middlesex, May 17 2009).

21. "Mera Joota Hai Japani—Shree 420," Adobe Flashplayer file, YouTube http://www.youtube.com/watch?v=C8lyrGroeyM (accessed May 31, 2009).

22. Touma, *The Music of the Arabs,* 38.

23. Amnon Shiloah, *Jewish Musical Traditions* (Detroit: Wayne State University Press, 1992).

24. Claude Lévi-Strauss, *The Raw and the Cooked: Introduction to a Science of Mythology* (London: Random House, 1994 [1964]), 18.

25. Barenboim, "In the Beginning Was Sound."

26. Shabi, *Not the Enemy,* 143.

27. Barenboim, "The Power of Music."

9 Off-Modern Homecoming in Art and Theory

SVETLANA BOYM

Do we know how to mediate between being homesick and being sick of home? What is the best medium for such a balancing act? Once we recognize the paradoxical desire for homecoming in ourselves, do we know how to acknowledge the nostalgia of the other?

During the first decade of the twenty-first century it became clearer than ever that nostalgia, like globalization, exists in the plural; it is crucial to know more not only about the elusive objects of nostalgia but also about elusive practices of power that use it. The word *nostalgia* comes from two Greek roots, *nostos*, "return home," and *algia*, longing. I define it as a longing for a home that no longer exists or has never existed.[1] Nostalgia is a sentiment of loss and displacement, but it is also a romance with one's own fantasy. Nostalgic love can only survive in a long-distance relationship. A cinematic image of nostalgia is a double exposure or a superimposition of two images—of home and abroad, of past and present, of dream and everyday life. Nostalgia is not merely an expression of local longing, but a result of a new modern understanding of time and space that made the division into "local" and "universal" possible. While the story that nostalgics tell is one of homecoming, the form of that story is hardly local. One can think of nostalgic stories as a series of migrating plots, hybrid and cross-cultural, that go beyond national attachments. Unlike melancholia, which confines itself to the planes of individual consciousness, nostalgia is about the relationship between individual biography and the biography of groups or nations, between personal and collective memory, individual home and collective homeland.

The key issue in the rites of return is a frequent confusion of time and place, of the time of individual life and the time of history. Nostalgia appears to be a longing for a place, but actually it is a yearning for a different time—the time of our childhood, the slower rhythms of our dreams. In a broader sense, nostalgia is rebellion against the modern idea of time, the time of history and progress. The nostalgic desires to obliterate history and turn it into private or collective mythology, to revisit time like space, refusing to surrender to the irreversibility of time that plagues the human condition.

Nostalgia is not always directed toward the past: sometimes it is a longing for a better time or a slower time, a time out of time, unencumbered by appointment books. In this sense, nostalgia is not always retrospective; it can be prospective as well. The fantasies of the past determined by the needs of the present have a direct impact on the realities of the future. It is this consideration of the future that forces us to take responsibility for our nostalgic tales.

While futuristic utopias might be out of fashion, nostalgia itself has a utopian dimension, only it is no longer directed toward the future. Sometimes it is not directed toward the past either, but rather sideways. The nostalgic feels stifled within the conventional confines of time and space. The most productive and creative side of nostalgic examination lies in what I think of as an "off-modern" dimension that invites us to explore lateral moves, zigzags, conjectural histories and paradoxes of homecoming.[2]

As an artist and intellectual, I believe that we have to begin with a critical, artistic reflection on our own rites of return, which opens our eyes to their complexity and allows us to acknowledge and confront the nostalgias of others. Some of the best critical theory on memory was written by immigrants of the second generation. Immigrants of the second generation (who either came to the new country as young children or are children of immigrants) share the frames of references, styles of writing, and syntax of longing with native populations, which makes their stories of quests for roots or longing for the recovery of personal history more understandable, explicit, and acceptable than the tongue-tied and accented tales of first-generation immigrants. Firsthand immigrant storytelling, like mine, is more convoluted, punctuated by untranslatable experiences as well as a mostly untranslatable sense of humor. An immigrant of the first genera-tion carries with her cultural bilingualism, actual experience of adult life in the "homeland" with its political and social complexities and incon-venient histories of dissent that offer her alternative perspectives on her new country. First-generation immigrant stories complicate the concept of multiculturalism and pluralism, revealing pluralities within national tra-ditions and multiple cultures within a single individual. Thus she might have more trouble with nostalgia or any discourse of return than does the immigrant of the second generation.

My personal rite of homecoming will be mediated by photography. Pho-tography for me is not an elegiac art, but rather a ludic art, an art of experi-mentation and not of documentation. Technology like nostalgia is only a form of mediation between us and the world, between the present and the past. We have to cheat the imperatives of technological progress and constant technological obsolescence. The project *Nostalgic Technologies* is about errands and errors; I collect photographic and computer errors and try to defy the understanding of photography as the art of mechanic or digital reproduction. In my work I often touch the image, producing literally a "touching picture" and sometimes a "moving picture." My proj-ect *The Unforeseen Past,* however, is not a sentimental "retouching" of the past but an attempt to interfere with the processes of mechanical and digital reproduction of the images in order to crack the elegiac patina of nostalgia.

The act of recording homecoming was never a simple one for me. I come from a family where in every generation, starting at least with my great-grandparents, the family homes (or any kind of modest living ac-commodations) were lost, destroyed, and expropriated. Sometimes they were remembered with affection and bitterness, but mostly they were willfully forgotten. Moreover, this happened several times during each family member's lifetime, and nobody was ever able to go back or recover anything except a few photographs with torn edges and pre-Photoshop se-pia. Perhaps this is not unusual for lower-middle-class Eastern European Jews who inhabited the outskirts of empires, but the story of multiple losses that happened before and after the Holocaust and occurred with every regime change is rarely told, with all its uncomfortable twists and turns that defy some contemporary theoretical plots of history. It belongs to the "off-modern" annals of parallel histories that are not fully documented in any photo album.

My paternal grandparents came from the Baltic region while my maternal grandparents came from Ukraine and Belorussia, and neither was allowed to live outside the Pale of Settlement before the revolution. So they moved to Petrograd-Leningrad, losing and never revisiting their original places of birth that were completely destroyed during the Second World War. The Soviet Union entered the war together with Nazi Germany after signing the infamous Molotov-Ribbentrop pact with Hitler and annexing the territories of Poland (Western Ukraine), Latvia, Lithuania, Estonia, and a part of Finland in 1939. My maternal great-grandmother stayed in Ukraine during the first weeks of the war and was executed. There was virtually no information about the execution of Jews and about the extent of the Nazi invasion; even after the Nazi invasion into the Soviet territory, Stalin didn't believe that Hitler would violate the Molotov-Ribbentrop pact and arrested several Polish Jews who escaped to the Soviet Union for spreading the "anti-German propaganda. My paternal grandfather worked in the Kirov factory as an engineer, but was later imprisoned by Stalin. My grandmother, a secondary school teacher, was arrested right after the war during the campaign against the "rootless cosmopolitans" (a major postwar purge by Stalin directed largely against Soviet Jews, with uncanny resonances of Hitler's anti-Semitic rhetoric), and spent six years in the Gulag. It turned out later that the unofficial reason for her arrest was the desire for home improvement on the part of a low-level KGB (NKVD) officer who was interested in annexing my grandmother's room in a small communal apartment, which he subsequently occupied.

Having grown up in another "communal apartment" in a historic building with an incredible art deco facade and squalid inner yard, in rather poor living conditions and with friendly if mostly intoxicated communal neighbors, I inherited some of my grandparents' stories.[3] While I had a deep attachment to the beautiful city of my birth, Leningrad–St. Petersburg, famously called "the foreigner in its own land," I ended up emigrating from it and coming back only after the fall of the Soviet Union, not to reclaim anything but just to confront the familiar ruins.

The first series of "picture-perfect" homecomings is called *Images Without Black*. When I returned to Leningrad in 1989, after a nine-year absence, I found my old house in a sad state of disrepair: not only the neo-baroque facade in the style of Russian art nouveau of the early twentieth

FIGURE 9.1   *Leaving Leningrad* (1989–2003); Svetlana Boym.

century, but even the inner yard and the back staircase that led to our communal apartment. I stood numb in front of the ruins; it was only when I pulled out my camera to take a picture that I discovered the word *death* written on the rusty pipe (figure 9.1). The graffiti was laconic and excessive at once. Later I found out that they were making a film in my half-demolished yard about the absurdist poet Daniil Kharms, whose books were illustrated by Vladimir Tatlin. I still don't know whether the graffiti was a part of the set or the work of an anonymous author. The story turned out to be more tragicomic than I expected.

After I returned to the United States, I printed the image of my home ruins once when my computer ran out of black ink. It was a cheap printer that could still bypass the instructions and thus realize its unforeseen technological potential. In order to make the printer work, I had to hit it (literally, I am afraid), and at the end it started working again, the lack of a black cartridge notwithstanding. Its unconscious spilled out in amazingly deviant and almost psychedelic colors that made each print unrepeatable. The image bore an uncanny resemblance to my home, but in it I managed to disrupt the rite of homecoming.

From still photographs I turned to the exploration of minimal movements that dwell on the mystery of human touch and unrepeatability. In

FIGURE 9.2   *Unforeseen Past* (2008), still; Svetlana Boym.

the project *Unforeseen Past: Touching Family Pictures,* each moving image records an act of touching a family photograph (figure 9.2). Touching images is a literalization of the metaphor. We remember to retouch, but forget the touch. Touch has become invisible and unforeseen.

For these images, I use a multiburst mode on my still camera, which never lets me freeze a single perfect moment. The syncopated image dwells on the glare and cracks of each old picture, laying bare photographic errors and passing ghosts. Occasionally my tired fingers cast a blood-tinged shadow from behind the photograph. The multiburst mode was created for the amateur sportsmen and Pilates addicts who now had the opportunity to check their imperfect form. For me this nearly obsolete low-tech function is poised between photography and cinema. It reminds us of the early days of cinema when recorded movement was still new. When I touch pictures, the transience of memory and the materiality of the photograph collide in an unforeseen fashion.

During my childhood I used to stare at the ceiling of our room in the communal apartment in the same building in Leningrad—a relic from another era (figure 9.3). Even when the house was ruined, this ceiling fragment survived, immune to all revolutions. A few bare wires hung down from the gaping hole where there once was a lamp.

FIGURE 9.3   *Unforeseen Past* (2009), installation; Svetlana Boym. *Madrid Centro de Arte Contemporaneo*

When I emigrated from the USSR, we were not allowed to carry family albums. Photographs with more than three people in the picture were considered a "suspicious grouping." Each picture we took with us thus became unique and unrepeatable. I began to rephotograph those pictures caught between two cultures—one of sparseness and the other of excess, one of archival obsession and the other of obsolescence. I still don't have a proper family album, but I constantly reframe photographs and play with foreign words that don't translate into my mother tongue. *Frame* comes from *from*, which means "forward," "ahead," and "advance"; I don't know how and why it evolved into the unfortunate direction of framing nostalgic introspection.

The "unforeseen past" in photographs is a contradiction in terms; the photographs in this case don't leave a transparent record of what had happened and of "being there," but document visual ambivalences. They open up the folders of lost time, questioning the security of the past and the affection of nostalgia. The unforeseen past is an uncanny double of the foreseeable future; it confuses the vectors of time and allows us to imagine a different present.

In the project *Global Transits and Portable Homes*, I engaged with a different way of "touching pictures," by interfering with the technological process and defying the understanding of photography as the art of mechanical or digital reproduction. This series is about leaving homes, foreign cities, and images behind and at the same time commemorating them.

St. Petersburg became for me one of the cities in transit (figure 9.4). I photograph modern architecture in partial ruins coming mostly from the boundaries of Europe—East and West. I traveled through former war zones in the former Yugoslavia, but I didn't want to do disaster tourism; I wanted to reflect on the art of everyday survival. I noticed that the shelled building in Sarajevo is inhabited again and the satellite dishes are spread out of the ruined balconies like desert flowers. I am interested in looking back at the photographs, rephotographing against all instructions,

FIGURE 9.4   *Leaving St. Petersburg* (1993–2008); Svetlana Boym.

FIGURE 9.5 *Leaving Sarajevo* (2000–2008); Svetlana Boym.

keeping in the glare and the passing shadows, occasionally dropping a
piece of trash or a flower on the old snapshot, leaving in all the blemishes
that a professional photographer would try to remove (figure 9.5). I don't
use superimpositions or computer manipulations but prefer the manual
labor of memory.

My images of portable homes are taken closer to my current home,
in Boston, right before and during the financial crisis of 2008; they are
windows of the closed real estate agencies that show foreclosed or sold
homes (figure 9.6) Printing each of these cities in transit and each of
these portable homes is a miniperformance. I pulled each picture manu-
ally out of the printer, leaving fragments of images, blotches of ink lines
of passage. As I was doing this, the printer was screaming at me "Pay attention! Communication error has occurred!" The rhythm of withdrawal

FIGURE 9.6   *Portable Home* (2008), Cambridge; Svetlana Boym.

is unrepeatable, and so is each print. This procedure goes against both the printer's instruction manual and the mass reproduction of photographic images. Printing becomes a transitory experience, and the picture is always incomplete. If we make failure into an artistic conceit, it can become a form of co-creation or collaboration with chance. The "off-modern" dimension of the project consists in reflecting on history on its outskirts as well as in the form of image making that allows us to rethink "new media" through estranging artistic techniques and not only through new technologies.

The practice of photography estranges the practice of writing and also allows for a certain renewal of vision, original wonder, and adventure of chance. Should the rite of return include the rite to detour? Perhaps such a detour—whether artistic, personal, or intellectual—is a more honest way of confronting the challenges of a lost home and of the nostalgic conflation between personal and collective history, between memory and politics.

Thinking further about difficult but necessary detours and about the prospective dimension of nostalgia, I developed the concept of the off-modern. In my view, the contemporary moment is not characterized by a pure "clash of cultures," but rather by the particular clash of the cultures of modernization. It can be described as a conflict of asynchronic modernities, of various projects of globalization that are often at odds with one another.

This is why I want to get away from the endless "ends" of art and history and the prepositions *post-*, *neo-*, *avant-*, and *trans-*, of the charismatic postcriticism that tries desperately to be "in." There is another option: not to be out, but off—as in off-stage, off-key, off-beat, and, occasionally,

FIGURE 9.7   *Multitasking with Clouds* (2008); Svetlana Boym.

FIGURE 9.8   *Multitasking with Clouds 2* (2009); Svetlana Boym.

off-color. Off-modern does not suggest a continuous history from antiquity to modernity to postmodernity and so on.[4] Instead, it confronts the radical breaks in tradition, the gaps of forgetting, the losses of common yardsticks, and the disorientations that occur in almost every generation. Off-modern reflection does not try to cure longing with belonging. Rather, it produces off-springs of thought out of those gaps and crossroads, opening up a third way of intellectual history of modernity. It involves exploration of the side alleys and lateral potentialities of the project of critical modernity. In other words, it opens into the "modernity of what if" rather than simply modernization as it is. The politics and aesthetics of the lateral moves that combine estrangement from the world with the estrangement for the world opens into another political history of a modernism that is barely known.

Off-modern approaches work both temporarily and spatially. They allow us to think about alternative genealogies and histories of modernity and at the same time invite us to look at the different shapes and forms of the modern experience all over the world, beyond the presumed Western center, as well as the complex reactions that modernity elicits. The *off* in off-modern designates both the belonging (albeit) eccentric to the critical project of modernity as well as its excess, the second emphatic *f*. In some ways, off-modern reflection returns to the unfinished business of critical modernity (figures 9.7–9.9). Off-modern genealogy often follows from unfulfilled projects, unbuilt architecture, shelved films, which nevertheless survive for a long time in the cultural imaginary. In spite of this poetics of failure, in some ways off-moderns are most faithful to the project of critical modernity and participate in its unsentimental reenchantment.

FIGURE 9.9   *Black Mirrors, Phantoms* (2009); Svetlana Boym.

One aspect of off-modern genealogy is that it is not teleological and includes the experience of freedom Hannah Arendt called "our forgotten heritage." In this sense, the experience of freedom is something fundamentally strange, a new beginning and "miracle of infinite improbability" that occurs regularly in the public world. Since freedom is one of the most abused words in present-day politics, it seems challenging for me to explore it as something "infinitely improbable." If we want to escape the banalization of freedom, we have to imagine its other history, the history of "what if"—of its unpredictable and unexplored plots. Arendt is an antinostalgic philosopher, so she emphasizes that this way of inhabiting the world is not about homecoming but about making an artificial home, not a home into which we were born but a home that we freely choose for ourselves, a home that contains a palimpsest of world culture.[5] Such an exploration of memory and freedom is fundamental for me both in theory and in artistic practice.

How do I reconcile my scholarly and my artistic lives? If, in the 1990s, many artists dreamed of becoming their own curators and borrowed from the theorists, now the theorists dream of becoming artists. Disappointed with their own disciplinary teleology, they emigrate into each other's territory. The lateral move. Neither backward nor forward: sideways. Not the nostalgic performing the rite of return, but the serious amateur, as Roland Barthes understood it, the one who knows how to lose, to unlearn, and to love.

Notes

1. See "The Off-Modern Manifesto" in Svetlana Boym, *Architecture of the Off-Modern* (Princeton: Princeton Architectural Press, 2008). For images and videos see www.svetlanaboym.com.

2. For a more detailed elaboration of the concept see Svetlana Boym, *The Future of Nostalgia* (New York: Basic Books, 2001). In the introduction to *The Future of Nostalgia*, I propose a distinction between two types of nostalgia—based on two types of aphasia—restorative and reflective. Restorative nostalgia stresses *nostos* ("home") and attempts a transhistorical reconstruction of the lost home. Reflective nostalgia thrives in *algia*, the longing itself, and delays the homecoming—wistfully, ironically, desperately. Restorative nostalgia does not think of itself as nostalgia but rather as truth and tradition; unable to come to terms with its own impossible longing, restorative nostalgics are hostile to the nostalgias of others. By contrast, reflective nostalgia dwells on the ambivalences of human longing and belonging and does not shy away from the contradictions of moder-

nity. Restorative nostalgia protects the absolute truth, while reflective nostalgia calls it into doubt, confronting both longings and paranoid delusions in one's own and the other's conception of an original home. Moreover, reflective nostalgia allows for a nondeterministic view of both the past and the future (xviii).

3. On the communal apartment as home, see Svetlana Boym, *Common Places: Mythologies of Everyday Life in Russia* (Cambridge: Harvard University Press, 1994). The story of my grandmother is told in detail in Svetlana Boym, "My Grandmother's Last Love," *Harvard Review* 21 (Spring 2002): 20–29.

4. Critic and writer Victor Shklovsky proposes the figure of the knight's move in chess that follows "the tortured road of the brave," preferring it to the master-slave dialectics of "dutiful pawns and kings." Victor Shklovsky, *The Knight's Move* (Champaign, IL: Dalkey Archive Press, 2007), and "Art as Technique," *Four Formalist Essays*, ed. and trans. Lee T. Lemon and Marion J. Reis (Lincoln: University of Nebraska Press: 1965), 3–24. For further elaboration see Svetlana Boym, *Another Freedom : The Alternative History of an Idea* (Chicago: University of Chicago Press, 2010).

5. Hannah Arendt, "What Is Freedom?" *Between Past and Future* (New York: Vintage, 1972).

10 Return to Nicaragua

The Aftermath of Hope

SUSAN MEISELAS

In Nicaragua I experienced an extraordinary optimism, a moment in which a whole society was mobilized, uniting together as they overthrew a dictatorship. The images I made came to stand in for that optimism. If I've returned to Nicaragua so often, it has been to see what has remained of that hope among present generations, born after the revolution.

The building that housed the newspaper *La Prensa* was bombed in the last month of the war, destroying their archive. To replace some of the visual evidence, I collected images made by a number of international photographers and brought them back to Nicaragua on the first anniversary of the overthrow of Somoza. Those images became part of the Museum of the Revolution, contributing to the documentation of a history that might otherwise have been lost.

The photographs I made during the popular insurrection from 1978–1979 have become the reference for a continued relationship and sustained engagement with the people and places I once framed. I see this work as part of an archive to reexamine, revisit, and perhaps rerender. Returning is a way to reconnect.

FIGURE 10.1   *Anastasio Somoza Portocarrero, with recruits of the elite infantry training school (EEBI)* (July 1978), from the series *Reframing History*, Managua, Nicaragua, July 2004; Susan Meiselas.

Initially I gathered the publications that had used my photographs to track the different contexts in which they were seen. It was as if each image had taken on a life of its own.

Five years after the insurrection, in 1984, I curated a small show, titled *Mediations*, presenting three parallel narratives: in the center, the sequenced pages from my book *Nicaragua: June 1978–July 1979* interrupted with a framed image that had been acquired by a museum and transformed into Art. Below were the outtakes from my selection process, and, above, I placed the tearsheets to show the images that had been chosen and published in popular international magazines.

FIGURE 10.2   Installation view from the exhibition Mediations, held at Side Gallery, Newcastle-on-Tyne, 1982–1983; Susan Meiselas.

In a sense, this is an interrogation, from and of a history; an attempt to remember and reread images. This process of inquiry continued ten years after the revolution, while making the film *Pictures from a Revolution*, which was a search for the people who were within the photographs that I had made, to find them and find out what had happened to them in the years that had intervened. My intention was to create a tension between the formal framed "iconic" image and the life that had gone on beyond it, following the trauma of a long war.

FIGURE 10.3   *Nicaragua: June 1978–July 1979* (New York: Pantheon, 1981), annotated with field notes by the subject while searching for people in the photographs for *Pictures from a Revolution* (1991); Susan Meiselas.

Fifteen years later, I returned with the project *Reframing History*, in which these photographs were again reexamined, as a marking of time, a point of departure and reflection. The concept was to create a public installation, in the streets, not a permanent museum, but a temporary crossroad. The 2004 project was a collaboration with the Institute of History at the University of Central America and took place for a month in Nicaragua, around the twenty-fifth anniversary of the triumph over Somoza.

FIGURE 10.4   *Youths practice throwing contact bombs in forest surrounding Monimbo* (June 1978), from the series *Reframing History*, Masaya, Nicaragua, July 2004; Susan Meiselas.

There were three phases to *Reframing History*: the most important for me was the dialogue initiated to create the actual installation of the photographs as murals in the landscape of four towns where they were first taken. The second phase was filming people *looking*, while gathering community reactions and recollections. The last phase was a further transformation, an exhibition throughout Europe and later New York with the murals and video creating a work of remembrance for a distant international audience who had initially experienced the war through some of these pictures.

Rather than remaining buried within an archive, the photographs were alive again. On-site, they ignited reflections that reaffirmed both my connection to Nicaragua and their own deepening historical value.

PART III

Rights of Return

11 Between Two Returns

AMIRA HASS

On April 11, 1987, the Jewish-Italian writer Primo Levi commit-ted suicide.[1] He leaped off the third-floor landing of his home at 75 Corso de Umberto, Turin, Italy. Levi survived Auschwitz where he had been in-terned on February 26, 1943, and liberated two years later on January 27, 1945. He was obliged to remain in the Soviet zone until October 1945; only then could he return to Italy, to Turin. Levi's was a concrete and natural return: to his country, his hometown, landscape, language, his own home and family. Levi was one of eighty-five hundred Italian Jews (out of forty-five thousand) who were shipped as cargo to death camps; seventy-nine hundred of them never returned.

For over thirty years, Levi argued for concrete return, making an active case for the diaspora, for the right of Jews to remain dispersed in their diaspora—a historical-philosophical statement that the natural place for Jews was their place of birth anywhere in the world and not some leg-endary homeland. This was a statement addressed to Zionists and anti-Semites alike. Levi's concept of citizenship was nonethnic, nonreligious, quite the opposite of the essence of Israeli citizenship. Was he conscious of what his return to Italy implied? I have no way of knowing.

In his "self-murder," as the German term *Selbstmord* would have it, Levi undid two returns: his concrete/literal return chosen in 1945 and another one that he did not weigh as a possibility: the mythological return to *Eretz Yisrael*, the Land of Israel. Did he want to tell us that no return was possible after Auschwitz? But in 1950, he, like Jews all over the world, had the legal right to immigrate to the two-year-old State of Israel, a foreseen, understandable move, five years after the German-European murder industry was dismantled, though its product, destruction, remained still and ever so concrete.

In July 1950, the Knesset, Israel's parliament, passed the "Law of Return," granting all Jews the right to "return" to a place they had never known, save for the Bible and other stories, perhaps. The law stipulated that "every Jew has the right to come to this country as an *oleh*. . . . An *oleh*'s visa shall be granted to every Jew who has expressed his desire to settle in Israel."[2]

After 1948, only three thousand Italian Jews exercised this right, to return to a place unknown to them. Several possible realities may account for this unusually small number (less than a tenth of the Italian Jewish community). The estrangement of Italian Jews from their place of birth by the German-European death industry was not as powerful and as widespread as it was in Poland, for example. There was not much time left for Nazi dictates to wreak total destruction upon that community, so deeply rooted in Italian soil. Furthermore, the newly born state in dire physical and economic conditions was obviously much less attractive than the optimistic, apparently stable, new Italian republic and, in particular, the fact that it was outside the Soviet zone, unlike Romania, for example, another fascist regime where a large part of the Jewish community was spared the fate of occupied Poland's Jews but chose to emigrate en masse.

From the beginning, the movement of "return" to the alleged ancestral homeland has navigated several competing drives: the personal-religious, the religion-based but secular and nationalist drive, inspired by the romantic ethnic nationalism of Germany and central Europe, and, eventually, the drive to escape racist persecution and discrimination, harsh economic conditions, and dictatorships. At times, two or all of the above could serve as relevant justifications, but the fact remains that only with the rise and success of genocidal anti-Semitism did Zionism stop being an ideological home for a minority of the Jews and begin to appeal to the majority (that is, the majority of the then decimated Jewish community) by offering Israel as a place to live.

According to the Law of Return, upon choosing Israel, a Jew was defined as neither a "returnee" nor an immigrant, but rather as an *oleh,* or, in the plural, *olim*. This word stems from the Hebrew infinitive "to mount," "to ascend," "to rise." It invokes the teaching of the Talmud that the land of Israel is higher than all other lands. That is why leaving it, on the other hand, is seen as a descent, *yerida*. In Zionist parlance, *descent* is a disparaging term, charged with spite and scorn, the opposite of ascent, *aliya*. Its original, scriptural use, however, did not carry any judgmental connotation. Ascent did not necessarily denote immigrating to and settling in the Land of Israel. A visit sufficed to be termed aliya. Only in Zionist jargon has aliya gained added value and become synonymous with immigration and settling in.

And the Law of Return continues: "Every Jew who has immigrated into this country before the coming into force of this Law, and every Jew who was born in this country, whether before or after the coming into force of this law, shall be deemed to be a person who has come to this country as an *oleh* under this Law."[3] It should be stressed that, grammatically, *oleh* does not designate a person who has completed an action, but rather one who is still in the process, a present-continuous, as it were. That is, the very birth of a Jew in the country makes him an oleh (and not simply a citizen, a resident) and entitles him, like a Jew who did in fact immigrate, to the spiritual, metatemporal, never ending status of permanent ascendancy. I was born in Jerusalem and thus shall to the last of my living days be an *olah*—forever ascending, not merely in the metatemporal but also in the metaspatial sense of the term.

Israel's legislators reserved the "return" for a collective act: the People returning to its ancestral homeland. Did the lawmakers shy away from actually defining each Jewish individual a returnee, even one who had never seen the country before? That is, were they simply unable to go so far as to conjure up linguistic and legalistic metareal situations? I cannot say. Perhaps they merely wanted to put to use every ancient term in their arsenal that would attest to a concrete, not merely imagined, continuity between the Land and the People.

Faysal Hourani, a Palestinian writer born in 1939 in Masmiya, a Palestinian village on the road connecting Jerusalem to Gaza, is a returnee. In 1948, the inhabitants of Masmiya had to flee the fighting as well as targeted attacks by Jewish troops. They have not been allowed to return since. Hourani's mother settled in Gaza as a refugee, while he, a nine-year-old boy, was sent to his dead father's parents who had fled and lived in exile in Damascus. In 1996 Hourani returned—not to his home village, which had become an Israeli community, but to Gaza. The Israelis authorized his entry into the country for the very first time after an absence of forty-eight years. Hourani was issued an ID by the Palestinian Authority, but this too could only be granted with Israeli authorization. To this very day no document of Palestinian civil status—birth, death, change of address—is valid and recognized unless it is registered in the computerized database of the Israeli Ministry of the Interior. Palestinian, not Israeli, terminology designates Hourani and the other several thousands of high-ranking PLO activists whom Israel allowed to reenter the country as returnees. As Hourani was born in the country, his return was literal, and the Palestinian term bears no trace of manipulative symbolism. If there was anything surreal about Hourani's return, it was the fact that he could not come back to his own home (razed long ago) or to the scenery of his childhood.

In Hourani's newly issued ID—printed by a Palestinian printer, yet authorized down to its last detail by the State of Israel—"Israel" is named as the place of his birth. But Israel did not exist when Hourani was born. Moreover, in the ID of an Israeli citizen (Jew or Palestinian) born in the country before the establishment of the state, namely, before 1948, his local place of birth would be specified as Jerusalem, Haifa, Tel Aviv. Evidently, the Zionist bureaucracy cannot acknowledge that a Palestinian refugee who now resides in the 1967 Occupied Territories has roots in a concrete place within what is now Israel proper. Would not that be a tacit recognition of his right to return?

Therefore, Palestinians whom Israel allows to "return" are obliged to partake in the metatemporal transformation of the country into the Jewish state, years before it actually became the State of Israel. In their actual return to their homeland, Palestinians must pay an added value tax: acknowledge the eternal status of Israel, the state that in 1948 expelled some seven hundred thousand of them (and later, after 1967, hundreds of thousands more by different means), robbed them of their lands, robbed their remaining family members of their lands and livelihood, and has been trying to downplay their existence in it ever since. The state defines them as "the Arab minority, the Arab sector," anything to avoid acknowledging their "Palestinian-hood." Strangely enough, "Israel" as the place of his birth is the only item on Hourani's ID that is not printed in both Hebrew and Arabic. It appears only in Hebrew. Could the Arabic script not bear this myth, this lie?

Zionist ideology does its best to concretize the alleged blood links supposedly shared by Jews all over the world and to tie them all to the soil of the Holy Land. But the very terminology used by the Israeli bureaucracy, in its law and in the wording of the Palestinian Authority–issued IDs, reveals the fabricated connection. What the Law of Return does not dare, namely, to combine return with subjects and personal pronouns, is done outright on a huge road sign at a junction around two miles east of the Palestinian town of Ramallah. This junction is controlled by an illegal unauthorized colonist outpost, an offshoot of nearby Beit El, no less illegal a colony. "We have returned home," the sign cries out. "Here in Beit El, 3800 years ago, The Land of Israel was promised to the People of Israel by the Creator of the World. Based on this promise we sit today in Haifa, Tel Aviv, Shilo and Hebron."

The proclamation is signed by the colony's local council. At the bottom of this spiritual sign a very concrete reference is made to its commercial sponsors: two supermarkets at Beit El and the firm that prints and posts these billboards. A checkpoint at the entry to Ramallah blocks the road leading to both the colony and the town. Only Palestinian notables, diplomats, and journalists are allowed through. Residents of Ramallah as well as of nearby villages on whose land the Beit El colony was built are not allowed to drive through it. Their daily commute from work is an ordeal. Take, for example, that young employee at the Palestinian Ministry of Education. He lives in Beitin, the alleged ancient site of Beit El that housed altars for Canaanite divinities, five minutes away from Ramallah. Because of the blocked roads, however, the drive to Ramallah and back takes him thirty minutes each way. But this is an aside, to give a sense of today's reality. It was in 1977 that the Jews "returned" to Beit El where Abraham built an altar 3,800 years ago. Or was it 3,802 years ago as the billboard placed there two years ago claims?

Among other places to which Jews have "returned" since 1967 is one called Halamish, some fifteen miles west of Ramallah. Like the Beit El colony, it was built in 1977. Local folklore tells of a certain American journalist who interviewed people in the village of Nabi Saleh, across the road from Halamish. "Since when have you lived here?" he is said to have asked one old man. The old man held the young reporter's hand and asked him to look around: "Do you see the wad (valley) below? From up here I used to watch Adam and Eve playing with each other." Obviously, the question echoed Zionist argumentation that Palestinians were new to the country, unlike Jews who had already been here back then, 3,772 years ago.

Another returnee, a Palestinian Marxist whose first name is Daoud, did not have to go back as far as Adam and Eve to claim his roots. Of all Arab peoples, he once told me, Palestinians are the ones who tend the most often to give their children biblical, Hebrew names: Daoud, Mussa, Sara, Maryam, Isaac, etc. Names are passed from grandfather to grandson, grandmother to granddaughter, for generations on end. His materialist conclusion: many of the Palestinians are descendants of the early Hebrews. Initial attempts by the Palestinian Ministry of Culture to connect Palestinians to a Canaanite past and ancestors do not seem to have taken hold. It suffices for most people to point at a house that was theirs and is now occupied by an Orthodox Jewish kindergarten or a Peace Now activist's family. Trees that grandparents had planted and cacti that marked their family's land off from their neighbors' are as good as written deeds of ownership. There is nothing fabricated or imagined in this continuity. In 1967, nineteen years after they had been expelled from their homes, old people could go back for the first time to see them. Having gone back, I was told by friends in Gaza, many returned to their refugee camps and died of a heart failure or, rather, of a broken heart. Only upon their return as visitors did they realize that a literal, permanent return was no longer possible.

I, too, had a grandfather, a great-grandfather actually, who died in the Holy Land, in Jerusalem—not of a broken heart though. His was a natural death of very old age. In fact, sometime in the late nineteenth or early twentieth century, he chose to emigrate from Sarajevo, Bosnia, in order to die in the Holy Land. Back then, so the family legend goes, he was already in his nineties. In the territories united under the Ottoman Empire, there were no borders to break up his journey. He mistakenly assumed he would die upon his arrival. I doubt whether he termed his journey a "return." My family's lost genealogical tree reaches back to the 1492 expulsion from Spain, not to Adam and Eve, not even to Sara's days; Sarajevo was the family's perfect home for generations. My mother used to joke that my great-grandfather's death, and the place where he was buried, the Mount of Olives cemetery, guaranteed our right to stay in the country in accordance with the original PLO charter of July 1968, which states that "those Jews who had normally resided in Palestine until the beginning of the Zionist invasion will be considered Palestinians." In my mother's and others' interpretation, the Zionist invasion was historically connected with the Balfour Declaration of 1917 that promised the Jewish people a national home in the land of Palestine.

Like Primo, my mother was a Levi. Like him, she survived a concentration camp, Bergen Belsen. Like Primo Levi, at first she opted for her right to return home, to Yugoslavia. As a Jew, so the joke goes, she was a real

Yugoslav: not Bosnian, not Serbian, and not Croatian. Her 1949 return to Israel was an escape. She fled from the terrible void she had found in her real homeland. I assume it was the same void that eventually made Primo Levi do what the Nazis failed to do: murder himself.

Some forty years later, my mother tried to undo this flight and return to Yugoslavia. It was still one Yugoslavia back then. My mother was already seventy years old. She had almost decided to rent a room in a Belgrade apartment when the landlady told her: "Through this window I could watch the Jews being rounded up and sent away." My mother took her yet unpacked suitcase and fled again, back to Paris, her already chosen diaspora for some ten years. In so doing, she voted for the right of Jews to live in the diaspora of their choice, not necessarily the diaspora of their birth. My mother's, then, was a temporary return to the diaspora and to the principle of people's right to live wherever they choose. She did come back to Israel in the early 1990s. This time, too, it was not a mythological return defined by a state law, but a concrete return to a concrete home. Perhaps the fact that she had a daughter played a role in her decision.

Twice I have been asked whether I have ever thought of "returning" to Sarajevo, meaning returning to live there. I instantly saw beyond the words, and the shock at being asked such a question prevented me from commenting on its absurd terminology. How could I return to a place where I had never lived and visited only twice as a tourist? One person who asked me this question was a Palestinian prisoner with whom I used to converse on a clandestine cellular phone smuggled into jail. Palestinian political prisoners in Israel, unlike criminal prisoners and Jewish-nation-alist prisoners, are not allowed to use pay phones to speak to their families, even when their constitutional right to have family visits is not being re-spected (as is the case now with all Gazan prisoners). The question would not have upset me so much had that same person not remarked just a few conversations earlier how a certain article of mine taught him new things: that not only Germany but other European societies had played their part in Judeocide and that the survivors, upon their return home, were often not welcomed by those societies. I thought I had finally met a Palestinian who grasped the refugeeness of Jews, including Israeli citizens. But his question made me realize how deeply ingrained the Palestinian concep-tion is that we, Israel-born Jews, do not really belong here.

Palestinians often ask me: "Where are you from?" I know very well what they mean, but I reply: "I am from Jerusalem, I was born there." "But no, no," they insist, "where did you really come from?" They insist on giving me imagined roots in places, languages, and landscapes that are totally strange to me. One woman, a returnee, but from a refugee family originally, admitted that before she had met me she told people: "If Amira is such a leftist and progressive and against the Occupation, she should go back to where she came from."

While I was upset and hurt by the prisoner's question, I was actually enraged when a French woman asked me a similar question. She was on one of those solidarity tours at the beginning of the current Palestinian uprising. Having read my articles and my book, she was all admiration and compliments. But then she asked me whether I thought of "return- ing" to Sarajevo. "Where?" I asked in disbelief. Then, as I realized there was nothing wrong with my ears, I shouted: "Return to a continent that threw us out of the globe, out of the world of the living?" I smelled an anti- Semite who was saying in fact: "You have no right to be where you are." She was a European, a Christian, ignoring the perfectly familiar history that placed me exactly where I am, her history. True, I am not an *olah* in the sense that the Law of Return imposes upon me. I am not uplifted by any sensation of permanent ascendance because of my being a Jewish- Israeli citizen. I wish my parents had emigrated elsewhere. But they did not, and Israel became my diaspora. I tried another diaspora for two years, but hurried back to the sunlight, vegetation, scents, language, and all the other things that make a home a home.

My father, too, fled the void he encountered in his Romanian home- town upon his return from four years in a Transnistria ghetto. Like my mother, he had never been a Zionist, and yet he found himself in Israel at the end of 1948, an oleh who, like my mother, gradually became more and more familiar with the Palestinians' plight and void. Sometime at the beginning of the First Intifada, perhaps in 1988, or 1989, he shared with me a dream he had had the previous night. His description was so vivid that I sometimes feel I actually dreamed it with him. In that dream we, my father and I, were standing on a hill facing east. Many thousands of people were walking toward us, going down the hills, up the mountains, and through the valleys. Holding my hand and overwhelmed with happi- ness, my father exclaimed: "Look, Amirale, look, they are coming back, they are coming back!" The return he dreamed was, of course, the return of the Palestinians. The dream told me, more than all of our past and future conversations, how tormented my father was with the implications of his mythological return to the Holy Land, or rather, the implications of his concrete flight from what used to be his home: namely, the dispossession of an entire people from its homeland. So he dreamed the solution: undoing history.

For years, many Palestinians believed it was possible to undo history and return home. On the declarative level, all Palestinian organizations still demand that the right of return of Palestinian refugees to their homes be included in any future peace settlement.

I suspect that, for many, admitting their fear that an actual return was impossible—at least in our lifetime—would be considered politically incorrect and a total breach of all commonly accepted rules. Back in 1994, my friends at Jabaliya refugee camp in the Gaza strip started expanding their former shack and replacing it with a massive three-story building made of concrete blocks, spacious enough for their entire family. "How come you only started building it now?" I asked their father. He surprised me by replying that now, with the Oslo Accords, he knew for certain that they would never return home.

Other villagers who cannot go back home were expelled in 1967—not 1948—from three villages west of Jerusalem. 'Imwas, Yalo, and Beit Nouba were located in an area that the Jewish army failed to conquer in 1948. Soldiers who occupied the villages at the end of the war ordered all inhabitants to leave for Ramallah. Then they demolished the solid stone houses with explosives or used bulldozers to raze them. Some people were said to have been killed inside their homes, others on the road, while fleeing. In 1973 the Jewish National Fund in Canada collected money to turn two of these destroyed villages, 'Imwas and Yalo, into a "national" park, called Canada Park. It is a highly popular recreation site among Israelis who return every now and then to relish its lush expanses and beautiful views. Some of the villagers were thus twice expelled: they had moved to those three villages in 1948 after having fled or been driven out of their original villages.

In March 1976, this group addressed the following letter to Israel's then Prime Minister (Rabin), Minister of Defense, and Chairman of the Knesset:

"Re: Request to Return to Our Villages"

Your excellencies,

As inhabitants of 'Imwas, Yalo and Beit Nouba, we have the honor to appeal to Your Excellencies in the hope that you will examine our legitimate request. We ask only for our legitimate humanitarian right to return to the villages from which we were driven and expelled. Before the war in 1967 we lived peacefully in our villages on the West Bank, Israeli border, with no problems with our Israeli neighbors. We were in no way a threat to security or a destabilizing presence in the area. For no reason, from the very beginning of the war, we were driven out from our villages, on foot, with our children and elderly. The Israeli army ordered us to leave our houses, telling us we could return after the war. Since that day, we have been unable to go back to our homes, but we live in the hope that one day it will be possible. We have appealed to the West Bank military administration but have received no reply to date. We are therefore referring our request to Your Excellencies as supreme authorities of the State of Israel. Our houses were completely demolished and there is nothing left of our village. We were forced to leave our land and houses, and everything was destroyed including our furniture, our livestock, and all our possessions, but we still hope to be able to return. . . . We are prepared to rebuild our houses ourselves without applying for compensations from the State, and we are full of hope that we shall be able to live once again as we have in the past, as peaceful neighbors.

Yours respectfully,
The residents of 'Imwas, Yalo and Beit Nouba

No one even took the trouble to reply. Thirty-one years later, on November 1, 2007, a relatively new Israeli group called Zochrot (Remembering) joined the villagers in their appeal to Ehud Barak, Israel's minister of defense, asking why the residents could not return to their homes. Being an Israeli group, they did get a reply this time from a senior adviser to the minister who, on March 20, 2008, bothered to write them as follows: "The return of the village inhabitants is not allowed for security considerations."

Not only can they not return either to their pre-1948 homes or to their post-1948 homes, but they are not even allowed to visit. Most of those 1967 refugees live in the Ramallah area; some of them in nearby villages. For the past seven years, Israel has been blocking the roads that lead to the three villages and their surrounding lands. The average Israeli is convinced that this area is Israel proper. There is no sign to indicate the opposite. The fate of these three villages epitomizes Israel's overall policy of consistent, serial dispossession throughout the years, since the state's inception. Much state violence has been exercised to make those acts of dispossession last, persist, and expand. The Law of Return is part and parcel of this violence, as it entitles every Jew on earth to more rights in this country than any Palestinian born in it possesses.

The mythological return of Jews has successfully made the literal return of Palestinians impossible. With the passing years, as many first-generation refugees age and die, the return home becomes increasingly transtemporal, metareal, as testified by Mahmoud Darwish's two poems with which I will end:

WE TRAVEL LIKE ALL PEOPLE

We travel like everyone else, but we return to nothing. As if travel were
a path of clouds. We buried our loved ones in the shade of clouds and between roots of trees.
We said to our wives: *Give birth for hundreds of years, so that we may end this journey within an hour of a country, within a meter of the impossible!*
We travel in the chariots of the Psalms, sleep in the tents of the prophets, and are born again in the language of Gypsies.
We measure space with a hoopoe's beak, and sing so that distance may forget us.
We cleanse the moonlight. Your road is long, so dream of seven women to bear
this long journey on your shoulders. Shake the trunks of palm trees for them.
You know the names, and which one will give birth to the Son of Galilee.
Ours is a country of words: Talk. Talk. Let me rest my road against a stone.
Ours is a country of words. Talk. Talk. Let me see an end to this journey.[4]

WHO AM I, WITHOUT EXILE?

. . . Nothing brings me back from this distance
to the oasis: neither war nor peace. . . .
. . . Nothing carries me, or loads me with an idea:

neither nostalgia, nor promise.
What shall I do? What shall I do without exile
And a long night of gazing at the water?

We have both been freed from the gravity of the land of identity.
What shall we do?
What shall we do without exile
And long nights of gazing at the water?[5]

Perhaps, because it is transtemporal, the Palestinians' return will materialize one day, and their exile will have become one of choice, not of coercion.

Ramallah–New York, April 2008

Notes

1. Whether or not Levi took his own life is subject to debate. For a discussion of the controversy surrounding the circumstances of Levi's death, see Carole Angier's *Double Bond: Primo Levi: A Biography* (New York: Farrar, Straus and Giroux, 2002).

2. State of Israel, "The Law of Return 5710 (1950)," Knesset, http://www.knesset.gov.il/laws/special/eng/return.htm.

3. Ibid.

4. Mahmud Darwish, "We Travel Like All People," in *Unfortunately, It Was Paradise: Selected Poems*, ed. and trans. Munir Akash and Carolyn Forché (Berkeley: University of California Press, 2003), 11.

5. Mahmud Darwish, excerpts from "Who Am I, Without Exile?" ibid., 113–14.

12 Adoption and Return

Transnational Genealogies, Maternal Legacies

MARGARET HOMANS

Is a transnational adoptee in the U.S. an exile, an immigrant, or just an American with a "different" face? Is she a victim of kidnap, or of racist or sexist expulsion, or is she the beneficiary of a rescue, or perhaps of a misguided "study abroad" plan gone awry? Did love alone motivate her relinquishment and adoption, or was she an object of exchange in a global market in human lives? Does her identity derive from her DNA, her "blood," her "birth culture," or her adoptive environment; from her point of origin, from her adoptive "fresh start," or from her unstable location in global circuits of migration and exchange? And, depending on how she may answer these questions—which reflect something of the dizzying array of unspoken norms and debated theories current among adoptees, their birth and adoptive parents, and the professionals and state agents on whose changing views their lives may hang—what does it mean for an adult adoptee to return to the country from which she departed as a baby, of whose language and customs she has no memory? To the unknown mother who has for decades been "an act of imagination"?[1] For those adopted as older children, taught in an assimilationist era to deny their memories, will a "roots trip" be a welcome return to the comfort of a once loved home, or will it only activate a painful sense of loss? What do adoptees seek when they go "home," and what is gained and what is lost in replacing a dream of reunion and belonging with the experience of return? Adoptees who undertake return trips can become caught in the contradictions not only between competing concepts of adoptive being in the U.S. but also between competing narratives of adoption produced by the U.S. and by their countries of origin. This essay reads a group of recent return memoirs by adult Korean adoptees raised in the U.S. to see what, at this historical moment, these contradictions can produce.

A "return" in the context of transnational adoption presupposes certain norms that are relatively new in the history of transnational adoption. In the 1960s, 1970s, and 1980s, successful adoption was understood to require a "clean break" from the past and the child was expected to assimilate completely; within this discourse "return" was unimaginable. By contrast, according to the Hague Convention on Protection of Children and Co-Operation in Respect of Intercountry Adoption (1993), although transnational adoption still means full membership in the adoptive family, parentless children now have the right, if they cannot be raised by a family in their nation of origin, to support for the formation of an identity linked to their culture of origin.[2] This widely recognized right, meshing as it does with current U.S. norms around ethnic identity, not only makes return trips imaginable but raises enormously high expectations for them. Many transnationally adopted individuals in the U.S. express a powerful need to reconnect with some aspect of their origin, whether by identifying culturally with their birth nation, by returning to their birthplace, or by searching for their birth parents. Some social theorists, however, have questioned the apparently seamless logic connecting this felt need to its apparently obvious sequelae: return, search, and reunion. In diaspora studies, for example, the origin may be understood to be not so much an actual geographical starting point as a back-formation created by the desires of diasporic subjects;[3] this can be the case for adoptees as well. Anthropologist Barbara Yngvesson explains how little can be taken for granted about the meaning of a place of origin. Of the painful story of an adoptee who returned to Korea and found her birth mother she writes, "this narrative illuminates the powerful pull of a discourse of identity and the 'returns' (to an origin) that identity requires, while at the same time pointing toward a more complex story of movement between (temporary) locations, of desire that is shaped by hegemonies of race, blood, and nation, and of the impossibility of ever fully belonging in the places where we find ourselves."[4] The place of origin seldom provides the returning adoptee with a simple sense of belonging; indeed, it can nightmarishly mirror the situation from which the adoptee seeks refuge. The expectations that motivate the return may depend on antiquated binary logics of home and away, foreign and familiar, even of self and other, that are belied by the global interconnectedness of adoption now.

Although adoptees' yearning for connection to the nation and culture of origin is widespread globally, its acute expression in the U.S. can be traced to peculiarly American contradictions around race, nationality, ethnicity, and blood.[5] Growing up in all-white communities in the 1960s, 1970s, and 1980s, the adult Korean adoptees who began producing memoirs in the 1990s were bound by two opposing unspoken laws: the imperative to assimilate in a society that believed itself to be color-blind and the iron law of racism that singles out skin color and facial configuration as the most salient factors in personal identity. Virtually all the memoirists discuss the violent racisms they encountered, despite their best efforts to conform and their parents' denials. This account is typical: "Raised by white parents in a predominantly white town, I considered myself to be white. Others saw me differently, though. People stared at me as if I were an alien and children asked if I could see through my "Chinese, slant eyes." The worst episodes were when teenage boys surrounded me on the school bus and yelled obscenities and racial slurs at me. My race shouldn't have mattered, I thought, because it didn't matter to my friends and family."[6]

How you look is what you are, these transplanted children quickly discovered, and yet their new families were devoted to denying difference. Saying "you are a [last name of adoptive family]" might be the only way they could express their love.[7] In Deann Borshay Liem's autobiographical film *First Person Plural* (2000), adoptive family members unapologetically recall acting out, in the name of love, what for Liem was the cruelty of color-blind adoption in a racist society. Able only to see that the child at the airport was Asian, failing to notice that she was not the child in the photos they had received over a period of years (an exchange of identities of great significance to the child herself), in her sister Denise's laughing recollection, "I think mother went up to the wrong person. . . . It didn't matter. I mean, one of 'em was ours [mother laughs]." Her brother Duncan congratulates himself on his blindness: "You don't have the family eyes, but I don't care; you got the family smile. Color and look doesn't make any difference. It's who y'are; you're my sister,"[8] while her father makes a joke of it. "People used to stare and . . . ask us, is she your daughter? . . . Then I would say, of course she is, we look just alike, don't we? [laughs]."[9] On leaving home for college, Liem fell into a "deep depression" on account of this denial and the uncompleted mourning for her birth family that accompanied it.

The racism from which these adoptees suffered often came in a specifically gendered form (as is true of life writing about U.S. domestic adoption, most of the memoirists are women). In the passage by Crystal Lee Hyun Joo Chappell quoted earlier, the teenage boys yell not just "racial slurs" but "obscenities" too. The visuality of American race and racism was exacerbated by the intensive policing of appearance for U.S. girls and women. Efforts to normalize their appearance (permed hair, makeup, eyelid surgery) are reported by women adoptees though rarely by men; many recall as children hating to be photographed or to see themselves in a mirror. *First Person Plural* documents, with vivid archival images, Liem's teenage efforts, as head cheerleader and prom queen, to create and maintain a "happy American façade" by rendering her face, hair, and body style white-American; but not even plastic surgery made her feel secure.[10] In her first memoir, *The Language of Blood* (2003), Jane Jeong Trenka reports an extreme form of sexualized racism when, in college, she is pursued for months by a white male stalker who calls her "nothing but a Korean in a white man's world,"[11] videotapes her through her dorm window, follows her to her parents' home, wrecks the house, and attempts to shoot her father. He is eventually jailed, his car having been found stocked with paraphernalia for a horrendous crime, including duct tape, vaseline, a loaded gun, a video camera with a tripod, and a shovel. This episode makes an enduring psychic scar, for Jane blames herself. The threat of sexual violence is hardly unique to Korean adoptees or to Asian women; specific to Trenka as a transracial adoptee is her psychic vulnerability.

Trenka's is an extreme case, yet it helps make visible the scopic sexist racism that troubled the young lives of so many children adopted from Korea and led them to dream of returning home to the (imaginary) true mother who would heal these wounds. Misled by denial, totally unprepared for the virulent biases that would surround them outside their homes, many adoptees grew alienated from their parents and communities. Looking different in a looks-based culture motivated many returns, as suggested by Katy Robinson's childhood letter to her adoptive mother, from her 2002 memoir *A Single Square Picture*: "Do you know what it feels like to have an Asian shell while longing to be white just like you? Well, I am not one of you. . . . I am Korean and I want to find out what that means."[12] Trenka, too, traces her initial desire to return to Korea in part to her harrowing experience with the stalker, and she attributes her recent choice to move there (in her second memoir) to her divorce from the husband who, like the stalker, turned out to care more for an eroticized "Asian woman" fantasy than for Jane herself. Korea is imagined as a place of nondifference and acceptance where sexist racism could not occur; the ebbing of assimilationist norms in the 1990s and the rise of identity politics, encouraging identification with racial and national origins, played a part too. At the same time, the South Korean government, recognizing in the children sent abroad a potential economic resource, encouraged return visits. In 1997 the Overseas Koreans Foundation was created, as part of the Ministry of Foreign Affairs and Trade, to promote "blood ties that cannot be severed."[13] Government-sponsored homeland tours flourished; a popular TV show staged reunions; individual families as well as the state sought forgiveness and financial help from their restored children.

These reunions and returns seldom match adoptees' hopes for acceptance and comfort. According to anthropologist Eleana Kim, the OKF has produced not more loyal Koreans but, instead, through the disidentification wrought by the government's inappropriate demands, a virtual "nation" made up of individuals from all over the world who gather periodically and identify with one another not as Koreans but as Korean adoptees.[14] Although "KAD nation" is a positive element in many lives,[15] it also names a form of permanent homelessness. In a study of young adult adoptees returning from Sweden to Chile, Yngvesson shows that seeing their homelands and meeting their birth mothers, instead of making them feel whole as they hoped, produced confusion, a "shaking up [of] identity" rather than a securing of it.[16] Similarly, Seoul is now home to a sizable floating community of returned adoptees (men and women), among whom Trenka writes of having lived for three years. In her haunting second memoir, *Fugitive Visions* (2009), they live fragile, marginal lives, cut off from their adoptive families yet unable or unwilling to assimilate into Korean life.[17] Prone to alcoholism, they meet in the English- and French- speaking bars; suicides, according to Trenka, are not uncommon. The scopic sexist racism that angered and harmed Korean adoptees in the U.S. is not remedied by their being in a place where, at last, they seem to look like everyone else. Many find themselves subjected to a nationalistic form of racism when disparaged for forgetting Korean language and customs and for looking American.[18] They also encounter Korean forms of androcentrism and sexism that they experience as even more toxic than those they suffered in the U.S.

Korean culture, like American, defines kinship primarily through "blood" or genetic ties. Whereas, in U.S. adoption discourse, blood kinship paradoxically becomes the dominant metaphor for severing a child's biological ties and reassigning her new kin, *"as if begotten,"*[19] among the Korean families in the memoirs, ties of blood are understood to be so strong as to be inviolable. Children who have lived for twenty or thirty years as members of U.S. families are greeted upon their return as if no break had occurred. Parents under economic and other kinds of stress placed children in orphanages and even agreed to their adoption abroad because they thought that only thus could their children be made safe, fed, and educated; they could not imagine or anticipate that their children would, by law and U.S. custom, cease to be theirs, often disappearing untraceably. "My mother," writes Trenka, "had no idea we would be separated for twenty-three years, that international adoption is not some kind of extended study-abroad program."[20] On returning, these adoptees encountered the powerful discourse of blood both as the expectation that they would now rejoin the family and resume being Korean—as if Korean language, cultural knowledge, and body style were in their blood—and as the expression of a patriarchal belief system that confounds their U.S. liberal feminist assumptions about personal freedom. They flee U.S. sexist racism only to find even more explicit sexisms in Korea, where among their parents' generations traditional (in this case, Confucian) gender norms and hierarchies are far more openly enforced than in the U.S. They find subservient, often abused, wives and mothers and the expectation that they too will give up their independent American ways to become Korean-female. "'It is good to be a man in Korea,'" a male Korean adoptee tells Katy Robinson; "'I need to find myself a good traditional Korean wife to take home with me.'"[21]

Many children were relinquished or abandoned for reasons of sexism. Boys are preferred, and girls might be mistreated or abandoned in situations where a boy might have been treasured and kept. Trenka and an older sister were sent to America because their mother, herself bearing disfiguring scars from her husband's violence, feared for her daughters' lives. "My own Umma told me that if she had kept me, I would have been either dead or a beggar. She told me stories of how my father beat me about the head and my head turned black and blue, how he threw me from a window, how she was homeless and slept on the streets."[22] Trenka notes the irony of her having, on account of her stalker, "experienced the fear that my mother had given me away to escape," a fear of misogynist violence that may have locally specific causes but whose effects cross national borders.[23] Time and again, adoptees learn that their birthmothers, left partnerless by death or by sexual betrayal, had to give them up because a single mother had no social standing and no way of earning a livelihood. Eleana Kim writes that, despite a 1991 change in the law giving some rights to mothers, "birth mothers . . . represent the most subordinated groups in an entrenched patriarchy and misogynistic state welfare system."[24] After the accidental death of her father, writes one adoptee, her mother "tried to support us by selling insurance, books and other things. She tried for almost three years . . . but like tens of thousands of single mothers in Korea's patrilineal society and poverty of the 1970s, she found it impossible and turned to U.S. adoption."[25] Still sadder, another adoptee's mother "left my dad because he was an alcoholic and beat her. She left to save her life. She couldn't take me with her because I was the property of my father."[26]

Although these assertions of male privilege and patriarchal authority stem from Korean law and tradition, the intensity and cruelty of their recent expression appears sometimes to be motivated by a defensive nationalism that responds to decades of imperial subjugation followed by divisive war and then the IMF crisis of the 1980s. Trenka, analyzing her father's violence in the context of a nation of failed, alcoholic men (all the beggars in Seoul, she says, are men), reports that, with their light skin, she and her sister were "assumed to be half-American in a public setting such as this, packed with . . . American soldiers carrying rifles who ate meat every day."[27] Her father raged against what he took to be his wife's unfaithfulness to him and to the nation and against the children who seemed to make it visible. In Liem's film, too, the older brother identifies the family honor with that of the nation when he delivers a face-saving speech that echoes the official South Korean line about foreign adoption: Deann was not "abandoned" but rather "sent away" to enjoy "better opportunities" and to get an education. The tearful mother at first parrots his words, dutifully supporting the young patriarch; yet at other times, departing from the script, she weeps and tells Deann that she has felt "endless heartache" and acknowledges that her daughter's "pain was indescribable."[28] Daughters returning to Korea often struggle to hear their mothers' broken, discredited voices behind the loudspeaker of public and private male authority.

Nonetheless, at least in adoptees' dreams, refound birth mothers and the cultural values linked to them may soothe away together the scopic

sexist racism of the U.S. and the patriarchal sexism of Korea. Rediscover-
ing the taste and smell of Korean food can provide the greatest pleasure
of a return trip, and returning adoptees tend to locate in outdoor food
markets their fantasies of suddenly recognizing and reuniting with their
lost birth mothers.[29] When families reunite, the mothers press home-
made food on their children. Touch, too, is often imagined as the sign of
maternal presence. Katy Robinson wistfully recalls "the way she combed
my hair and cut my bangs, pasting down wisps of hair with a lick of her
finger."[30] One short return memoir ends with two dreamscapes in which
the writer is climbing a mountain in the dark and sees, first, herself as a
baby, glowing blue in the moonlight; then, closing her eyes and praying
to the mother she never found, she holds her hand out in the dark, and,
"after a while, I feel her grasp my hand."[31] Trenka, who does find refuge
with her mother and sisters in *The Language of Blood*, describes a nearly
womblike contact that mutes the visual and accentuates intimate bodily
contact and care. On arriving at the Seoul airport, released from the visual violence of "cameras flashing in shocking explosions," she writes,
"I was pushed onto a bus with my mother," who cannot stop weeping
and who "clutched my hand tightly and didn't let go." The bus ride is
like a journey down the birth canal for both of them: "In my memory, we
are suspended together in the blackness, all by ourselves, with nothing
to say, no words to say it." Umma's stories about her perilous babyhood
penetrate her daughter physically, and she reinforces them with touch.
"She showed me her breasts to tell me that she loved me and had nursed
me. I touched her old woman's depleted breasts, as she asked. *Touch me
here, where I gave myself to you. I made you with my own body*, she seemed
to say."[32] When Umma gives her daughter a bath, "the water is warm as
birthwater"; Umma squats, in laboring position, and "washes me hard
and quickly, with so much ardor it hurts, and I become a child again." The
bath, like the bus ride, enacts her rebirth as her mother's baby, and these
deep physical pleasures seem to repair the injury of abandonment.

Are maternal feeding and touch sufficient remedies for the suffering
inflicted on adoptees by androcentric regimes? For the highly articulate,
communicative daughters who author these memoirs, they can be both
comforting and frustrating. The mothers refuse to honor adult boundaries. On her first visit to Seoul, Trenka expects to spend an "orderly week"
with her tour group before turning her attention to her birth family, but
Umma keeps appearing at the hotel room of "her baby," "bearing plastic
bags crammed full of tomatoes and watermelon—far more than I could

ever eat."[33] Especially when there is no or little shared language, mother and daughter resort to tears and caresses, forms of communication that wear thin after the first overwhelming moments. As David Eng points out, Liem manages her confusion about having both a Korean and an American mother by distributing, one to each, the roles of preoedipal and of symbolic mother, but neither is satisfactory.[34] Liem's American family inhabits a scopic symbolic domain: the film opens with a survey of her father's art photographs, and that she herself is making a film aligns her with her father's viewpoint, despite the harm she sustained from the U.S. culture of the gaze. When she visits her birth family, by contrast, "my body remembers something, but my mind is resistant," her communications with her mother are limited to the semiotic (touches, hugs, and tears), and she finds herself unable to relearn Korean. The rediscovery of the pre-oedipal mother turns from a source of comfort into a source of frustration.

Although Trenka (unlike Liem) celebrates the restoration of her pre-oedipal mother, it cannot last. By the time of her third visit to Korea, her mother is dying of metastatic brain cancer, which appears in the narrative as the result of long years of abuse and poverty. She requires the constant care of her daughters, and Trenka moves into the hospital with her sisters to reciprocate Umma's wordless maternal care. "I rubbed your back, where you had carried me," she writes. "I came to know your body" and to learn that "I am a daughter after your body and after your heart. Even if I fail to create you again with words, I will carry you with me, in the language of blood."[35] This semiotic "language of blood" links the returned daughter to the preoedipal mother. The father was the violent intruder who inscribed his dominion in the form of scars on the mother's and sisters' bodies. The language of blood, by contrast, is the wordless bond between mother and daughter that transcends their geographic and linguistic distance. But this relationship can be perfected only after Umma's death, when linguistic and cultural barriers fall away. Toward the end of the memoir Trenka writes: "Now that you are dead, you are more near to me. You've always been so far away, halfway across the earth in your basement apartment in Seoul, me here in Minnesota trying so hard to learn your language and failing. . . . But now I talk to you all the time. I talk to you in English, and I think I hear you talking to me in English, or in emotions, or maybe it is something else, but I can understand it. I have dreams now. They are in Korean, and they must be from you."[36] The memoir ends with a lyrical vision of Umma taking her daughter's hand—"Umma's hand is hot and plump, the way it used to be, and she holds on too tight, the way she always did"—and flying, together with Trenka's new baby daughter, like butterflies into a gorgeously evoked stratosphere.[37] The language of blood here is translated from maternal bodily contact into the writer's distinctive literary style, in which she does "create [her mother] again with words." An alternative to silencing paternal force, this maternal language authorizes Trenka's emergent voice. But the maternal language itself is impermanent, going unmentioned in Trenka's second memoir.

How different Trenka's "language of blood" is from the language of "blood" in Katy Robinson's *A Single Square Picture*, where blood refers to the patriarchal preoccupation with bloodlines, blood descent, scopic identity (son and grandson are carbon copies of the father), legitimate birth, and the violent control of women's lives upon which these preoccupations depend. Robinson reads the Korean bloodline in an explicitly feminist framework. "I am grateful I didn't have to grow up a dutiful girl in Korea," she writes home to her American mother; "I am reading a collection of folktales and the moral of every story is for the wife to sacrifice herself for her husband and in-laws."[38] She discovers that Korean gender hierarchy accounts both for her relinquishment (at age seven) by her unmarried mother and for her difficulty now in locating her birth mother. Welcomed effusively to Korea by her birth father and his son, her (legitimate) older half-brother, she feels estranged by their sentimental presumptions of intimacy ("Your brother loves you very much," a translator tells Robinson; "since you and your brother share the same blood, he feels very close to you") combined with their "heartless[ness]," her term for their active efforts to keep her from finding her birth mother (140, 197). For father and son, the birth mother represents a threat to what is, after all, a fragile patriarchal authority. Robinson's memoir is populated by women who were forced to accept their husbands' and lovers' infidelities and their socially and economically devastating desertions. To the men—like the South Korean government itself, which in 1998 apologized for allowing foreign adoptions and then went on permitting the practice—these outcomes exhibit both their masculine prerogative (of which they are proud) and masculine shame (the father keeps confessing his failures as a father). The resulting culturally sanctioned disparagement of women Robinson experiences firsthand: as she prepares to meet her father, her local hosts require her to "comply with the standards of a proper *Korean* daughter, demanding that she dress up, curl her hair, apply makeup, and purchase a deferential gift" (43). Often in her father's company she feels infantilized; "I felt my independence and my American identity dissolve with each passing second I spent with him" (119). Father and son control Robinson's actions while in Korea by appropriating her search for her mother: they promise to make inquiries but fail to do so. By having "erased" her mother, Robinson thinks, they believe they can erase paternal shame (197).

Finally Robinson understands that her mother may not want to be found, for the same reason she gave her child up: the exposure of the illegitimate birth could compromise whatever new life she has been able to arrange. When Robinson recalls and speculates about her birth mother, and when she meets other abused wives and mothers, she counters their "erasure" by recalling and imagining touch, taste, smell, and sound. In her memory of the airport where she is to board the plane for America, when her mother is told to let her daughter go, "her hand releases my fingers, shoots up my arm, and grips my shoulder. As she does this, I feel a shot of panic travel up my chest. . . . But another eternity passes before my mother releases her clawlike grip on my shoulder bone and moves her hand to cover her eyes" (3). Sharing bodily sensations, mother and daughter cannot part, but they do. Trying to soothe herself, she "clung to the scent of roasted seaweed and peppery kimchee, the feel of my grandmother's body next to mine, and the last look on my mother's face." (Later, in the U.S., staring at a Polaroid taken in the airport, she cannot recognize herself.) In her fantasy of reunion her mother holds her and "answers all my questions as if reading my mind, [with] no need for a translator" (132–133). Very like Trenka's "language of blood," this dream of unalienated, unmediated contact with her mother's mind and body always ends "with a sense of completion and wholeness."

Although Robinson never meets her mother, she acquires a "surrogate Korean mother" (her father's first wife) who, like Trenka's Umma, pinches, squeezes, and pats her and stuffs her with food (206). Robinson, in turn, trying to tell her she is beautiful, mispronounces the Korean word and calls her "delicious" (211). But the squeezing, delicious mother represents not so much the long-sought mother of Katy's hopes as the patriarchal system that both creates and destroys her. The grandmother and her daughter-in-law never sit down to eat with her son, Robinson's half-brother, who barks orders into the kitchen and never offers to help. Robinson is horrified by the two women's traditional Korean female servitude and by the grandmother's continued shame and grief over having been deserted thirty years before. The grandmother disintegrates in tears because the presence of the mistress's daughter reminds her of their family's "demoted status" and "reopen[s] old wounds" (215, 220). As in *First*

Person Plural, the nurturing, preoedipal mother reveals her lack of social power, her pathetic and understandable yet deeply unappealing loyalty to the father's law.

Robinson soon develops a symptom. Her vision blurs; she has a detached retina. This turn of events is linked both literally and figuratively to her search for her mother, which she now must abandon. The Korean doctor says her condition is hereditary; with excellent eyesight on her father's side, her weak eyes must come from her mother. Only by falling ill, evidently, can she gain accurate information about her mother. This "sick joke" anticipates the irony that Trenka's greatest intimacy with her Umma is occasioned by Umma's fatal illness (250). Delirious, lying together on the floor and stroking her daughter's hair, Umma calls her *ipun eggi* or "pretty baby," her mind going back to her daughter's birth twenty-five years earlier.[39] Although Trenka takes great pleasure in this revelation of her mother's love, for Robinson, Korean motherhood, including the maternal touches, tastes, and smells that were once so laden with positive value, begins to lose its aura of safety and comfort. A farewell visit to the half-brother revives the image of the grandmother as domestic slave, doing too much hand laundry, making too much kimchee. Finally, Robinson reviews her fragmentary memories of her mother: she "can almost feel the warmth of her love," yet their closeness is also frightening. Late one night, she recalls, she awoke to hear her mother and grandmother arguing about her and then saw her mother run to the bathroom to vomit on the floor. "Seeing my mother slumped over like that, still sobbing as she choked and spat, suddenly flipped my own stomach upside down. I sensed her desperation and knew that it somehow involved me. I ran to the bathroom and found myself squatting next to my mother, getting sick just as she had a moment earlier" (295). This remembered bodily connection, the mother's legacy, is about damage as much as about love.

The mother's death in *The Language of Blood*, her remoteness in *First Person Plural* (Liem says she now "admit[s] she's not my mother"), her erasure and Robinson's resignation about it in *A Single Square Picture*: found or not, the long-sought birthmother in each case cannot resolve the daughter's battles either with American scopic sexist racisms or with Korean nationalist patriarchy. Through these frustrating returns, the daughters come to understand the violence that damaged their mothers' lives, that necessitated their own relinquishment and adoption, and that lives on in the persistence of the sexual double standard and of cultural biases toward sons. The birthmothers and grandmothers want married daughters with grandchildren, to continue the family line and to bear the burden of gender that has formed and deformed their own lives. And the memoirists generously comply, even as they frame their compliance in terms that gently underscore the unbridgeable distance between them. Liem's film ends, in figurative compliance, with a still shot of Liem and her husband and baby, as if the filmmaker had stepped momentarily from behind the camera to sign her work as wife and mother. Robinson and Trenka likewise incorporate figurative babies into their self-definitions as writers. In her memoir's last lines, Robinson mentally resolves her ambivalence about the longed-for-yet-dangerous maternal body by identifying not with her birthmother's body but with her stories. She imagines her birthmother with the younger children Robinson hopes she bore, patient with them because she "understands the ache of first love and the fickle hearts of handsome men much more than her children will ever know. Her children will doubt her, just as she doubted her own mother and my children will someday doubt me"; being able to pass on her mother's and grandmother's stories makes a "cycle that will connect generations of women, Korean and American" (297). Like Trenka, she can manage the heartbreaking absence of her birth mother by positioning her as the authorizing ground of her writing. The publication of Trenka's second memoir treats Umma as a distant memory and has nothing to say of the desired grandchild, but it confirms Trenka's vocation as a writer. While Robinson shapes her maternal genealogy into an engine of narrative continuity, Trenka turns the maternal "language of blood" into lyrical prose. As Mei-Ling Hopgood writes at the conclusion of her memoir of returning to her birth home in Taiwan (and, like Trenka and Robinson, of discovering a brutal, patriarchal father and a worn-out, unreachable mother): "I offer my voice to the chorus of ancestors. I am not the son who can perpetuate the family name, but I can tell our story. I am not the heir that Ba wanted, but I, too, can be a keeper of our history. I choose to continue the narrative in my own way."[40] In their own ways, the Korean memoirists transform ambiguous maternal legacies into strong claims to a creative future and new legacies for younger generations of transnational adoptees.

Notes

1. Laurel Kendall, "Birth Mothers and Imaginary Lives," in Toby Alice Volkman, ed., *Cultures of Transnational Adoption* (Durham: Duke University Press, 2005), 162–181, quotation 164.

2. See Toby Alice Volkman, "Introduction: New Geographies of Kinship," in Volkman, *Cultures of Transnational Adoption*, 1–22, discussion 5; or Barbara Yngvesson, *Belonging in an Adopted World: Race, Identity, and Transnational Adoption* (Chicago: University of Chicago Press, 2010), 19.

3. For example, see Stuart Hall, "The Local and the Global: Globalization and Ethnicity," in A. D. King, ed., *Culture, Globalization, and the World-System* (Minneapolis: University of Minnesota Press, 1997).

4. Yngvesson, *Belonging*, 163.

5. Anthropologist Signe Howell notes that transnational adoptees in Norway seldom express the intense wish to reconnect with their origins, which, she believes, is the product of American preoccupations with autonomous individuality and with race, in concert with the essentializing discourses of "psycho-technocrats" (social workers and other state-authorized experts) who, at this historical moment, have established "biogenetic connectedness as the mainstay of kinship." Signe Howell, "Return Journeys and the Search for Roots: Contradictory Values Concerning Identity," in Diana Marre and Laura Briggs, eds., *International Adoption: Global Inequities and the Circulation of Children* (New York: New York University Press, 2009), 256–270, this discussion 258–261.

6. Crystal Lee Hyun Joo Chappell, "Now I'm Found," in Tonya Bishoff and Jo Rankin, eds., *Seeds from a Silent Tree: An Anthology by Korean Adoptees* (Glendale, CA: Pandal, 1997), 124–135, quotation 126.

7. Barb Lee, director, *Adopted* (Carbondale, CO: Point Made Films, 2008).

8. Deann Borshay Liem, director, *First Person Plural* (San Francisco: National Asian American Telecommunications Association, 2000).

9. Deann Borshay [Liem], "Remembering the Way Home: A Documentary Video Proposal," in *Seeds from a Silent Tree*, 116–120, quotation 117. The quotation in the next sentence is from 118.

10. Liem, *First Person Plural*; Liem, "Remembering the Way Home," 118.

11. Jane Jeong Trenka, *The Language of Blood: A Memoir* (St. Paul, MN: Borealis, 2003), 73.

12. Katy Robinson, *A Single Square Picture: A Korean Adoptee's Search for Her Roots* (New York: Berkley, 2002), 36.

13. Eleana Kim, "Wedding Citizenship and Culture: Korean Adoptees and the Global Family of Korea," in *Cultures of Transnational Adoption*, 49–80, quotation 62.

14. Kim, "Wedding Citizenship and Culture," 59–60, 71.

15. For example, see Sunny Jo, "The Making of KAD Nation," in Jane Jeong Trenka, Julia Chinyere Oparah, and Sun Yung Shin, eds., *Outsiders Within: Writing on Transracial Adoption* (Cambridge: South End, 2006), 285–290.

16. Barbara Yngvesson, "Going 'Home': Adoption, Loss of Bearings, and the Mythology of Roots," in *Cultures of Transnational Adoption*, 25–48, 32.

17. Jane Jeong Trenka, *Fugitive Visions: An Adoptee's Return to Korea* (St Paul, MN: Graywolf, 2009).

18. See, for example, Leah Kim Sieck, "A True Daughter," in Susan Soon-Keum Cox, ed., *Voices from Another Place: A Collection of Works from a Generation Born*

in Korea and Adopted to Other Countries (St. Paul: Yeong and Yeong, 1999), 84–91, this point 85; or Eleana Kim, "Wedding Citizenship and Culture," 65–66.

19. Janet Carsten, *After Kinship* (Cambridge: Cambridge University Press, 2004), 149, citing Judith Schachter Modell, *Kinship with Strangers: Adoption and Interpretations of Kinship in American Culture* (Berkeley: University of California Press, 2004), 4.

20. Trenka, *Fugitive Visions*, 98.

21. Robinson, *A Single Square Picture*, 175.

22. Trenka, *The Language of Blood*, 200.

23. Trenka, *The Language of Blood*, 69.

24. Kim, "Wedding Citizenship and Culture," 72; for a somewhat more optimistic view of Korean birthmothers' situations, see Kendall, "Birth Mothers and Imaginary Lives."

25. Chappell, "Now I'm Found," 131.

26. Mea Han Nelson-Wang, "Purpose," in Cox, *Voices from Another Place*, 64–66, quotation 64; for a similar story, see Tonya Keith, "A Journey Back," in Cox, *Voices from Another Place*, 32–40.

27. Trenka, *Fugitive Visions*, 134–135.

28. Liem, *First Person Plural*.

29. For example, see Kimberly Kyung Hee Stock, "My *Han*," in Cox, *Voices from Another Place*, 96–104, this point 96.

30. Robinson, *A Single Square Picture*, 294.

31. Sieck, "A True Daughter," 91.

32. Trenka, *The Language of Blood*, 102. The quotation in the next sentence is from 107.

33. Trenka, *The Language of Blood*, 100, 99.

34. David Eng, "Transnational Adoption and Queer Diasporas," *Social Text* 76 (2003): 1–37.

35. Trenka, *The Language of Blood*, 139–40.

36. Trenka, *The Language of Blood*, 192.

37. Trenka, *The Language of Blood*, 220.

38. Robinson, *A Single Square Picture*, 184.

39. Trenka, *The Language of Blood*, 150.

40. Mei-Ling Hopgood, *Lucky Girl: A Memoir* (Chapel Hill: Algonquin, 2009), 244.

13   Foreign Correspondence

SONALI THAKKAR

I'm on a train moving slowly through the Frankfurt suburbs, on my way to the nearby town of Mainz, where I'm teaching English and American literature to German undergraduates for the year. There's a copy of that day's *Frankfurter Allgemeine Zeitung* sitting folded on my lap. On the front page are several compelling headlines: a piece on Romanian-German author Herta Müller, who's just won the literature Nobel for her writing on dictatorship and migration; an article on China's controversial "honoured guest" status at the Frankfurt Book Fair, which has just opened that day; and an update on the fate of Thilo Sarrazin—a highly public figure in Germany's historically left SPD party who's caused a scandal by asserting that Turks and Arabs in Berlin, along with various other members of the "underclass," are contributing to the city's economic stagnation and cultural decline and must be either radically assimilated or denied recognition as members of the body politic.[1] As if in counterpoint to Sarrazin's claims, there's also a prominently placed op-ed by political journalist Stefan Dietrich. It argues that immigrants have long since left the fringes to become part of society and active participants in the political discourse about migration. They are not the mute objects of immigration policy: they are here to stay and they play a role in transforming the public debate.[2]

These two positions—that migrants are a policy problem requiring po-litical elites to find forceful or even coercive solutions and that migrants are interlocutors and agents of transformation—are both mainstays of contemporary immigration politics in liberal democracies. Seeing them recapitulated on this newspaper page, I'm reminded of Ama Ata Aidoo's 1977 prose poem *Our Sister Killjoy*, not because it adopts either of these perspectives but because it proposes a very different understanding of the political stakes of migration.[3]

A Ghanaian feminist author and scholar, Aidoo writes critically about African and transnational feminisms in the period after decolonization as well as about the African diaspora. *Our Sister Killjoy* brings together these themes, and critics describe it as a formally innovative feminist and anti-colonial provocation. The work narrates the journey of a young Ghanaian woman called Sissie to Germany and England. Sissie's voyage is not one of exile or economic migration. Instead, less predictably, she heads off on what resembles a student exchange or one of those overseas friendship-and-goodwill programs for youth, this one sponsored by the postwar Ger-man government's international largesse and its desire "to make good again."[4] But, unlike an exchange, the travel only goes one way: from Africa to Europe. Sissie's German benefactors understand her journey as a varia-tion on the colonial civilizing mission; it is an educative opportunity for a promising young woman from Africa to enrich her character and pros-pects through an encounter with European culture.

Sisse also eventually travels to England, and the narrator addresses its strange pull on her imagination, noting, "Germany is overseas. / The United States is overseas. / But England is another thing." It is the place that Sissie reluctantly acknowledges as "her colonial home."[5] In Germany, which of course does not share England's specific colonial history with Ghana, she is seemingly unencumbered by such unwanted affinities. Yet the colonial dynamic with which *Our Sister Killjoy* is concerned encom-passes Germany as well, and Germany provides the impetus for the entire journey and is the focus of the first half of the book. Barbara Mennel notes that in *Our Sister Killjoy* "England functions as the imperial center and Germany as its displacement," upsetting the familiar postcolonial binary of colony and metropole, while from a German studies perspective the text is "considered neither German nor migrant literature."[6] The work's eccentric interest in Germany is likely why I think of it as I sit on the train, crossing the Rhine. That, and its resonance for me, as I too was once a youthful visitor to Germany: a teenage Rotary exchange student who arrived with barely a few words of German. Now I've come back a decade later for a second extended visit, this time nominally as a teacher, but really in order to learn more about contemporary German debates on migration and multiculturalism—debates that Aidoo's more than thirty-year-old text illuminates in surprising ways.

It's around 1967 as Sissie's journey gets underway, and she finds herself in a quaint-sinister Bavarian village where she plants trees, embodies difference, and reaffirms to herself what she seemingly knows before she's even left: that she's a woman whose place is at home. I use that phrase not in the narrow sense of an enforced reproductive domesticity (if anything, Sissie's commitment to the idea of home is what complicates the text's heteroromantic subplot) but to try to get at what makes the work so unsettling: namely, that it valorizes Sissie's radical political commitment to Africa and its decolonization in a way that at times shades into something disturbingly like nativism, a conviction that a life in the diaspora is no life at all.

Believing that "for the slave, there is nothing at the centre but worse slavery," Sissie is baffled and infuriated by the Ghanaians and other Africans she meets in England who have remained abroad. The African diaspora in Europe and elsewhere is an intractable problem for her—one that gives her "many sleepless nights trying to understand why, after finishing their studies, our brothers and sisters stay here and stay and stay."[7] If, as I'm suggesting, the op-ed in the *FAZ* reaffirms to its German audience that immigrants are there to stay—hardly news—it's because reiterating this point is politically potent. For migrants and their advocates, asserting that their presence is lasting and persistent effectively forces the issue of migrant rights, challenging convenient fictions that migrant workers, illegal aliens, and others are transient, temporary visitors who will or must be forced to leave. As the massive demonstrations in spring 2006 for migrant rights in the United States showed, the quotidian act of staying put becomes a measure of migrants' *staying power*—a staying power that eventually demands acknowledgment and recognition.

But in Sissie's formulation, staying is no political affirmation. It loosens the bonds of attachment and weakens political consciousness and accountability. The real work is to be done at home, and she "plead[s] [that] instead of forever gathering together and virtuously spouting such beautiful radical analyses of the situation at home we should simply hurry back."[8] When Sissie speaks uncomprehendingly of those who "stay here and stay and stay," her repetition of the term implies that those who choose not to return are traveling further and further away by remaining where they are. This image—of moving away while staying put—appears in the text itself, but inverted, as a figure for the futility of diasporic attempts at upward mobility. Migration, she muses, is one aspect of "the general illusion of how well an unfree population think they can do for themselves [*sic*]. Running very fast just to remain where they are."[9]

Even those who *do* return are not exempt from her disdain; them she suspects of merely not having had "the courage to be a coward enough to stay forever in England."[10] There's a powerful germ of critique at the heart of her rhetoric that can't be dismissed, for what Sissie deplores here is what Gayatri Chakravorty Spivak has described as the collusion of transnational economic migrants with global capital.[11] Or, as Bruce Robbins puts it, it sometimes seems "that upward mobility can happen only as betrayal of those left behind."[12] Such issues of complicity and opportunism are charged and salient, and the text addresses them poignantly, including in the form of fragments of coaxing letters from home that ask: "When are you coming?" "if only you were here," "apart from you, who else do we have?"[13] What's questionable, though, is Sissie's conviction that such migratory dispersion can be corrected, presumably by gathering one's resolve, bringing one's loyalties in line, and making the morally correct choice to go home, even as she recognizes that these migrations are the historically produced results of colonial and postcolonial upheavals.

And what's back home at the end of Sissie's dusty rainbow? She admits to a preening young doctor who resists returning that "the rewards [at home] would not be much. Hardly anything. . . . It will be humble expressions of humbler means. A hen. A cockerel. An old woman would carry you eggs laid by home-reared chicken [*sic*]. A widow might bring you her last tuber of yam. . . . Most of the time, it will be plain old verbal 'thank-you' very timidly said, and in silence, a blessing of the womb that bore you."[14] Bracketing for a moment Sissie's recourse to images of home-reared eggs and fertile wombs, what's striking is her certainty in the plausibility of return, her conviction that return is a matter of moral courage and political will. Her insistent desire to reverse migratory currents in the name of "group survival" must be read in the context of subsequent accounts of diaspora that take as their starting point the impossibility, even undesirability, of a return to origins.[15] Instead, they sketch the political possibilities of diasporic rupture rather than its reversal, stressing new forms of identity and practices of memory and translation that both recognize and delicately bridge the temporal and spatial divide.[16] Paul Gilroy has proposed diaspora as a rejoinder to essentializing discourses of racial solidarity and authenticity, suggesting instead the notion of a diasporic consciousness that remembers the ruptures of "loss, exile, and journeying," rather than conjuring up "a lost past" and "a culture of compensation that would restore access to it."[17] Sissie, in contrast, understands the relation between diaspora and home as simultaneously parasitical and neglectful; diaspora indicates the willful renunciation of belonging and history, rather than the existence of fragile continuities or imaginative bonds. While Gilroy and other theorists of diaspora question a telos of homecoming, Sissie worries: "We have been scattered. We wander too far. We are in danger of getting completely lost. We must not allow this to happen."[18] Her words are hortatory but also elegiac. Indeed, they render uncertain any possible distinction between Sissie's return as an act of political conviction and other forms of return that stem from nostalgia and the wish to recuperate loss.

It is these nostalgic or recuperative modes of return with which we're more familiar—modes in which return is deferred, foreclosed, or traumatic—frequently generated in works of migration literature and exile or narratives of traumatic memory. Among that constellation of stories on the front page of the newspaper, all of which are in some way stories about returning and staying, I pause on the headline "Herta Müller in Transylvania." Earlier that day, at the Frankfurt Book Fair, I'd heard Müller speak about her newest book, *Atemschaukel*, in an interview for the television channel Arte.[19] First, a series of photographs flashed up on a screen— photos of her journey to Ukraine with poet Oskar Pastior in 2004. It is his story of imprisonment in Soviet camps that the novel revisits, and, as Müller explained in the interview, early in their collaborative project they undertook literally to revisit that landscape—a journey of return.[20] The journey is fraught, for Pastior has never before returned, and they fear he may not be able to bear it. But instead, she explains, the journey is a type of *Heimkehr*, a term that most properly implies a homecoming, but also emphasizes the act of returning or circling back.

Yet in this instance, too, the full measure of what such a return might mean remains incalculable, for Oskar Pastior dies before they can write the book and before he has a chance to return again, as he wishes too. What's left, Müller says, is the task of writing the story—a task that falls to her. Describing herself as the story's *Werkzeug* or instrument, Müller also functions as its medium, transforming the belated and unfinished return into narrative. In such instances of diasporic or exilic loss, what's salvageable may be return as a narrative trope that allows for explorations of fiction making and self-fashioning, substituting narrative open-endedness for return's presumed closure.

Yet such substitution is never symmetrical or compensatory. In *Lose Your Mother: A Journey Along the Atlantic Slave Route*, Saidiya Hartman addresses the absence of a legible archive of slavery and the Middle Passage, tracing the consequences for disrupted genealogies.[21] She attends to the archival aporia, in part by engaging in forms of narrative reinvention.[22] Such narrative work doesn't aim to console with the illusion of narrative fullness, but rather seeks to draw attention to failures and gaps of transmission, echoing Gilroy's emphasis on diasporic memory work as tracking what is lost without imagining it can be recovered.

But, despite its focus on historical gaps and fragments, Hartman's book coheres powerfully around the narrative frame of her own journey along the slave routes of West Africa. Her travel narrative retraces, or returns to, the forced footsteps of other travelers in the hopes of making their presence legible. It is a terrain she describes as "both an existent territory" and a "figurative realm of an imagined past." She travels, therefore, to find out what is knowable, as well as to investigate how one might narrate or speak of what is not.[23]

I stress this point because *Our Sister Killjoy*, like *Lose Your Mother* and Müller's account of return, is also self-consciously a narrative of travel. It may seem obvious to suggest that return narratives are travel narratives, for return in the literal (rather than metaphorical) sense seemingly demands a journey. But what's telling is how the text adopts or revises certain tropes and generic conventions. Hildegard Hoeller has observed that the depiction of travel in *Our Sister Killjoy* echoes aspects of Joseph Conrad's *Heart of Darkness*, among them the parallel that Sissie, like Marlow, "sees herself travelling towards a heart of darkness of violence, savagery, ignorance, and lust."[24] Hoeller draws multiple connections between Marlow and Sissie's modes of travel, and asks about the two texts' shared use of an "economy of stereotype"[25]—Toni Morrison's term for a repertoire of racialized images that "allows the writer a quick and easy image without the responsibility of specificity, accuracy, or even narratively useful description."[26] Yet, rich as Hoeller's connections are, *Heart of Darkness* tells of journeys that generate self-knowledge so terrible that one either can't return home (Kurtz) or returns profoundly transformed (Marlow), while *Our Sister Killjoy* is more skeptical of travel as a mode of self-discovery and transformation. The text is bookended by Sissie's two journeys, the first of which takes her from Africa to Europe, "organised in such a way that they passed over the bit of Africa left in their way in the dead hours of the night," and the second that returns her home so that she wakes to see the coastline of Africa, "warm and green."[27] The circularity of a journey that ends where it began is represented as a fulfillment and completion: a "complete sweetness" that returns Sissie to herself, rather than suggesting a self made anew (133). As far as Sissie is concerned, the original purpose for African students to travel to Europe was to "come to these alien places, study what we can of what they know and then go back home" (120). There's something defensive about this plan, for it seems to suggest that the goal is to acquire knowledge without being transformed by it. *Self*-knowledge might be dangerous and may interfere with the simplicity, even purity, of this knowledge-gathering mission.

This is not to suggest that Sissie's journey doesn't generate new forms of knowing and new knowledge, but it's difficult to determine whether what Sissie learns is generated by the journey or by the return home. Throughout the text, the narrative of Sissie's experiences in Europe is contextualized by what she's learned subsequently or, as the text puts it over and over again, "by knowledge gained *since*" (36; my emphasis). It's not clear what relationship the text posits between the experience of the journey and some supplemental knowledge that eventually renders it narratable. In fact, one of the most suggestive aspects of Sissie's experience abroad—her homoerotic relationship with a German woman named Marija—resists narration and inclusion in the traveler's report: "do you go back to your village in Africa and say . . . from the beginning of your story that you met a married woman?" Sissie wonders (65). While the narrative of the travel falters and questions its own legitimacy, the direction of Sissie's travel remains steadfastly directed at a return home, or Heimkehr.

Unlike Hartman's narrative, where even a literal journey is a "return" only in a metaphorical sense, or Müller's account of a journey that returns to an unhomely site of trauma, the correspondence between "home" and "return" is unambiguous in *Our Sister Killjoy*. Home is the point of departure, and the point of departure is the final destination. John Zilcosky has observed that the defining characteristic of travel narratives may be their uncertainty about truth and fiction; the difficulty of authenticating the traveler's account is amplified by the self's attempt "to find itself through displacement."[28] Aidoo is certainly conscious of the opportunities travel presents for reimagining one's circumstances and refashioning the self.

In Europe, Sissie polices the accounts of those who've returned home with fantastic tales of Europe's wonders, comparing their stories to the reality to find "They lied. / They lied. / They lied. / The Been-tos lied." Yet Sissie herself is not above a little judicious redaction, thinking guiltily of her mother, "To whom she sent / Shamefully / Expurgated versions of / Her travel tales" (90, 60). Sissie recognizes her missives home as *tales* that cannot be corroborated and for which she's unlikely to be held accountable.

What differentiates a narrative of travel from a narrative of migration? To the extent that travel narratives assume an eventual return home—or at least assumes a home from which one has traveled—the distinction may be that, unlike the migrant, the traveler seemingly makes no lasting claims or impositions. Sissie is a traveler, a guest who is just passing through and who won't insist on staying. In that sense, *Our Sister Killjoy's* adherence to the conventions of a travel narrative not only affirms Sissie's return as an ethical and political necessity, it also casts that return as generically inevitable.

Even as narratives of travel and those of migration might tentatively be distinguished on such a basis, they share an interest in how individuals reimagine the kinds of social bonds in which they're enmeshed and reconfigure the communities to which they're accountable. Sissie falters at the thought of relating her encounter with Marija at home, contrasting the seeming implausibility of this relationship to the supposed solidity of the familial relations she's temporarily left behind. But, when the lines of accountability and the inevitability of return are less certain, there may be opportunities for the emergence of what Edward Said describes as *affiliative* relations, which transcend genealogy, kinship, and the presumably "natural continuity" of *filiative* relations between "one generation and the next."[29] Said generates these terms by thinking about exile and displacement, which suggests that one politically optimistic implication of such displacement may be the possibility of decisively reimagining stories of origin. Yet, as he acknowledges, the seemingly more expansive quality of affiliative relations based on adherence to shared values, common institutions, or compensatory communities constantly threatens to fold back into the filial.[30] This is an observation that is in keeping with the logic of diaspora, which pairs geographical displacement with cultural continuity and transmission. Continuity, frequently framed as intergenerational familial transmission, is what supposedly allows for the transmission of identity *despite* dislocation. It is this emphasis on cultural reproduction as familial reproduction that makes diasporic discourse so dependent on family forms.[31]

The connections between familial reproduction and cultural continuity are certainly striking in *Our Sister Killjoy*, yet part of what Sissie questions while abroad is the familial status of members of the diaspora. That's not quite the same as interrogating the usefulness of kinship relations as a figure for national or ethnic belonging, but it does open up a fissure. By questioning their belonging and, by extension, the terms of her intimacy or familiarity with them, she also opens the question of what other kinds of intimacy or affiliation may be possible in their place. Relating to Marija why she's called Sissie, she explains that it is not for the usual reason of a dearth of girls in the family, but "because of something else. Some other reason . . . to do with school and being with many boys who treated me like their sister" (28). Sissie cannot quite put this relation into words. Twice she describes it as somehow otherwise ("something else," "some other reason") before finally specifying that to be "Sissie" is not to be a sister but to be nonetheless treated like one.

But Sissie's quasi-familial position cannot hold when she travels abroad. Superficially, such familiarizing and familial names are the mode by which she and others like her hail and recognize one another in passing encounters at train stations and transit points: "She said, 'Hi Brother.' / He said, 'Hi Sister.' / 'I am from Surinam.' / 'I am from Ghana'" (80). But, in England, she confronts boys with whom she was educated, or boys like those boys, who've pursued the paths of upward mobility open to them; forestalling their return home and deferring their responsibilities. When Sissie confronts them, they respond with empty invocations of not only her name—Sissie, My Sister—but also other names. For as Sissie observes, "For most, it was the mother thing. Everybody claimed that he wanted to make sure he did 'something' for 'My Mother'" (123). Among these newly minted members of the diaspora, familial ties aren't guarantees of attachment or cultural continuity. Instead, they are placeholders—emptied-out names that are called upon to signify a continued and decorous attachment to home. Over the course of this exchange, "Sissie" increasingly reveals itself to be the sign of a vanishing relation.

It's not clear what might replace it. One possibility is that a space opens up for a relation with a man whose first words to her are an invitation to rename herself otherwise: "I know everyone calls you Sissie, but what is your name?"—a question that remains unanswered (131).

Certainly, Sissie's ambiguous and challenging relationship with the hapless German *Hausfrau* Marija does not compensate for the withering of these familial bonds. The relationship is ambiguous and challenging because, as Gay Wilentz suggests, Sissie's violent rejection of Marija seems swiftly and even brutally to foreclose their homoerotic encounter and its suggestiveness[32]—ambiguous and challenging, too, because, as Hoeller argues, Marija shades toward the cartoonish, a seemingly vulgar portrayal of a provincial bumpkin who, when it comes to worldliness, is virtually "illiterate," in contrast to Sissie's sophisticated historical consciousness.[33] It is true that Sissie's rejection of Marija's kiss appears to coincide with a longing for a home that's familiar and safe, far from the seeming perversity of a place "where not so long ago human beings stoked their own funeral pyres with other human beings, where now a young Aryan housewife kisses a young black woman with such desperation, right in the middle of her own nuptial chamber" (64). But Marija's touch arouses fear, pleasure, anguish, and regret; Wilentz and Hoeller's well-founded observations don't fully capture the two women's relationship and its tentative tenderness.

Ann Cvetkovich, noting the insistence with which heteronormative "models of sexual reproduction govern those of cultural reproduction," so that "each generation is expected to produce another like itself," suggests that queer accounts of migration and diaspora might disrupt such assumptions, generating other "bonds of affect and affiliation that are not biological or natural."[34] The suggestion of interracial and homoerotic desire in *Our Sister Killjoy* seems to reflect these questions, especially in light of the text's concern with the disintegration of filiative bonds under the pressures of diasporic distance (though Aidoo's thoroughgoing critique of diaspora is no more mollified by the possibility of a queer diasporic relation than it is by any other version of diasporic life).

But what's more interesting, even, than how a queer diasporic narrative disrupts the text's sometimes strident rhetoric of scattered families in need of reuniting, are the multiple challenges that Sissie and Marija's relationship poses: not just homoerotic and interracial but encompassing something yet more fraught. That is, the seeming perversity of an empathic bond between a young African woman attuned to the violence of fascism and imperialism and a German who, as Hoeller suggests, is almost (but to my mind not quite) reduced to a stereotypical representation of an entire nation of brutish, ignorant racists. It's this vexing peculiarity that's suggested in the passage I quoted earlier, which reports with seeming incredulity the kiss between "a young Aryan housewife" and "a young black woman."

In fact, the text demonstrates a hyperalertness to Germany's catastrophic recent history, perhaps most strikingly through Sissie's awareness of the historic phantoms that crowd the landscape. For her, Munich is not the crown of Bavaria but is, instead, "The Original Adolf of the pub-brawls / and mobsters who were looking for / a Führer," is "Prime Minister Chamberlain / Hurrying from his island home to / Appease, / While freshly-widowed Yiddish Mamas wondered / What Kosher pots and pans / Could be saved or not" (81). But *why?* The text turns repeatedly to this history to unveil what's hidden, denied, and unthought, but, even as Sissie draws on this history with knowledgeable ease and familiarity, it's not really clear how she understands her relation to it or what connections she draws between imperialist and fascist histories. Despite the singularity of the text's vision and Sissie's remarkable ability to intuit the unmarked violence of the landscape, she never explicitly articulates what kinds of solidarity, mutual recognition, or shared forms of suffering might exist among those brutalized by the different historical violence of slavery, imperialism, and genocide.

To try to answer this question, and to press toward a discussion of one more mode of return that's quite different from those I've touched on thus far, I want to turn one last time to the assemblage of stories in the newspaper. There's nothing intrinsically special about that date or paper—it's a snapshot of a day on which issues of migration and difference, as is not infrequently the case, are somehow front-page news. Specifically, I want to focus on the story describing the ongoing consequences to Thilo Sarrazin, former Berlin finance minister and a major figure at the Bundesbank, of the interview he gave to the cultural journal *Lettre International* as part of the journal's special issue on Berlin twenty years after the fall of the wall. Sarrazin argues that Berlin has struggled in its reconstruction efforts post-1989, lagging according to economic markers and failing to attract the right kind of people to the city. Berlin, he explains, has never again achieved the heights it reached before the war, in part because the city cannot compensate for what it lost with the expulsion of its Jewish population. Their disappearance, he mourns, marked the passing of a classically bourgeois culture oriented toward achievement and accomplishment.[35] This wistful description of a pre-1930s German Jewish community, representing the apotheosis of a culture that's now lost, he contrasts to Germany's present-day minorities. Turks and Arabs in particular, whose numbers he explains have risen thanks to incorrect policies, have no "productive function apart from selling fruits and vegetables."[36] It is not that he minds migrants—quite the opposite. It would please him if it were Eastern European Jews "with an IQ 15% higher than that of the German population" who were taking over Germany with their higher birth rates, but what he cannot abide is the specter of the Turks doing the same, when all they "regularly produce is new little headscarf girls."[37]

I reproduce Sarrazin's comments in some detail not in order to wallow in their awfulness, but to get at what's rhetorically specific about the way he frames the problem. His emphasis on birth rates, IQs, and population statistics adopts the brutally biopolitical language of a racist thinking that manifests itself in demographic calculations and eugenicist population improvement schemes. That he advances this point not only by referring nostalgically to a prewar German Jewish minority annihilated under the sign of those same racist logics but also by trying to reanimate the language of Jewish "racial" characteristics (characteristics that, today, would supposedly improve rather than degrade the German *Bevölkerung*) is a depressing confirmation of what Paul Gilroy has argued are the common threads of racist thought and rhetoric across different histories of violence.[38]

Our Sister Killjoy makes these connections via its insistent turn to the history of German National Socialism and the Holocaust. As a *guest*, Sissie's presence may be of "phenomenal" interest and fascination, everything about her "exotic" and "charming," but such attraction can turn just as quickly into something else, as she knows (43, 47). Indeed, the text emphasizes that racialized bodies are not just expelled but also made useful, subtly suggesting an echo between Nazi medical experiments in the Bavarian forests, "just hearing of which should get a grown-up man urinating on himself," and, later, Sissie's horror at the news of Dr. Christian Barnard's forays into heart transplantation in 1960s apartheid South Africa—experiments that Sissie suspects depend heavily on the disposability of black South African bodies (44, 95–101). Aidoo's attentiveness to the continuities between National Socialist and colonial racisms in the era of decolonization, which she suggests in the form of correspondences and echoes rather than two-dimensional commonalities, encourages us to think critically about Sarrazin's historically disingenuous comments in the present. What political maneuvers are effected when previously cast-out Others are rehabilitated and instrumentalized as today's friendly ghosts and are rhetorically positioned so as to shame and disparage new Others?

Sarrazin is willing to spell it out, asserting the rightful consequences for those who are not properly productive and do not constitute the right kind of "human capital": one needn't "recognize" them, he declares, so long as they make themselves unworthy of recognition.[39] The question of recognition is at work in Sissie's logic as well. Even as she recites the reasons for return as a series of joys and modest rewards that are ends in themselves and therefore ought to be morally persuasive, she also counterposes them to the impossibility of achieving recognition abroad, saying "we would burn out our brawn and brains trying to prove what you describe as 'our worth' and we won't get a flicker of recognition from those cold blue eyes" (130). Sissie is in the grip of her own stereotypes and clichés, but her words reveal that the forms of return with which the text is most concerned—that is, return as an act of political conviction and social accountability—are locked in a tense and mostly silent contest with a racism that demands Others not stay and that refuses to recognize them. Sissie must return home, not just because her loyalties demand it but also because she feels herself unwelcome and unwanted elsewhere. In one of the work's devastating passages, the words that Sissie has incessantly repeated throughout the text—"finish and hurry back," "go home"—move uncannily from her mouth to other mouths, facilitated by the form of the text, which moves between prose and poetry, allowing for the unexpected circulation and repetition of words and phrases that suddenly signify differently:

Frozen fingers in winter,
Cheap nigger-food from Shepherds Bush
Hot faces in hiding from
Sneering mouths that wonder
When
You are going to
Finish, and go back home . . .

(104)

Racist demands to "go back to where you came from" and the ceaseless repetition of jeering calls for racially categorized Others to "go home" are also calls for a form of return. It is also *this* mode of return that *Our Sister Killjoy* implicitly addresses—a mode of return that takes us in a direction quite different from return as an act of political conviction or return as an acknowledgment of familial and social bonds or return as a foreclosed, traumatic journey or even return as a mode of fiction making. It asks us to think about return as an outcome of the failure of recognition—of return as racism's imperative.

Notes

I am grateful to Sherally Munshi and Knut Sennekamp for their many helpful comments on an earlier version of this essay.

1. Thilo Sarrazin, "Thilo Sarrazin im Gespräch: Klasse statt Masse," *Lettre International* 86 (Autumn 2009), 198.

2. Stefan Dietrich, "Alle mischen mit," *Frankfurter Allgemeine Zeitung,* October 14, 2009.

3. Ama Ata Aidoo, *Our Sister Killjoy* (White Plains, NY: Longman USA, 2004).

4. Ibid., 8.

5. Ibid., 85.

6. Barbara Mennel, "'Germany Is Full of Germans Now': Germanness in Ama Ata Aidoo's *Our Sister Killjoy* and Chantal Akerman's *Meetings with Anna*," in Patricia Herminghouse and Magda Mueller, eds., *Gender and Germanness: Cultural Productions of Nation* (Providence: Berghahn, 1997), 245 and 238.

7. Aidoo, *Our Sister Killjoy,* 120.

8. Ibid., 121.

9. Ibid., 89.

10. Ibid., 107.

11. See, on this issue in Spivak's work, Bruce Robbins, "Soul Making: Gayatri Spivak on Upward Mobility," *Cultural Studies* 17, no. 1 (2003): 16–26; and Gayatri Chakravorty Spivak, *A Critique of Post-Colonial Reason: Toward a History of the Vanishing Present* (Cambridge: Harvard University Press, 1999), 357.

12. Robbins, "Soul Making," 17.

13. Aidoo, *Our Sister Killjoy,* 104–6.

14. Ibid., 130.

15. Ibid., 114.

16. See Daniel and Jonathan Boyarin's argument for diasporic dispersion as the grounds for political identity: "Diaspora: Generation and the Ground of Jewish Identity," *Critical Inquiry* 19, no. 4 (Summer 1993), 693–725; and, more recently, Brent Edwards's argument that diaspora depends on transnational practices of reading, writing, and translation: *The Practice of Diaspora: Literature,*

Translation and the Rise of Black Internationalism (Cambridge: Harvard University Press, 2003).

17. Paul Gilroy, *The Black Atlantic: Modernity and Double Consciousness* (Cambridge: Harvard University Press, 1993), 198.

18. Aidoo, *Our Sister Killjoy*, 118.

19. Herta Müller, *Atemschaukel* (Munich: Carl Hanser, 2009).

20. Herta Müller, "Grenzgänger: Schreiben und Erinnern: Felicitas von Lovenberg (*Frankfurter Allgemeine Zeitung*) im Gespräch mit Herta Müller (*Atemschaukel*)," Interview, Robert Bosch Stiftung and ARTE Deutschtland, Frankfurt Book Fair, October 14, 2009. This interview is available as an embedded video on Arte's website: http://www.arte.tv/de/Kultur-entdecken/Literatur/2894430 .html.

21. Saidiya Hartman, *Lose Your Mother: A Journey Along the Atlantic Slave Route* (New York: Farrar, Straus and Giroux, 2007).

22. See, for instance, her reimagining of the life and death of an unnamed woman murdered aboard the ship *Recovery;* ibid., 136–53.

23. Ibid., 9.

24. Hildegard Hoeller, "Ama Ata Aidoo's *Heart of Darkness,*" *Research in African Literatures* 35, no. 1 (Spring 2004): 135.

25. Ibid., 136.

26. Toni Morrison, *Playing in the Dark: Whiteness and the Literary Imagination* (Cambridge: Harvard University Press, 1992), 67, see also 58.

27. Aidoo, *Our Sister Killjoy*, 10, 133.

28. John Zilcosky, "Writing Travel," in John Zilcosky, ed., *Writing Travel: The Poetics and Politics of the Modern Journey* (Toronto: University of Toronto Press, 2008), 9, 7.

29. Edward Said, *The World, the Text, and the Critic* (Cambridge: Harvard University Press, 1983), 16.

30. Ibid., 19–20.

31. To offer just one striking example, when Arjun Appadurai poses the question of "reproduction" in a transnational context, he tellingly describes the problem of "cultural transmission" as synonymous with the question of how "small groups, especially families . . . deal with these new global realities as they seek to reproduce themselves," despite pressures under which "generations easily divide." Arjun Appadurai, "Disjuncture and Difference in the Global Cultural Economy," in Bruce Robbins, ed., *The Phantom Public Sphere* (Minneapolis: University of Minnesota Press, 1993), 228.

32. Gay Wilentz, "The Politics of Exile: Reflections of a Black-Eyed Squint in *Our Sister Killjoy,*" in Ada Uzoamaka Azodo and Gay Wilentz, eds., *Emerging Perspectives on Ama Ata Aidoo* (Trenton: Africa World Press, 1999), 84.

33. Hoeller, "Ama Ata Aidoo's *Heart of Darkness,*" 136.

34. Ann Cvetkovich, *An Archive of Feelings: Trauma, Sexuality, and Lesbian Public Cultures* (Durham: Duke University Press, 2003), 122.

35. Sarrazin, "Thilo Sarrazin im Gespräch," 197.

36. Ibid., 198.

37. Ibid., 199.

38. Paul Gilroy, *Against Race: Imagining Political Culture Beyond the Color Line* (Cambridge: Harvard University Press, 2000).

39. Sarrazin, "Thilo Sarrazin im Gespräch," 198, 199.

14   "O Give Me a Home"

PATRICIA J. WILLIAMS

One definition of trauma is that it is an injury so great that no words can capture or describe it. Faced with the insufficiency of language, the victim performs or experiences that horror over and over again in the form of dreams or flashbacks or acting out. Hurricane Katrina was and continues to be an unparalleled trauma upon the body of American society. Many people have described it as the greatest natural disaster in our history, but there was little that was "natural" or inevitable about it. The wound that Katrina left resulted from a complicated intersection of social forces: from the failure to heed many years' worth of warnings about the disreputable condition of the levees to the failure to initiate mandatory evacuation proceedings well before the storm hit, from the corruption that rendered regional government so perpetually ineffectual to the corporate muggery that has left this richly endowed arable delta impoverished and poisoned, from the cruel and inhuman conditions in "Angola" Penitentiary to the school system that was and remains little more than a prison industrial complex itself.

Except as a matter of degree (or as a matter of pure size), all this is familiar. Indeed, it is so entirely familiar that it practically seems predestined. Public and low-income housing razed to make way for corporate interests. Elderly left unattended on their deathbeds. Homeless children with more weapons than hope. . . . A diaspora of broken families hunting for kin: Have you seen my mother? Have you seen my brother? This is a picture of my fiancée. . . . The chilling ghostliness of such reiteration is not about what has already happened; ghosts are most frightening when they drift from memory to the visible present and become the lens for our future. The horrors of Katrina form an ongoing narrative of national distress, of aimless migration, of homelessness, of exile. If the Puritan jeremiads envisioned our nation as a Promised Land, a New Canaan, a latter-day Jerusalem, our twenty-first century jeremiad is rewriting itself as paradise lost: as a tale of broken covenants, of much crying in the wilderness, of New Orleanians being swallowed up by a sea of red ink, without trace, without mourning, without cultural memory.

Close on the heels of the hurricane came revelations of national patterns of predatory lending and our massive home foreclosure crisis. A bitter, confused, if thoroughly American narrative began to swirl: doom is nigh, what a sucker you've been, and now no one's going to save you. . . . You didn't pack for eternal exile? Well it's your own dumb fault.

Homelessness rather than nudity is the great shame of the post-Edenic state. Against this backdrop, the peculiar locution of *homeland security* becomes a threatened terrain to be hunkered down inside but not lived within. The "homeland" is a Swiss cheese of unguarded portals, disposable trailer parks, promiscuous doorways, and floodgates that don't work—yet simultaneously and curiously devoid of real houses or real homes. In contrast, the simplicity of home becomes a site for nostalgia, the old country before famine, flood, or pogrom, an imaginary geography of tremendous contradiction, of ambivalence and flight, of (up)rootedness and romance, of magic and superstition.

This theme of the terrible sublimity of loss dominates our literary and political figurations and, unless addressed, or until healed, no doubt will continue to. It is the plot line of the Timothy LaHaye's *Left Behind* series as well as the tension in Toni Morrison's *Beloved* and Longfellow's *Evangeline*. It runs through the babble on Fox News, in television dramas like *24*, in Samuel Huntington's book *Clash of Civilizations*, and in journalist Robert Kaplan's doomsday political futurism. It shapes our domestic police practices and informs our global war on terror. There's a certain Schadenfreude to it, the frisson of a well-rehearsed nightmare, the creed, the screed, the Greek chorus, the litany of woe, the passion play whose dark moral law haunts us ceaselessly.

When I think about the human disaster that has unfolded in the wake of Hurricane Katrina, there are two moments that stand out in my mind. The first is George W. Bush's press conference in Mississippi on September 2, 2005, during which he bounced uneasily from foot to foot like he couldn't wait to get out of there, looking sullen and furrowed, observing with tense jocularity that Trent Lott's house had been lost, too, and that "we" were going to rebuild him "a fantastic house" and that he, our president, was looking forward to rocking on the porch when that day came to pass. The second moment was the now famous interview with Homeland Security chief Michael Chertoff on National Public Radio. Media junkie that I am, I had the TV and the radio on at the same time. As pictures of the horrific conditions at the convention center, including the image of the body of that poor old woman who had passed away in her wheelchair, were being broadcast to the world, Chertoff was insisting that he had no knowledge of any extreme conditions or deaths at the center. "Our reporter has seen [it]," insisted the host. "I can't argue with you about what your reporter tells you," said Chertoff with snappish impatience. I confess that I found myself filtering this horror through a very personal lens. It overlapped with the task of clearing out and selling the house I grew up in, in Massachusetts, the house my mother was born in, my grandmother's house, a house that had belonged to my family for a hundred years. My distress at having to give it up is confused with the scenes of Katrina's devastation that most of us—if not Chertoff—were witnessing. Against that appalling backdrop, I found myself clinging to a sense of place, even though I was not truly or traumatically displaced. Mine was an African American family that owned a home in times when so few did.

So I still think hard about this as I look at the continuing devastation of the Ninth Ward, an area that, before the storm, had more African American property owners than anyplace else in Louisiana. As I drove back and forth from the house I grew up in, carrying out pictures of my college graduation and my Latin notes from seventh grade, I heard a woman on the radio describe how jarring it was to see the media describe her neighborhood as one driven by poverty and desperation. She was about to get her MBA; her brother already had his MBA; their extended family owned nine homes there; they all had insurance and owned cars in which they had fled for their lives. But it was the Ninth Ward; it was indeed being dubbed "poverty-stricken," "corrupt," "drug-ridden," and politicians like Dennis Hastert were talking about bulldozing the entire area. The Ninth Ward and Gentilly and other black neighborhoods haven't been entirely

bulldozed in the years since. But, despite all the talk about rights of return, the only thing that's happened since—at least in the way of publicly
funded reconstruction—has been the planting of a few strips of grass in
front of still empty buildings. Millions of dollars have gone into setting
up charter schools in the suburbs, and tens of millions have been spent
on metal detectors for the few public schools remaining within in the city
limits. The budget for books, meanwhile, has been infinitesimal.

And so I still think about what might have happened had I not been
engaged in the relatively leisurely process of packing up my memories but
had rather been forced to run for my life. In particular, the documentation
of people being "sorted" in the shelters should give us pause. The elderly
were taken from their families, the sick from their caretakers, newborns
from their mothers, and, because men were apparently segregated from
women, husbands from wives, mothers from sons. I heard one unidenti-
fied local authority on the radio saying that when people were evacuated
to other states they were not told where they were going, so as to make
them less unruly. And there were accounts of white foreign nationals air-
lifted out "secretly" by National Guardsmen and warned not to go into the
shelters because it was too dangerous for them. To some extent, this sorting and separation is what already happens in homeless shelters in many
places around the country. Hurricane Katrina merely made that reality, at
least momentarily, impossible to repress.

The rationalization of such practices proceeds unchecked, however. A
few days into the seething mess at the Convention Center, a sociologist
named Betty Hearn Morrow opined on NPR that it was less traumatic for
people in distress to be grouped by their own kind. "That's just human
nature," said Morrow. Putting people into groups reinforces a sense of familiarity and security, so they should be relocated "according to their backgrounds." She gave an example of sorting people from Guatemala and
Nicaragua and explained how that would help keep the peace—though
she did not explain how separating Americans from Americans would
do the same. My ears pricked up at this take on civil society; I wondered
what "kind" I might appear to be in an evacuation. My son has been over
six feet tall since he was thirteen. If we were fleeing without any identification, would anyone believe he's a child? Would we be put on separate
buses to unknown compass points? Would I be herded off to the camp for
middle-aged law professors? And, if that's too scary to contemplate, would
it really becalm me with a sense of "familiarity" to be penned up and
marched off with a group of other black women of my "background?"

According to Mayor Michael Bloomberg, the City of New York, where I live now, has been divided into grids in case of catastrophe. People would be ordered from their homes, or taken by force if necessary, and marshaled along preset routes to reception centers where they would be identified by Social Security number and then relocated. I want to be a good citizen, part of the orderliness of a well-managed response to disaster. But with the images of New Orleans in mind, why on earth would any of us stream willingly toward chaos? If it is true that families may be broken up as a means of crowd control, then perhaps just a little public discussion is in order. And if it is true that white foreign nationals are a higher priority than black solid citizens, to what then do we pledge allegiance?

At homeland insecurity, new categories of suspect profiles bubble forth. Race, ethnicity, religion, a fortiori—but the list churns on with up-to-the-minute brands of scoundrel like an endless ticker tape: unusually clean-shaven men, men with long beards, people wearing heavy clothing or shoes with thick soles or big hats, women carrying large handbags, unknown delivery men bearing oversized packages, kids with backpacks or violin cases, sweaty people, cool-as-a-sly-cucumber people, people with cameras, people praying aloud, people who blink too much or not enough, men with thick waists, women pretending to be pregnant, people who spend too much time in public libraries, men reeking of rosewater—on and on it goes. Apparently, we are also to be on the lookout for the great masses of the unshaved, unwashed, and unperfumed, to wit, "vagrants who seem out of place"—an almost calculatedly redundant designation—for fear they might be terrorists posing as "homeless people, shoe-shiners, street vendors or street sweepers."

In our once celestial cities, whose denizens are now deemed dangerous, one hears calls for house-to-house searches, shoot-to-kill policies and protection from "too many" civil rights. Debates rage about "political correctness" rather than whether this isn't beginning to look like martial law or an effective immunization of police from discriminatory behavior, scattershot decision making as well as deadly mistake. I ponder this global game of Gotcha. It is a traumatically insistent re-presentation of a violent past as well as a prefiguration of devastations to come. With this endless looping, our civic domesticity becomes ever more embittered, tainted by the obsession with enemies amongst us whose voices speak like the ghost of Hamlet's father, whose shapes we profess to "know" instinctively and in defiance of fancy rituals of politeness, legal niceties, book learning, or empirical knowledge.

This interrelationship of homelessness, suspicion, and citizenship found its most interesting expression in the all-too-brief debate about whether the half-million people displaced by Hurricane Katrina ought to be categorized as "evacuees" or "refugees." This nomenclature was more than semantic—as some experienced disaster aid workers knew only too well, it might have made a difference. Under international law, a refugee is someone who has fled their country of origin because of violence or persecution based on race, caste, ethnicity, political belief, or religion. When refugee status is granted, allowing admission to the United States, it automatically confers entitlement to resettlement aid, such as sponsorship, housing, medical treatment, employment opportunities, psychological counseling, and food stamps. According to most experts, the victims of Hurricane Katrina would probably have been better off classified as refugees, even though their removal was entirely domestic. "After half a century of experience, the public-private partnership that resettles refugees nationwide is like a well-oiled machine compared with the new apparatus being invented on the fly for Katrina survivors. And the refugee agencies want to help."[1]

By contrast, "evacuees," whether by war, famine, flood, earthquake or tsunami, are considered merely "internally displaced" and thus are not subject to the same automatic benefits. They must rely on a patchwork of mostly charitable or religious or Red Cross–initiated responses—in other words, whatever hodgepodge can be thrown together at the moment of the disaster in question. In the wake of Katrina, this meant that any potential right to resettlement or return was left to lopsided market forces and disastrous political decisions allowing nothing less than prospecting in the old flood-ravaged neighborhoods by developers and other monied interests. Perhaps most hurtful of all, the Federal Emergency Management Agency had been reorganized as a subdivision of the Department of Homeland Security shortly before the hurricane. Not only was Michael Brown, the head of FEMA, woefully inexperienced in disaster management, the entire Department of Homeland Security seemed prepared exclusively for war rather than recuperation. Thus a great deal of time and precious resources were wasted—mistaking flight for riot; need for greed; and the scramble to high ground for all-out invasion.

I spent a few days in New Orleans recently. Four years after the hurricane, it is still a city in mourning, more riven than ever. An estimated 30 to 40 percent of the population has not returned, most because they have not been able to. Landlords have refused to accept out-of-state housing vouchers from renters trying to return. Rents have soared because of the decreased housing stock. Yet the New Orleans City Council recently OK'd the demolition of virtually all the surviving stock of public housing—large brick-and-mortar buildings, all minimally damaged, all eminently reparable. (The tenants were never even permitted to go back in and retrieve their belongings.)

Today, the Lower Ninth Ward is an eerily lush plain of overgrown sadness. Of the fourteen thousand residents before the storm, only about eight hundred remain. One of the more intriguing embellishments upon this expansive devastation, however, is the flutter of hundreds of little signs affixed to the remaining lampposts: "Easy terms! Refinance with us!" "Want to rebuild? No money down!" Local newspapers are full of disturbingly gushy articles about realtors who slaver over the historic row houses still standing in largely black and poor areas. They see the next Soho! The new Chelsea! To hasten the process of what one half calls gentrification and the other half feels as dispossession, the city has passed an "antiblight" ordinance. Little signs have been planted in front of houses where only the walls remain. "Do you know where this owner is?" These signs pass as public notice: found owners are slapped with antiblight fines. Failure to pay results in forfeiture of the land.

A year after Katrina, flooding caused levees to burst again, this time on the upper Mississippi, making mud of Cedar Rapids, Iowa. Rush Limbaugh snickered that the residents there weren't "whining" about their condition like those noisy New Orleanians. Well, it's quiet in New Orleans now, a terrible brew of frustration beyond words and utter exhaustion. If it is just as quiet in the largely white floodplains of the upper Mississippi, we should not take that for a good thing in an economy as troubled as ours. The collapsed levees in Iowa and Missouri are signs of the same deeply broken infrastructure, even if the corruption that allowed it is not as visible, as cruel, or as racially inflected as in New Orleans.

American mobility depends upon the equity accumulated in its homes and the stability lent by reasonable rental stocks. The failure to make affordable housing a right has, in the long run of the last half century, hurt all Americans, leaving us with ravaged "inner cities" and strip-malled "havens" of suburban blight. There are, as I see it, two models competing for our future unfolding on the street. Model Number One: while walking in the Eighth and Ninth Wards, I saw scores of volunteers from all over North America, a rainbow coalition skewed heavily to young people and college students, working for organizations like Habitat for Humanity.

They were sweating in the broiling sun, hard at work, hammers in hand. Model Number Two: I overheard a conversation between two middle-aged men apparently touring the area "for deals." The first was wearing an Obama T-shirt. The second said amiably, "So, you're for Obama." No, replied the first man; he was "a liberal" but hadn't decided yet. Turns out he was just wearing the shirt to ingratiate himself with the natives—although *ingratiate* was not the word he used.

Alas, poor us. The course we pursue may be politically disastrous, academically wrong, strategically flawed, statistically disproved—a cacophony of finger-pointing and calls to 911—but our narratives instruct us to be stubborn guardians of the faith. At our collective peril do we remain enchanted by homiletic hokum about sifting wheat from chaff.

Notes

1. N. Bernstein, "Feeling Empathy, Refugee Groups Reaching Out to Victims of Hurricane," *New York Times*, September 18, 2005, 37, 42.

Images from New Orleans
Keith Calhoun and Chandra McCormick

FIGURE 14.1   *After the secondline* (2007); Keith Calhoun.

FIGURE 14.2   *Father with his kids, George Brown Convention Center* (2005); Chandra McCormick.

FIGURE 14.3   *Family, three generations, George Brown Convention Center* (2005); Keith Calhoun.

FIGURE 14.4   *Disaster in Lower 9th Ward* (2006); Keith Calhoun.

FIGURE 14.5   *New Orleans family now living in Houston, TX* (2007); Keith Calhoun.

15 The Politics of Return

When Rights Become Rites

ELAZAR BARKAN

The Problem with Rights

A rights-based approach to protecting refugees poses the dilemma of which rights ought to be defended. Increasingly, this involves weighing the right to protection (of life) against other rights. For example, in the 1990s the conflicts and contradictions of a rights-based approach were clearly at play in Georgia and Bosnia. In Georgia the refugees who fled the Gali region were encouraged by the UN to return to their homes. Their return, which did not happen, would have placed them in a precarious situation. Here the call for return privileged one right (the right to return) over another right (the right to protection). During the Bosnian war the rights dilemma involved the evacuation of minorities. Providing evacuation assistance to refugees, thus honoring their right to protection, conflicted with their right to stay in their homes. While evacuation assistance might have appeared to collude with the newly termed *ethnic cleansing* (as the displacement became known), encouraging the refugees to stay would have ignored the danger to their lives. The right to one's home, then, was in conflict with the right to security. In both Georgia and Bosnia, saving lives conflicted with the right to stay and the right to return. These are only two of many cases where the rights dilemma challenges the international community and human rights advocates. How to address this issue?

The international community has resisted embracing a principled solution, which in practice often translates into absence of decision making. In principle, the international answer is both protection and return. This, however, evades rather than addresses reality. A more nuanced analysis of the history of refugee crises presents an opportunity to differentiate between types of displacement, and such differentiation may facilitate general policy guidelines. These, in turn, may not only provide more protection and greater respect for refugees' rights but also improve their welfare.

The Right to Return

The Universal Declaration of Human Rights (UDHR) states that "everyone has the right to leave any country, including his own, and to return to his country."[1] This right "to return" has become central in international policies that aim to resolve refugee displacement. It is understood as universal and comprehensive, not politically situated. In practice, however, that is not the case. Although the displaced person's right to return is presented as a universal category, like so many other rights, it is most clearly visible when it is breached. Further, whereas repatriation is presented as an individual right, the right to return is violated as a group right. Most refugees who are displaced as members of groups are caught up in the unresolved dilemma of a struggle over sovereignty. And, while self-determination is a recognized right, the international community has continuously privileged sovereignty over group rights and over the right to secede, categories into which minority claims to repatriation often fall.

The statement Sadako Ogata, the United Nations high commissioner for refugees, issued on June 16, 2003, at the World Conference on Human Rights in Vienna remains a prescient description of both the refugee situation and of the right to return. While Mrs. Ogata underscored the refugees' "right to seek and enjoy asylum, the right to return and the right to remain," she also stressed that the right to asylum, which has been fundamental since the 1951 United Nations Refugee Convention and its 1967 protocol, has come under stress because of the expansion of the number of refugees.[2] Asylum was not working any longer as a solution to the mass displacement problem. Indeed, the violence against refugees became a critical global challenge. Too many "people who are fleeing violence and human rights abuses at home are confronted with danger, rejection at frontiers or legal obstacles in their search for asylum."[3] Conceding that the right to asylum can go only so far in addressing the structural challenges of mass displacement, Ogata turned to the right to return. She presented asylum as "protection," the right to remain in one's own country as "prevention," and the right to return as the solution. "The responsibility lies with the countries of origin to do what is necessary to enable refugees to freely exercise this right," Ogata asserted and argued that "there should be both peace and respect for their [refugees'] human rights."[4] She also pointed out that "assuring these requires a comprehensive approach that addresses the political, security, human rights, humanitarian and development aspects of the problem."[5] Surely, if the country of origin had been interested and capable of exercising that responsibility in the first place, the displacement would not have taken place. Presenting the right to return as a solution should strike us as wishful thinking more than as policy.

While the refugee problem is presented as political and structural (too many refugees), the solution postulated by Ogata was aspirational: peace, development, and respect for rights. If prevention does not work and protection is inadequate, the proposed (rhetorical) solution becomes a *rite*— not a political answer. The demand for repatriation is directed at the very political entities who are responsible for the displacement, and who refuse to accommodate return. In the rite of declaring the right to return as a solution, the "natural" right is presented as a "positive" right, as though the rhetorical declaration of a right embedded it with the commitment and force of the international community. Thus Ogata created an impression that the refugee crisis is a violation of specific well-established rights rather than the consequence of the world community's unwillingness (or inability) to take action and assume obligations that would address refugee crises in a politically viable way. Ogata's presentation is conventional rather than novel. Without a roadmap for concrete specific crises, declaring world peace as a solution can hardly constitute a policy. When naming and shaming become the sum total of political theater, we have to wonder if a rhetoric of the right to return has become no more than a rite performed by its advocates and politicians alike.

Advocates of the right to return view it in an inclusive manner, extending it to those whom the United Nations High Commissioner for Refugees (UNHCR) today designates as "persons of concern." The international legal conviction is that the right to return represents customary international law and applies in cases of mass uprooting. This includes individuals as well as groups, those who were citizens of a state and those who came from the disputed territory. The prevailing sense of the legal right to return makes no explicit reference to nationality or citizenship, invoking instead the right to freedom of movement. For example, consider the presentation by Amnesty International: "The argument that large-scale displacements are excluded from the right to return is contradicted by international *practice*, as evidenced in consistent calls by UN bodies for the return of large numbers of refugees and displaced, such as Palestinians, Afghans and Greek Cypriots and, in the case of the former Yugoslavia, by the enforcement of the right to return in the Dayton Agreement."[6] "Practice" in this case is equated with rhetorical claims ("calls by UN bodies") and not with implementation and institutionalization required to deliver actual results. The question of repatriation raises a host of issues, including property restitution and compensation; group versus individual rights; and, most important, the question of conflicting rights, such as security conflict with aspects of freedom or the provision of vital needs. An African saying that a path is made by walking through the tall elephant grass may well be an apt metaphor. Minority return has yet to approach the grass, let alone establish a clear path.

Minority and Majority Refugees

A historical survey of the twentieth century clearly shows that there are two classes of refugees in matters of repatriation: majority and minority. In an accommodating political context, the former are able to repatriate; the latter hardly ever do. When the former return, the question of right is not raised; rather, it is part of a political solution. In contrast, in the few cases when a minority is able to return, as, for example, were the Tutsi in Rwanda, repatriation is the result of political force and military victory, not of rights. It is only when minority refugees cannot come back home that return becomes a question of rights discourse. By "minority" I mean to designate a specific political entity within a territory: these are "minorities" from a state perspective. In Bosnia the Serbs are a minority in the federation, while the Bosniacs are a minority in Republika Srpska. The Serbs are a majority in Serbia but a minority in Kosovo. The political independence of Kosovo, whether recognized or not, means that the

Serbs are a minority in the republic/province. Georgians became minority in the seceding Abkhazia and South Ossetia. The Palestinians are a minority in Israel. The Jews were a minority in mandate Palestine. The Germans were a minority in Eastern European states after World War II. Millions of Muslims from India and Hindi from Pakistan were expelled as minorities when the two countries came into existence. The list is long, and while other cases in Africa and Asia are less well known in the West, they are subject to similar political forces. Historically, minorities once displaced remain displaced even after the conflict is over; the memory of the ethnic animosity remains a barrier. I know of no example of successful minority repatriation as part of a conflict resolution process, contrary claims about Bosnia notwithstanding.

It was in response to ethnic cleansing in Bosnia that the most concerted and sustained effort of minority repatriation was made. This new position transformed repatriation from a policy into a vocally announced right, but the legal position did not shift and the international political will did not materialize. The new assertion was enhanced by the notion of "never again" and the commitment to prevent and reverse ethnic cleansing and genocide. In the short period since the right/rite had been asserted, both commitments have been broken too many times.

Yet, after almost a decade of failed efforts at minority repatriation and reintegration of communities in Bosnia, the international community declared success. Despite an enormous investment of resources, Bosnia, the most prominent case of minority repatriation, remains ethnically segregated. Although repatriation into previously mixed communities was officially recorded, it did not really take place. Many registered "returnees" have come back briefly to claim property, but, even under international supervision, very few of them were actually able to settle in their previous homes or communities. Moreover, it was mostly the old who returned; the young with families and children, those who would shape the future, never came back. The communities, then, were hardly ever rebuilt or reintegrated. Ethnic cleansing was not reversed. Yet these problems were not recognized. Neither were their consequences for the refugees in the Balkans (in and beyond Bosnia) evaluated nor their implications for other crises considered. Instead, without any real effort at implementation, rites of repatriation and "never again" have been rhetorically asserted. Because the international community focused on the rite of political righteousness rather than on the real challenge of rebuilding the refugees' lives (for example, allowing for reparation and maintaining the right of citizenship while enabling them to acquire a new identity), displacement, horrific and traumatic in itself, was made even more difficult.

More recently, the recognition that a political solution might be preferable to verbal commitment to repatriation has been translated into peace plans and/or resettling of refugees and internally displaced persons (IDPs). Notable examples include Kofi Annan's EU-endorsed plan for Cyprus and the implementation of UN policies that acknowledge the preference of resettlement in Georgia. In Iraq, where mayhem makes it difficult to speak of any rights, the wide spread of ethnic cleansing, not only of Christians but also of Sunni and Shia, makes it all too evident that repatriation is not even contemplated. While over the last generation the formal prohibition against displacement has been strengthened, the commitment to repatriate minority refugees has remained ineffective, in most cases limited to rhetoric rather than implemented in international law.

The Uses and Abuses of the Right to Return

Every time the right of return is invoked, the rights of some collide with the rights of others, local and universal principles inherently conflict with one another, and individual and group rights present irreconcilable choices. This is particularly true of minority groups that never return to states and regions from which they were displaced and in which, after their return, they would be in a minority. Given the historical and empirical evidence that minority groups are not repatriated based upon the right of return, what is its significance? Can an international right, or norm, be said to exist if it is never implemented? Do norms shift with different types of populations despite the "universality" of rights? If the right is not attainable, what consequences does it bear for refugees?

The observation that minority repatriation rarely succeeds says nothing about its desirability or lack thereof. Further, this generalized observation does not even begin to explicate the specificity of what such a declared right to return might be, whether repatriation means return to homes, homeland, state, or region. The historical failure of minority repatriation, however, has to be considered as a factor in an analysis of the implication the right to return carries for refugee rehabilitation. There may well be sound arguments to maintain the demand for a right, even if it is merely a rhetorical device or a moral force. But it would presumably be helpful to understand the political context and the plausibility of implementing the right. In face of deprivation, some may prefer to perform the rite of claiming national or group rights of return, but such a rhetorical assertion should not be confused with a solution to the refugee problem.

It should be made absolutely clear that my analysis of the unlikely repatriation of minorities does not specify under what circumstances such a right might be plausible. I will suggest a few thoughts. But, first, one ought to appreciate the context: although the right to return is frequently declared universal, it is the reverse when it comes to minority physical repatriation. As soon as the right to return comes in conflict with issues of self-determination and sovereignty, it is not honored.

The insistence on the right of return as a solution has ramifications for the policies advocated by and for refugees and thus bears directly on their prospective well-being. If history is a guide, and minority refugees are unlikely to be repatriated, other forms of addressing the problem must be advanced. This does not mean necessarily giving up the aspiration or the politics of return. Rather, the implausibility of return should become a part of the political calculus. If the refugees believe that repatriation is a right and a possibility, their attitude may well be different than if they realize that their return would be an unprecedented achievement, not an expected outcome. Having recognized the low probability of return, some may still choose to maintain the struggle for repatriation; others may opt for resettlement instead. Either way, the acknowledgment of the claim's aspirational nature and its status as a rite rather than a right would lead the refugees, as well as their advocates and the international community in general, to a different set of considerations.[7]

The Palestinian and Israeli Rights of Return

The Palestinian-Israeli conflict is the iconic case of return's likelihood to animate multilayered animosity and conflict. The Jewish return to Zion is the core of Zionism and the center of Israeli national self-construction, while the Palestinian expulsion and quest to return has been the most prominent and protracted refugee crisis since World War II. The question of return is at the heart of several conflicts between Israel and Arab states, between incompatible demands for national self-determination, as well as between national goals and individual well-being. Jews consider themselves displaced for millennia and so the idea of "return" propelled the Jewish national struggle for self-determination. This goal materialized after the Holocaust when, in lieu of accepting Jewish refugee survivors housed in displaced persons camps across Europe, various states supported the creation of the state of Israel. "Return" was a solution to Europe's unwillingness to accommodate Holocaust survivors, a policy that matched Zionist national aspirations.

The Jewish claims for repatriation, however, did not stop with the achievement of self-determination and an independent state in 1948. Two decades later (after the 1967 war), they metastasized into occupation and settlements under a continuous rhetorical cover of return to ancient land and the use of force. The "return" to pre-1967 "Israel proper" and to the occupied territories was the return of "Jewish" identity to a site, not the return of individuals or their immediate descendants who have been displaced. If "rights" were reclaimed, it was by means of force, motivated by nationalist drive, not due to international law or implementation of refugees' right to return. The category was the right to national self-determination (even if contested) rather than the right of individuals to their homes.

The suffering of the Palestinian refugees and the demand for return is at the heart of the international debate over repatriation. The question of return has animated Palestinian politics ever since the 1948 war and has been part of the international discussions about resolving the Palestinian-Israeli conflict ever since Count Bernadotte, the first UN representative to the conflict, focused on return as a priority. While "return" has been a long-standing Palestinian and Arab demand, the construction of return as a right is much more recent and associated mostly with the changed policies by the Palestine Liberation Organization (PLO) in the late 1980s. In the preceding four decades, the dominant Palestinian goal was to reverse the Nakba (the 1948 "catastrophe") by military victory and to replace Israel with a Palestinian state. Only after the PLO came to accept peace negotiations with Israel and formulated its goal of establishing an independent state next to Israel within the 1967 borders did return as a question of "right" emerge. The repatriation of the 1948 refugees and their descendants was an essential part of the newly envisioned solution.

Consequently, for the next two decades, the right to return, as well as its alternatives, was central to inner Palestinian politics and to the "peace process." Today, the Palestinian Authority accepts (albeit implicitly) the improbability of the refugees' actual return. Although the Palestinian Authority invokes the right to return, it has declared in many ways that such a right has to be resolved politically: that is, the Palestinian Authority demands a principled recognition of the right, yet is willing to leave it "unimplemented" in favor of a political solution.

At present, the mainstream Palestinian leadership understands that a literal interpretation of the right to return is unproductive to Palestinian national interests and probably to the refugees themselves. The valence of a right that exists aspirationally as a rite without a political signifier is a fascinating manifestation of political rituals and of the role and limits of political performance. Insofar as the struggle to recognize an unimplementable right affects the well-being of millions of refugees born into a life of displacement, the right to return raises a host of critical issues that need to be addressed by advocates and politicians alike. Timeline is critical: according to Jewish lore the longing to return lasted two millennia.

The right of return, however, has assumed a mythological force that makes its contestation unthinkable for many Israelis and for most Palestinians. In the last few years, creative solutions to transform the *rite* of return to the homes from which the refugees were uprooted to a *right* of return to any location within an independent Palestinian state—homeland—have been getting more recognition and legitimization. As the positive content of the "right of return" has never been formulated at the international level, it will be up to negotiators to define its exact meaning. Were peace negotiations to conclude with an independent Palestinian state and such a state to include provision for the return of refugees and their descendants, the question will still remain: How can the right of return be implemented?

The formal recognition of the right to return would require the future state of Palestine to establish specific immigration policies. The Palestinian state might follow the example of an increasing number of countries that privilege giving citizenship to immigrants of the majority ethnicity as "returnees." The list of countries that embraced *jus sanguinis* (right by blood to citizenship) includes China, India, Germany, and many ex-communist countries; especially noteworthy are the cases of newly established countries that emerged from a previous larger political units, such as the Baltic states or the former Yugoslavia. But perhaps even more pertinent is the case of the Law of Return in Israel, the core of Israeli citizenship.

Beyond Rites

The right of return has been constructed as a rite for different reasons by human rights advocates, refugee advocates, and politicians. Pursuing rights by naming and shaming is the conventional tool of human rights advocacy, and in this the claim of a right to return is unexceptional. Neither is it unique for being aspirational. The same can be said of a whole lot of rights struggles, including demands for protection by refugee advocates and demands for sovereignty by minority groups. The right of return, however, becomes more a rite than a right when politicians support the demand rhetorically and use it as an easy escape from finding an actual solution to a real crisis. By shifting the politics into the realm of rites, the politicians may satisfy their public performance needs but do very little to actually redress the deprivation of the displaced. This dilemma is at the heart of human rights as it becomes central to global politics. Almost twenty years ago, in 1993, the Second World Conference on Human Rights in Vienna, in its Declaration and Program of Action, adopted the statement that "all human rights are universal, indivisible, interdependent and interrelated."[8] This assertion has become the central dogma of human rights advocacy. One of the many justifications for this position is the claim that all rights are indispensable to protect and enhance the same basic values. But this general holistic worldview continuously clashes with the predicaments presented by rights that conflict with one another. Human well-being and rights do not easily cohere. It is in that sense that the right/rite of return is at the heart of human rights.

The rationale for describing the demand of minority reparation as a rite is the dissonance between the empirical evidence and the claims advanced by the right's supporters and politicians. One could imagine an aspiration of return that is not a rite, yet is not implemented, when it is presented as an aspiration. To desire something, even unachievable, is not a ritual. It is the essence of politics. To advocate and lobby for a goal is anything but a ritual. To aspire to equality is one thing. To claim equality exists as the rationale for rejecting discrimination is another matter. Yet to assume that an aspiration (return) is a reality and to argue for its further implementation in the form of specific policies falls into the category of ritual rather than politics.

Religious rites are obviously the source for such taxonomy. Political rites inform activities that are motivated by beliefs without empirical support. An example of such a belief is the mantra that unregulated free markets are natural and optimal in all situations, a claim that fails to account for ample evidence to the contrary. The demand for minority repatriation falls into this category of belief as well. Not because it would be wrong if it succeeded, but because it's a mirage. The right to return may well be argued on moral grounds, possibly justified by Realpolitik, it can but hardly be implemented by claiming it is a norm.

A rite presents a false solution to real-world deprivation. The misleading notion that return can resolve the displacement problems leaves minority refugees in a limbo that, at times, lasts for decades. If resolving the refugees' deprivation becomes the primary goal, it may have to be decoupled from the ultimate settlement of a conflict. At the very least, refugees should be able to move out of refugee camps and allow their children to start anew. While such ad hoc political solutions cannot repair the legacy of displacement and will continue to call for redress, and while deep-seated cultural and historical memories of violation are likely to influence the future politics of the conflict, refugees will still be better off if their physical needs are addressed in the short run.

The possibility of return should not be rejected a priori, but it should be treated as a matter of policy rather than rites. Prevention of displacement should remain the first priority, but once it fails and an ethnic conflict leads to displacement, there is an urgent need for alternative solutions. The challenge, then, is to transform the rite of return into a policy that would aim to resolve conflict, redress deprivation, and rehabilitate refugees' lives by facilitating resettlement, reparations, and compensation. If they are to effectively solve the refugee impasse, new alternative policies must aim to reconcile the desirability of minority repatriation and the complexity of the right to return.

Notes

1. United Nations, *The Universal Declaration of Human Rights*, Art. 13.2, http://www.un.org/en/documents/udhr/.

2. Office of the United Nations High Commissioner for Human Rights, *Vienna Declaration and Programme of Action*, UN doc. A/CONF157/23, http://www.unhchr.ch/huridocda/huridoca.nsf/%28symbol%29/a.conf.157.23.en.

UNHCR declared 1992 the "Year of Voluntary Repatriation." Mrs. Ogata, then UN high commissioner for refugees, "reaffirmed her determination to pursue every opportunity in 1992 for voluntary *repatriation* as the *preferred solution* to refugee problems." UN High Commissioner for Refugees, *Discussion Note on*

Protection Aspects of Voluntary Repatriation, April 1, 1992, EC/1992/SCP/CRP.3, http://www.unhcr.org/refworld/docid/3ae68cd314.html.

3. Ibid.

4. Ibid.

5. Ibid.

6. Amnesty International, *Bhutan: Nationality, Expulsion, Statelessness, and the Right to Return,* ASA14/001/2000, September 1, 2000, http://www.amnesty.org/en/library/info/ASA14/001/2000/en.

7. Howard Adelman and Elazar Barkan, *No Return, No Refuge: Rites and Rights in Minority Repatriation* (New York: Columbia University Press, 2011). A global comparative study of refugee repatriation and lack of return during the twentieth century.

8. Office of the United Nations High Commissioner for Human Rights, *Vienna Declaration.*

PART IV

Sites of Return and the New Tourism of Witness

16　Sites of Conscience

Lighting Up Dark Tourism

LIZ ŠEVČENKO

It's been nearly a decade since the United Nations recognized the Global Code of Ethics for Tourism, a set of principles to ensure "tourism's contribution to mutual understanding and respect between peoples and societies."[1] In the same moment, a small group of historic site directors came together to explore whether tourism had a more active role to play: to inspire visitors to address injustices they encountered at home and abroad. This group identified themselves as Sites of Conscience, making a specific commitment to "draw connections between past and present," "stimulate dialogue on pressing social issues," "promote democratic and humanitarian values," and "share opportunities for public involvement in issues the site raises." Convened by New York's Lower East Side Tenement Museum, they included sites as diverse as the Gulag Museum in Russia, preserving a Stalinist labor camp; the District Six Museum in South Africa, remembering forced removals under apartheid; and the Workhouse in England, exploring Britain's attempts to deal with poverty from the nineteenth century to the present. At the end of their first meeting, they decided to form the International Coalition of Sites of Conscience to help each other transform historic sites from places of passive learning to centers for people to become engaged in shaping the most urgent problems they face today. To do this, they needed to reimagine both tourism and tourists and grapple with challenging contradictions in each of their cultural contexts. What would a Sites of Conscience tourism look like? Could tourism—so strongly associated with passive, if respectful, observation—inspire activism?

Soon after the coalition was founded to grapple with these questions, Arthur Frommer published a syndicated column strongly promoting Sites of Conscience tourism. "I urge you to study the message of museums of conscience," he insisted, "and then to schedule a visit to one or more of them on your next trip." Frommer characterized Sites of Conscience as "shocking museums . . . dwelling on the . . . tragedies that humankind has suffered, the horrors and the cruelty." Their value lay in their darkness, as "repositories of humankind's foibles and crimes," and represented an important new way of exploring new places. Travelers could find a new understanding of both themselves and others by learning about a country's local struggles with global moral questions. Citing the ways the Slave House in Senegal raised questions around slavery and its legacies, or the Terezín Memorial in Czech Republic around genocide, Frommer asked, "What more important issues could possibly be placed before any visitor to the cities in which these museums are found?" These sites could help tourists "absorb lessons that may perhaps enable us in our own societies to avoid similar enormities."[2]

While the coalition's fledgling museum collective counted itself lucky to have one of the industry's international leaders trumpet its cause, Frommer's characterization of Sites of Conscience and its tourism reinforced some of the stereotypes Sites of Conscience were struggling against. First, sites in the coalition were exploring broader ideas of what could inspire conscience: was it only extreme tragedy and persecution? What role did stories of resistance, daily life and culture, or even complicity play? Further, Frommer's Sites of Conscience tourism still assumed fairly passive roles for both museums and visitors: sites needed only place an issue before visitors, and visitors needed only absorb it and hopefully avoid committing crimes against humanity. The question Sites of Conscience were grappling with was whether they had the potential as tourist destinations to inspire a more active global citizenry. To address this question, they had to develop a different experience of "return"—one that would use a journey back to catalyze action moving forward.

For example, in some cases, returning to a site of abuse mobilized survivors to demand restitution for past injustice in the form of material reparations or prosecutions. District Six was a thriving, culturally diverse working-class neighborhood in Cape Town. Under the Group Areas Act of 1966, it was razed to the ground to make way for a whites-only district. The District Six Museum began by inviting the thousands of people who had lost their homes and community to return to a Methodist church still standing near the destroyed neighborhood. The floor of the church was covered with a giant map of the former District Six. Ex-residents were invited to place themselves back in the neighborhood by marking their memories on the map—where they lived, worked, played. The process of gathering and reconnecting with former neighbors and sharing what they had lost, both emotionally and materially, served as a critical catalyst for organizing a movement to reclaim land as part of restitution for apartheid. Ex-residents launched a land reparations movement that succeeded in winning title back for many displaced people. One of the land courts that granted title back to displaced residents was held at the museum.

In Argentina victims conducted "returns" to sites of torture and detention to demand legal accountability for these crimes. After the restoration of democracy, amnesty was declared for any agents of the military dictatorship, leaving the fates of thousands of disappeared people unknown and uninvestigated. Families of the disappeared returned to sites across the city of Buenos Aires where their loved ones had last been seen. These sites—ranging from back rooms of local police stations to the massive Naval Academy campus—were places people passed every day, hidden in plain view, secretly co-opted by the state for detention, torture, and disappearance. Families worked to make the sites and their stories visible to a public and a state eager to move on, holding repeated public demonstrations and marking the sites with temporary art. After years of struggle, the amnesty law was overturned and prosecutions began. Sites that had been identified by the returns of the families became some of the starting points for investigation, with archaeological excavations yielding critical evidence for the trials.

If returning to sites of abuse has mobilized direct survivors to take action, what about those visiting for the first time? It's precisely the presumption of tourists' passivity and disengagement that's led many survivor communities to reject tourism to the most sacred of their sites as inherently voyeuristic. This is particularly true when part of a site's social mission is to create a healing space for survivors: when it promises a therapeutic experience of return to a site of trauma. In Argentina, after President Néstor Kirchner declared the most emblematic site of torture and detention under the dictatorship, the Naval Academy in Buenos Aires (Escuela de las Mecánicas de la Armada, or ESMA), as a "Space for Memory and Human Rights," many survivors and victims' families successfully lobbied for the massive campus to be kept closed to all but those with a direct experience of the site. Others argued that a new generation, one with no memory or experience of state terrorism, would need to see and learn from the site in order to prevent such practices in the future.[3] The District Six Museum in South Africa faces a related dilemma. The museum was first developed by ex-residents as a site of return and recovery of a lost community, collaborating with organizations providing both personal redress (counseling services) and collective reparations (land reclamation). But the museum soon became a celebrated destination for international tourists eager to learn about the human experience of apartheid. The museum now struggles with how, in its very small space, it can both maintain a respectful, private atmosphere for its primary community of ex-residents to mourn losses and celebrate endurance while sharing the lessons of this resistance movement with foreigners. But both the District Six Museum and the ESMA Space for Human Rights were explicitly founded to ensure that the abuses they remember do not recur. While deeply committed to social healing, both wrestle with the question: can a mission of preventing future atrocities be fulfilled without tourism?

The image of the invasive, voyeuristic tourist has been solidified in the growing debate over "dark tourism" or "trauma tourism," the practice of visiting sites of tragedy and suffering. Here public places remembering difficult histories have often been critiqued as trivializing or exploiting suffering.[4] But Sites of Conscience, as the coalition's founders conceived of them, are not inherently sites of tragedy. Instead, founders believed that conscience can and must be inspired by the full range of human experience and ethical dilemmas. Sites of Conscience include museums exploring social change movements, such as the Eleanor Roosevelt National Historic Site, and daily experience with social issues, such as the Lower East Side Tenement Museum. Many Sites of Conscience that do remember atrocities resist being understood simply as sites of suffering, as they might be labeled under the "dark tourism" framework, sharing instead many layers of stories, including resistance, the struggles of daily life, as well as blurrier moments of complicity or cowardice.

Sites of Conscience, then, do not only offer a return to a moment of trauma for those who experienced it. They can also invite a return to a crossroads: to a moment or a series of moments when individuals, states, and societies grappled with questions we are still grappling with today and made decisions we are still living with. The British National Trust's Workhouse invites visitors to tour this rare surviving example of the system of grim buildings built in the Victorian era to shelter Britain's "worthy poor" and deter the "idle and profligate." In use through the 1970s, when it served as a shelter for homeless mothers, the building was both a witness and an instrument of dozens of different approaches to social welfare. After touring recreations of an 1830s and a 1970s bedroom, visitors are invited to a concluding exhibit titled, "What Now, What Next?" Through chalkboards, bulletin boards, and interactive kiosks, the exhibit asks visitors to respond to a series of questions about social welfare policy past and present, including, "How do you define poverty? What solutions to poverty have been tried before? Is what we are doing now better, or worse? What new solutions might we try?" The space includes temporary exhibits on different organizations addressing social welfare issues today, with information about how visitors can participate in their efforts. Most recently, the Workhouse has developed a public dialogue program in which trained facilitators open conversations on personal experiences and opinions on supporting people in need.

A Sites of Conscience tourism practice would need to harness the possibilities these sites have to mobilize both local and international engagement in the legacies of their histories. These practices would need to maintain a deep commitment to those most in need of healing, such as immediate victims of a recent atrocity. But ultimately it will need to challenge strict dichotomies of insider and outsider, of returning and visiting, and open different forms of ownership of the site—and therefore responsibility for the issues it raises. Outsiders in one place are insiders in another and can participate in effecting change in their own localities or contexts. A Sites of Conscience tourism needs to imagine everyone as active participants or stakeholders—recognizing not everyone has the same stake and that each has a different role to play. The potential of the site is to activate all these participants to address the issues in their own contexts.

Sites of Conscience in a variety of different contexts have creatively exploited overlaps between insider and outsider, "tourist" and "local" in an attempt to inspire tolerance and activism in all visitors to the site. The most obvious examples are sites that treat "outsider" visitors not as people there to learn the story of others, but as people with an active role to play in shaping human rights both locally and globally. These sites call attention to the role of international actors in shaping what happened there and what continues to happen in the country, opening responsibility and possibility for social action to people with a variety of relationships to the site's history. The Villa Grimaldi Peace Park outside Santiago in Chile remembers a secret torture and detention center from the Pinochet dictatorship. Tours led by survivors and students connect individual stories of prisoners and guards to the larger international forces that placed them there—including the role the U.S. played in training secret police. Tours also raise questions about how societies allow human rights violations to take place under their noses as well as the strong role international actors can play in resisting abuse, such as when Pinochet was finally arrested in London. For some survivor guides, the site's mission is to inspire a commitment to human rights in everyone, raising awareness of international visitors' unwitting support for these practices and inspiring them to be more aware of the actions of their government both inside and outside their country.[5]

The Liberation War Museum in Dhaka remembers the genocide against Bengali people during Bangladesh's struggle for independence in 1971. Although its audience is primarily local school children, they devote a significant section of the main exhibit to the involvement of the U.S. in supporting Pakistan and of India in supporting Bangladesh. The museum also celebrates popular foreign support for the Bangladeshi cause, hosting annual commemorations of George Harrison's concert for Bangladesh and recalling the power of collective citizen action in bringing public attention to the issue.

Sites remembering creative social action have as important a role to play in inspiring this kind of conscience as those remembering human destruction. The National Civil Rights Museum at the Lorraine Motel in Memphis not only features over two centuries of struggle for African American civil rights but also connects visitors to new struggles in Memphis and around the world. A permanent exhibit on global human rights includes a video titled "We Want to Be Free," featuring social movements in South America, Russia, China, and the U.S., as well as kiosks through which visitors can explore other issues and movements further. The museum collaborates with Memphis's M. K. Gandhi Institute and a wide range of social justice organizations on an annual conference on nonviolence that uses the histories of Gandhi and King as the starting point for workshops in which youth identify the most pressing issues they are facing in Memphis today—gun violence was one—and how they might organize to address them. In addition to inviting movement "insiders" to return to the iconic balcony where King's body fell, the museum invites a broader public to return to a moment when so many took action.

In other cases, sites challenge ideas of insider and outsider to create common ground among people with different backgrounds and encourage a common possibility for participating in social change. The heart of the Lower East Side Tenement Museum is a five-story apartment building at 97 Orchard Street where more than seven thousand immigrants from over twenty different nations lived between 1863 and 1935. Millions of European Americans trace their roots—real or imagined—back to the Lower East Side and "return" to the neighborhood to reconnect with this mythical old world in the new.[6] They arrive to discover streets filled with people from China, the Dominican Republic, Bangladesh, and over thirty other countries quite different than those of their ancestors'—40 percent of the neighborhood's residents are foreign born, and more than 60 percent speak a language other than English at home. Who is the immigrant, the tourist, the outsider to this place, and who is the local? This can cause confusion and consternation among some visitors. As Josephine Baldizzi Esposito, a former resident of 97 Orchard Street put it, "It was one of my dreams to get back into that house. . . . When I came in contact with immigrants coming here now. . . . I would say, 'Oh my God, what country am I in? These are all foreign people. What are they all doing here?' Then I realized that these poor immigrants now are doing the same things my parents did."[7]

The museum hopes all visitors will experience such an epiphany—that the site can serve as a common ground for people who share both a sense of insider connection to the place and an experience or memory of feeling excluded. To achieve this goal, museum tours invite visitors to reflect on connections between the stories of different generations of immigrants in an attempt to forge understanding between people with different backgrounds and challenge anti-immigrant stereotypes. The museum's programs also seek to give those who have been made to feel like outsiders a sense of belonging and, specifically, a sense of agency and entitlement to organize for change. In Shared Journeys, the museum brings people learning English to "meet" their historic counterparts—immigrant families who lived at 97 Orchard Street a century ago—and learn how they organized to improve conditions for future generations of immigrants.

The museum also recognizes that outsiders coming to the neighborhood may be passive observers of the local scene but are actors in their own spheres. To that end, they try to use the specific history of the local

place to raise awareness of its connection to issues in visitors' own contexts and what visitors can do about them. In Kitchen Conversations, visitors from Atlanta to Australia are invited to participate in discussions over
tea about their personal experiences with immigration. In these facilitated
dialogues, visitors are asked to share stories and opinions of immigrants
and immigration issues in their own communities and reflect together
on whether and how it should be different. At the conclusion of the discussion, participants receive "10 Ways to Make a Difference," a pamphlet
describing how individuals in different communities effected change for
immigrants.

Other sites bring together people from very different parts of the world
to develop a sense of collective responsibility to be exercised differently
in each of their different contexts. The Monte Sole Peace School outside
of Bologna remembers the massacre of area villagers by Nazi troops and
Italian Fascist forces on September 29 and October 5, 1944, as part of a
campaign of terror toward the end of the war to suppress partisan resistance. Up to 770 people, mostly women and children, were killed. Now
converted into a nature park, this silent and peaceful landscape pays testament to the terrible violence against civilian populations in this region
during World War II. The Peace School Foundation of Monte Sole "pro-
motes training and peace education projects, non-violent transformation
of conflicts, respect for human rights and peaceful coexistence among
different people and cultures, and a society without xenophobia, racism
and any other kind of violence towards human beings and their environment." The school began by bringing youth representing two groups in
conflict—such as Israelis and Palestinians—to "return" to the scene of
conflict at Monte Sole, deconstruct the mechanisms of violence, and discuss how to address the current violence between their communities. But
confronting the problem directly proved too difficult, the divides between
the two groups too hard to bridge. Instead, the school invited two other
groups of youth to join, local Italians and Germans, representing nations
involved in the Monte Sole violence who had long since made peace. In
the resulting "Peace and Four Voices" camp, all participants were simultaneously locals and tourists: the Italians may have been "locals" to the site
itself but were tourists to the experience of violent conflict, while their Palestinian cohorts were outsiders to the place but not the issues. Educators
designed workshops that facilitated exchange of the varied experiences of
both violence and peace within each group of youth as the starting point
for all four groups to work together to identify how to confront conflict

in their own communities. Perhaps because this playing field was more level—or precisely because it was more variegated—educators found dialogue could finally open.[8]

As generations pass, and new social challenges emerge, Sites of Conscience will need to continually expand the moral of their story—mining the complexities and questions of their histories to confront new issues that arise. But this again can infringe in painful ways on the healing of immediate survivors. On the one hand, many survivors' groups are committed to imparting the lessons of their experience to a new generation. On the other hand, a class of fifth graders—gum chewing, gaping, and giggling—can desecrate a space faster than any imagined dark tourist. Some sites have found that as long as the story is confined to the past, to the experience of the adult narrating it, the issues threaten to remain abstract and irrelevant. Instead, sites like the Villa Grimaldi Peace Park have worked with teachers and students to identify the most pressing concerns in the classroom today and are developing new tours of the site that draw more direct connections between the history of the site and the challenges young people now face, such as violence among students or racial discrimination. One of the most devastating legacies of the dictatorship for young people today is a severely impoverished culture of activism, as youth who organized against the Pinochet state were disappeared, tortured, and detained. To address this, Villa Grimaldi's newest programs draw on successful examples of youth activism to help young people design a project they can implement in school to address the issues they have identified as most critical for them. Some survivors may have been appalled at comparing the systematic torture they experienced to bullying in the school yard. But Villa Grimaldi's educators believe that the site must be appropriated by different generations for different reasons if the goal of "Never Again" is to be reached.[9]

As Sites tap into aspects of their histories and face new realities, new groups of stakeholders may challenge the old for primary personal connection to the site. In 1995 the justices of the new South African Constitutional Court decided to build their court building on the very spot where justice had been most perverted under apartheid, the Old Fort Prison. The justices envisioned a public space where people could visit a museum about the history of the prison and learn of struggle for justice in the apartheid era and then visit the new Constitutional Court and observe the justices debating questions facing South Africa today. The Old Fort Prison held high-profile movement leaders like Nelson Mandela and

Mahatma Gandhi. But it also held ordinary people who committed acts that were criminalized under apartheid, such as traveling without a pass, and people who committed crimes like murder or robbery that were still against the law in the new South Africa. So which lessons of the prison's past were best for the present? On what foundation did the justices want to build a new South African conscience?

The team charged with developing the museum began by inviting all these types of former prisoners, as well as former guards, to return to the site, share their stories, and physically "map" their experience by identifying how different spots on the site were used. The team discovered dramatic differences between the past experiences of different categories of prisoners as well as between their views on how democracy had affected their lives since. They decided to capture these differences in their first exhibit by profiling diverse individual prisoners held at the Old Fort for dramatically different reasons. This provoked "strong debate," as one museum team member remembers: "Should the story of a murderer be represented alongside far more noble people who had fought for their freedom and been unjustly imprisoned?"[10] Where growing numbers of South African heritage sites celebrated anti-apartheid leaders and drew a stark line between South Africa's apartheid past and its democratic present, the Constitution Hill museum team recognized that for many South Africans, both those who suffered and those who benefitted from apartheid, the past was still very much unresolved. Rather than building a linear narrative celebrating the end of injustice, the museum team sought to create a space for diverse South Africans to grapple, in an ongoing way, with how justice should now be defined. In the exhibit space, above the profile of the different prisoners hung the question "Who is a Criminal?" Visitors are invited to write their responses to the question and post them on a wall of the exhibit. Instead of creating an exclusive site of physical return for those who suffered at the Old Fort, the team invited South African society to return together to the place and time when the country was battling over this key question, one still unresolved today. After touring the museum, visitors can enter the Constitutional Court and observe justices debating the same question in new forms.

The museum continually looks to new aspects of apartheid's history to provide perspective on the latest debates before the court. As its marketing director explained, "Just like South African society itself, [Constitution Hill] will never be completed, for every generation of visitors will add its own experiences and memories to the site."[11] In the wake of the court's decisions on gay marriage, the museum opened an exhibit on the struggles of LGBT communities in South Africa's past and present—a history that had made little appearance in the increasingly coherent national narrative supported by other museums and school curricula. Nor had it emerged as a story of the museum's primary stakeholder community of ex-prisoners. In fact, many survivors of the Old Fort Prison, and many other South Africans, might not agree that apartheid was fought in order to bring gay people the right to marry. In continuing to raise questions of conscience, once marginalized stakeholders may appear as new "tourists" in national narratives.

These dialogues were held as part of Constitution Hill's *lekgotla* programs. *Lekgotla* refers to a practice of gathering villagers under a shady tree to address community issues. Drawing on this cultural memory and reference, Constitution Hill developed a range of structures for modern lekgotla on a variety of issues raised at the site, all of which took place in the plaza between the court and the historic prison, between old and new visions of justice. The *lekgotla* were not intended to bring specific conclusions or resolutions but rather to create a space for people to gain new perspective and understanding of the issues and one another, to understand their rights and responsibilities under the constitution, and to be inspired to participate as citizens. The goal was to model democratic engagement on the site that could be replicated in society. Lekgotla structures included conversations between school children, talks and Q&A with ex-prisoners or others with direct experience, discussions between community leaders or policy makers on certain issues, or discussions between people with differences of perspective on an issue, such as whether homosexuality or gay marriage is a right to be protected like racial equality.

Tourism to historic sites that raise challenging social issues should neither be dismissed as unethical nor embraced as a guarantee of Never Again. Instead, deliberate practices must be developed to harness the potential of these sites to inspire civic engagement. Sites of Conscience are working together to develop a wide diversity of such practices, sharing some common principles, including

- Posing open-ended questions on the implications of the past for the present and providing space and time for a variety of stakeholders to respond.

- Supporting different opportunities for those who hold a different stake in the site—such as immediate survivors, school children, and international tourists—to experience the space separately. This could be at different times—such as holding closed ceremonies for survivors on certain critical anniversaries—or different spaces—such as separating exhibit and dialogue rooms from reflection and memorial rooms.
- In addition, opening structured opportunities for engagement between and among "insiders" and "outsiders" on common questions.
- Developing youth programs that teach new generations about what happened at the site in the past, then inviting them to identify for themselves what legacies of the sites' histories they live with today, what lessons the site offers to help them address those legacies, and what actions can be taken.
- Providing information or opportunities for people to become involved in shaping the issues of greatest concern to them today. Some sites provide visitors with lists of organizations that address the issues from different perspectives; others register people to vote on-site; others work with specific groups to design and carry out an action.

These practices will always struggle with the contradictory needs of those who need to mourn and those who seek to engage and debate. But these practices must begin with an expanded and critical notion of tourist and local, insider and outsider, that implicates everyone in both the problem and the solution. This requires an organic approach to heritage, one that recognizes the meaning of each site is not fixed, rather its legacies evolve with each passing day. A "conscience" tourism needs to continually return to the questions heritage sites pose for us to find new answers for our ever changing present.

Notes

1. World Tourism Organization, "Global Codes of Ethics for Tourism," 1999, http://www.gdrc.org/uem/eco-tour/principles.html.
2. Arthur Frommer, "Tourists Turning from Art to 'Museums of Conscience,'" SFGate.com, August 28, 2005.

3. Sebastian Brett, Louis Bickford, Marcela Rios, and Liz Ševčenko, "Memorialization and Democracy: State Policy and Civic Action" (2007), 9, http://www.sites ofconscience.org/wp-content/documents/publications/memorialization-en.pdf.

4. Michael Foley, and John Lennon, *Dark Tourism: The Attraction of Death and Disaster* (London: Continuum, 2000).

5. Brett et al., *Memorialization and Democracy*, 16.

6. Hasia Diner, *Lower East Side Memories: A Jewish Place in America* (Princeton: Princeton University Press, 2000).

7. Lower East Side Tenement Museum, *A Tenement Story* (New York: Lower East Side Tenement Museum, 2003), 4.

8. Nadia Baiesi, Marzia Gigli, Elena Monicelli, Roberta Pillozoli, "Places of Memory as Tools for Education: The Peace in Four Voices Camp at Monte Sole," *Public Historian* 30, no. 1 (2008).

9. "Never Again" has emerged as a slogan used by a wide variety of groups to convey remembering an atrocity in order to prevent its repetition in the future. Originally popularized in reference to remembering the Holocaust—some credit Jewish Defense League founder Meir Kahane's 1972 book *Never Again! A Program for Survival*, though it has since been used by Jewish leaders from other perspectives. When Abraham Foxman, national director of the Anti-Defamation League, titled his book 2003 book *Never Again? The Threat of the New Anti-Semitism*, he told the *Jewish Daily Forward* that some had assured him the phrase was for Holocaust survivors alone. Foxman himself believed that "We, the Jewish people, do not have a patent on that phrase." Beth Schwartzapfel, "Never Again, Again," *Jewish Daily Forward*, October 6, 2006. Regardless of Kahane's or Foxman's views, the phrase has been adopted by many different groups, not only referring to acts of genocide, but other large-scale human rights abuses: perhaps most famously, it was used as the title of the 1984 report on Argentina's National Commission on the Disappearance of Persons. Moving further from the original meaning, former Attorney General John Ashcroft used the phrase in the title of his 2006 book on 9/11.

10. Lauren Segal, ed., *Number Four: The Making of Constitution Hill* (London: Penguin, 2006), 127.

11. Ibid., 219.

Rise and go to the town of the killings and you'll come to the yards
and with your eyes and your own hand feel the fence
and on the trees and on the stones and plaster of the walls
the congealed blood and hardened brains of the dead.
  —Hayim Nahman Bialik, "City of the Killings"

17 Kishinev Redux

Pogrom, Purim, Patrimony

NANCY K. MILLER

What I believed as a child: we came from Russia. Russia, a vast, far-away, almost mythical kingdom, ruled by bad czars, filled with mean peasants, who lived in the forest with wolves, and even meaner Cossacks, who, when they weren't riding horses, or maybe while they were riding horses, specialized in physical attacks on Jews called pogroms: overall a place one left, if one was a Jew, as soon as possible. The fairy-tale-like simplicity of this geography and its inhabitants did not include a longing to return. No one ever talked about going back there, wherever back there actually was.

Before I traveled to Eastern Europe, I would have been unable to locate the city of Kishinev on a modern map. Kishinev itself was a place name that came belatedly, when I was already a middle-aged adult, as an overlay to my childhood vision of the Russian Empire. It wasn't yet Chisinau, the capital of Moldova, consistently referred to in the media as the poorest country in Europe, known for sex trafficking, the illegal sale of bodily organs, and Twitter-assisted post-Soviet political turmoil. But why was I going to Kishinev, and why did I think that we—my father's side of the family, the Kipnis side—came from there?

Not long before his death in 1989, my father gave me a few mono-grammed forks and spoons, which he described as "silverware from our family in Russia." Around the same time, he also gave me a photocopy he had made of the index to the *New York Times* with references to the 1903 Kishinev pogrom checked in the margins, as well as a map of Bessarabia with Kishinev circled in red. I do not remember asking my father directly where his parents came from, nor do I recall ever hearing accounts of their immigration to the United States. And so, when he died, the matter of where we were from remained just that: a fixed, generic, third-generation Jewish template—a classic American narrative of immigration followed by assimilation. For the next ten years, as had been true of my life before his death, I was not particularly interested in knowing more, beyond the vague sense that the *where* in Russia we were from was Kishinev.

I probably would have remained locked in my ignorance about the specifics of my Eastern European origins if an enterprising real estate agent had not, in the year 2000, reached my sister and me with the news that we had inherited property in a village on the outskirts of Jerusalem from our paternal grandparents. The property amounted to two dunams—two tiny plots of a quarter acre each, bought in my grandmother's name. This startling information led to an encounter with the other heir to my grandmother's dunams, my father's nephew, his older and only sibling's son, who was living in Memphis, Tennessee. In the year 2000 I met my cousin Julian Kipnis for the first time as well as his daughter, Sarah Castleberry. Through Sarah, who had already become fascinated with family history, I discovered a Web site devoted to our family name that included the ship's manifests for a multitude of Kipnis immigrants. On the manifest for my grandparents and uncle, under the category "last permanent residence," was written by hand: Kishiniew. I was instantly hooked by the possibility of finding out more about this family, the Kipnises, whose existence had always been shrouded in a kind of dark silence.[1] The encounter with my newly met cousin sent me back to the haphazard collection of objects and ephemera that I had taken from my parents' apartment after my father's death and that I had saved without quite knowing why.

Sorting through my father's papers I found a formal portrait of his parents and older brother. The name of the studio and its location in Kishinev were prominently identified on the front and back of the image. Based on what I took to be the age of the little boy (my unmet uncle) standing between my grandparents, I guessed that the photograph had been taken in 1903, which was also the year of the pogrom (figure 17.1).

Widely reported throughout the world, the Kishinev pogrom stood as a turning point in Jewish history, not only in Russia.[2] Perhaps, I thought,

FIGURE 17.1 Rafael, Shulem, and Sheyndel Kipnis, Kishinev, circa 1903. *Miller Archive*

these ancestors of mine had actually witnessed the event as immortalized in Bialik's famous 1904 poem, "City of the Killings," and Israel Zangwill's 1908 play, remembered now mainly for its title, *The Melting Pot*.[3] My grandparents and uncle left Russia for America in 1906.

Although only a handful of biographical facts about the trio had been transmitted to me, the photograph, the newspaper references to the pogrom, and the map, led me to link the Kipnis family name with Kishinev. There was something uncannily suggestive about the way the names of the family and the city seemed to mirror each other, the resemblance carried by the initial letter K, and the overlapping sounds of the syllables (*Kip/Kish/nis/nev*). I began, largely unconsciously, to identify the family enigma with the history of the city and to wonder whether the place itself could reveal what my father had failed to put into words. I began to feel that the pogrom belonged to me.

In the spring of 2008, almost impulsively, I decided to make the trip that would bring me to the city where my grandparents had resided before their emigration, despite the fact that I knew I was not likely ever to learn exactly where and how they lived or to meet anyone who had known them. The photograph no longer satisfied my longing to know more about them, nor did the ship's manifest. By the time I made the pilgrimage to the site of the pogrom, large numbers of third-generation descendants of the vast emigration from Russia at the turn of the twentieth century had, like me, begun looking for the towns their ancestors had left, and Web-based organizations like Jewishgen.org had set up Internet engines to facilitate the journey of return. Indeed, it was through a reference from www.Jewishgen .org that I found my guide Natasha.

Initially, I resisted calling my journey a "roots-seeking trip," as Natasha always referred to the itinerary, but I can't deny that the category fit my desire: "Amerikanka looking for babushka."[4] I had become not just curious but consumed with curiosity to see for myself the part of the world my father's parents—and his brother—had left behind and to follow the path of the pogrom. By e-mail Natasha explained to me that if I wanted genealogical information from the Moldovan archives I would have to engage a specialist. Even before I arrived in town, the archivist she recommended had already found records for one of my great-grandfather's cousins in Kishinev—his marriage and profession—as well as a document about a child who had lived only three days before dying of convulsions, the son of Refuel (my grandfather's name) from Tulchin, a small town now in

Ukraine; more evidence that I, we, they, somehow were from there, from this corner of Bessarabia, as it was called then.

I immediately located the position of this cousin on a branch of the tree that an American genealogist with Kipnis ancestors had made for me years earlier and looked again at the ship's manifest that I had already downloaded from Ancestry.com. The man, his wife, and his children left for New York from Odessa, a few weeks after my grandparents left Kishinev, on the same ship from Rotterdam, and were headed for the home of my grandfather Raphael Kipnis at 96 Allen Street in New York. The building no longer exists, but at the time it shared a courtyard, back to back, with 97 Orchard Street, the current home of the Tenement Museum of the Lower East Side. Side by side, back to back, this approximation of past locations has something of the ambiguities connecting biographies to locations that Svetlana Boym has designated as the off-modern, a detour from the predictable histories of the straight line.[5]

I went to Kishinev and followed the path of the pogrom as described in Bialik's poem, but it was only the *second* trip I made to the city—the one that could properly be called a return—that helped me understand my puzzling compulsion to make the first journey, a compulsion (abetted by technology) shared by thousands of fellow questers across the world, descendants of immigrants for whom, like me, the image, the screen, and the archive do not seem to be enough. We seem to want, though we might not put it that way, the real thing.

Not long after getting back to New York in May 2008 from my first trip to Kishinev, Aleksandar Hemon published *The Lazarus Project* and, at the same time, my sister handed over an album of photographs from Russia that had belonged to my grandmother.[6] Together, these unexpected occurrences illuminated both the meaning of my individual quest and the wider phenomenon expressed in rites of return: the genre, as it were, of the experience and the modes by which we return, think we return, and think about returning. The book and the album sent me back for a closer look.

Lazarus Averbach survives the 1903 pogrom in Kishinev and emigrates to the safety of America, only to be murdered a few years later in Chicago. In the novel, Brik, the narrator, tries to unravel Lazarus's story and embarks on detective-like travels to Eastern Europe to reconstruct the immigrant's pogrom past. When Brik and his travel companion, Rora, a photographer, both Bosnian like the author, neither Jewish, arrive in Moldova, they set out to research the pogrom: "the two of us who could never have experienced the pogrom went to the Chisinau Jewish Community Center to find someone who had never experienced it and would tell us about it." I was overcome with a sense of anxiety. Here was my own private adventure somehow scooped and transformed into literature through an artful postmodern scrim. What was the novelist doing to my pogrom? Naturally, Brik and Rora's guide is a Philip Rothian character, a beautiful, if slightly bored young woman, pale, with "deep, mournful eyes" (229). The two men ask her about the pogrom, which she dutifully recounts, and then are led to an adjacent room where they gaze in horror at a display of photographs: "bearded, mauled corpses lined up on the hospital floor, the glassy eyes facing the ceiling stiffly: a pile of battered bodies; a child with its mouth agape; a throng of bandaged, terrified survivors" (230). The description seemed familiar. I'd seen many of those same images online, illustrating the historical event. But I did not see them on my visit. What I saw on display about the pogrom that I too was researching as a character in my own story was an arch in the one-room museum around which collaged photographs had been pasted. The strongest image I remembered was that of young men clutching the Torah scrolls desecrated during the rioting. Had my guide failed to show me these other photographs? Had I seen them and forgotten?

As I raced through the pages of the novel, I had the uncomfortable sensation that Hemon's fiction was challenging my memory and even my sense of reality. In the novel, for instance, the two characters leave the display of pogrom photographs and move further into the room. Behind an alcove they see "a couple of dummies in Orthodox Jewish attire, positioned around an empty table, their eyes wide open, their hands resting on the table's edge" (231). I traveled back in my mind, looking at the photographs I had taken, and coming up blank. I started to distrust my reliability as the narrator of my memoir. I sent Natasha a frantic e-mail telling her about the novel and asking her whether we had seen these rooms. How could I have missed the pogrom exhibit? Surely I would have noticed these "dummies" meant to represent, the novel's guide explains, "a Jewish family from the time of the pogrom" (232). Could I have already forgotten what I had seen only weeks before? But maybe my panic was misplaced. After all, this was a novel: fiction not memoir. Maybe Hemon had invented the whole thing. I hated myself for being so literal minded. I was a professor of literature and knew about genre.

Natasha wrote back about the dummies: "Yes, and Purim figures. It's in the JCC, with the library where Olga [the librarian] showed you around." Natasha attached two pictures she had taken of our visit: "Please see yourself and the puppets." But these puppets are Purim figures, Queen Esther and King Ahashuerus, not dummies dressed as Orthodox Jews. Did Hemon and I visit the same place? I turned to Olga, laying out my confusion. "Aleksandar Hemon is correct in his description," the librarian began. And the dummies? "The dummies in Orthodox attire just symbolized the atmosphere of an average Jewish home," she said. I held my breath, stunned by this confirmation of my memory lapse. Finally, toward the end of her long, detailed message, Olga explained that before 2005—presumably when Hemon had visited the city—the museum and therefore the exhibit were located across the street from its current location: "So you couldn't have seen the described artifacts." I had missed not only the dummies but also, Olga added, the "exposition devoted to the Pogrom with map, names of the victims, and a large picture of Torah Scrolls damaged by the looters." I couldn't have seen what I didn't see! My heart exploded with relief.

A few weeks later, Olga sent me photographs from the exhibit Hemon described. I see the dummies, I see a beautiful young woman who might have been the guide in the novel, pointing to the photographs of the pogrom. The dummies. The husband is dressed in a long, black gabardine coat, like a Hasidic Jew. His large hat, much too big for his head, is scrunched down around his ears, in front of which curl significant side locks; his bushy, untrimmed beard and full mustache complete the representation of the Orthodox Jew, his gaze resolutely turned away from modernity. His wife's hair is covered with a black shawl knotted around her shoulders; dressed in a full, white blouse, a knitted vest, and long flowing skirt with an embroidered pattern around the hem, she looks like a Ukrainian peasant.

Compared to the dummies, the photograph of my grandparents taken in Kishinev shows a couple who have distanced themselves from the styles of Bessarabian Orthodoxy. My grandfather has trimmed his beard and poses hatless, in street clothes. My grandmother does not cover her hair and is wearing a fitted blouse and elegant taffeta skirt. The couple looks European, Victorian.

In my grandmother's album I found two studio cards from Kishinev photography studios. These were portraits of friends, who have inscribed across the back of their portraits messages of farewell in Russian, dated a few months before my grandparents' departure from Kishinev. In posture and affect the friends resemble the characters in period representations of

Chekhov. One reads: "To my dear friend R. Kipnis with his wife, from G. and E. Frein. May you remember us fondly." I know nothing about these people, but what their faces, fashion, and words tell me is that, far from the caricatures of the dummies, Rafael and his wife belonged to a circle who knew there was a future beyond the pogroms. Three months later my grandparents would sail for America. My grandmother was pregnant, or about to be, with my father.

The photographs from the dear friends, their gesture of farewell, confirmed to me what I had traveled to find the first time but hadn't: something beyond the ship's manifest and beyond the family portrait. My second trip to Kishinev was to see not just the site of the pogrom again but to see for the first time the place that my grandparents had left as members of what I had since learned was a vast middle class of petit bourgeois Jews. The tenements of the Lower East Side must have been something of a comedown for the upwardly mobile Bessarabian Kipnises, if they lived anywhere near their friend Mr. Samuel Grigory Traub, "in his private dwelling house . . . in the upper, newly built part of the town." Or perhaps they lived near the photography studio located, it says on the card stock, "near the water pump house."

In my return to Kishinev, I was following an impulse I could not fully explain to myself, but it was hard to resist the self-diagnosis that I had succumbed to Freud's account of the "repetition compulsion" in *Beyond the Pleasure Principle*."[7] In the *fort/da* story, Freud famously describes how a child tries to master an anxiety over loss through a game, a game that allows him to repeat through a symbolic act a feeling—the fear of his mother's absence, of losing his mother—that threatens his sense of security. Repetition in this sense is a pleasurable way for the child to master the terror of loss beyond his control. For those of us for whom the past is often what novelist Kiran Desai named "the inheritance of loss," returning to the scene of where something important was lost can feel comforting.[8] As adult returnees, like the child playing with the spool, we try to fool ourselves with time travel: we can't really recapture the past with its losses, but we can go back to its places. Playing with loss becomes a way to deal with one of the crucial features of these rites of return, and that is a confrontation with what we are missing. Sometimes this is something literal: trying to see, find, discover what we have missed—that is, overlooked. But also something symbolic: recognizing what's irretrievably missing.

I wanted to know where they lived. I'm not going to know that. But, because of the studio cards, on my return I'm going to walk past the street where one of the city's two water pumps was located. I'm going to walk past the street where the water pump is no more but where the friends who were already missing my grandparents had their photograph taken. On my repeat pilgrimage, I'm going to follow the poem more carefully because now I finally understand the route the *pogromchiks* took and that I had walked through in a daze the first time, overwhelmed by the strangeness of the topography in which I had found myself. I'm starting to understand what is next to what, what is far, what is close. The river Byck, which marked the border of the poor section of town at the time of the pogrom, in 2009 is barely a rivulet and often entirely dry.

With the screen of the novel doubled by images from the exhibit I hadn't seen, my effort to fathom the city's past sometimes felt like a replay of childhood trips to the Museum of Natural History where we were instructed to gaze at dioramas of lost worlds and foreign peoples. But on this occasion, when I crossed the threshold of the Jewish Cultural Center, something felt immediately different, even though the exhibits had not changed. As I walked through the rooms with Olga, I experienced the pleasure of familiarity, repetition. I could double-check some of the details for my book, but I was at ease—not even taking photographs.

Toward the end of our time together, Olga mysteriously left the small performance space for the children's theatrical productions we had revisited, saying she would be back, saying something, I thought, about "doors." I waited. When she returned she was carrying three dolls (the doors): Hemon's dummies, and, in fact, handmade puppets the size of small children. Olga quickly reconfigured the scene that had been the centerpiece of the exhibit I had missed, seating the puppets on chairs around a small table, which was covered with a festive Sabbath cloth, set with candlesticks and a ceremonial kiddush cup, all against the background of a painting representing a Kishinev streetscape from the era of the pogrom. In this reconstructed, improvised version, husband and wife are joined by their daughter, Ora. Olga danced with the daughter doll to show me how the puppets could be used. I don't know what I would have made of this scene had I encountered it on my first visit. I wasn't put off, though, as were the characters in Hemon's novel, by the sight of these figures in an earlier choreography, "a couple of dummies," awkwardly positioned in their chairs.

Instead, on this return visit to the tiny museum setting, I was moved by what I perceived as the affect driving the curatorial decisions: the twin effort to touch the visitor from abroad, but at the same time to engage the small children living in the city who participate in the center's activities. In a minor, miniature key, the Kishinev Jewish Cultural Center echoes the efforts made by museums of conscience like the Tenement Museum in Manhattan to reproduce the material setting in which earlier generations lived.[9]

Through many layers of remove and mediation, the props, the puppets and domestic artifacts, all rehearse the holidays that by definition recur in a kind of perpetual present tense: the weekly Sabbath, the annual Purim. When Olga the librarian danced with Ora the doll, I felt the poignant physical effort to keep alive through ritual something important that was irremediably past except as remembrance or as symbolic performance. You can play in the rooms that contain the local exhibits, as the children do, reenacting the story of Purim—Purim as the story of a pogrom averted—but the adults are summoned to remember the pogrom as tragic history. Those who remained were not rescued, Queen Esther notwithstanding. Watching the dance, I suddenly collapsed inside like the balloons wilting on the stage behind the dolls, a whoosh of intensely held-in breath that I could finally let go. I had been working too hard at all of this, my compulsion to document, to find the exact spot, to keep returning until I got it right. These were the rites. By their stylized artifice, the puppets forced me to realize that the historical people they stood in for would be real to me *only* as actors in shared rituals, celebrating a long history of survival, as well as loss, a history that extended to all the descendants who wished to see themselves as part of it. Maybe as a good daughter of Freud, my anxiety subsided on this visit because I was returned to childhood memories of a Judaism already lost to me, through assimilation over two generations. Maybe what I had been trying to find was a way to compensate for my indifference to the narrative that I'm now starting to see has shaped me all along. Let's say that's part of it, searching for the path of a lost history whose effects nonetheless remain embedded in me. But how much can this process of return give meaning in retrospect to all that I didn't know and don't know still?

On this second visit to Kishinev, a broader uncertainty that had accompanied me throughout my quest also began to ease, and this was a troubling anxiety about the story itself that I was constructing to put in the place of my ignorance. I had experienced this uncertainty both on the site, as it were, and as I carried out the research on my lost family at a distance, in my head and on paper, as a kind of dissatisfaction or dissonance: insufficient information or approximate pieces of knowledge. I sometimes called this feeling of frustration by a term from mathematics that had caught my fancy early on in the process as a metaphor for the outcome of my quest: *asymptotic*. As plotted on a graph, an asymptote is a line that a curve forever approaches. The curve and the line look as though they will ultimately meet, but in the end, they never touch. Nicely for me, the word *symptom* shares the root of this term—which makes a kind of circular sense; my symptom was frustration at what did not meet (literally, did not fall together). But, given the nature of the enterprise, the failure to coincide with the thing itself was inevitable.

How close, then, was close enough? I wanted to discover my grandparents' records in the archive; instead I had to make do with their second cousin, the way in nineteenth-century novels the protagonist has to tolerate poor relations. On this return visit I began to internalize this information differently: the second cousin offered lateral confirmation—a sidebar of evidence, but confirmation all the same—of my family's passage in this city, good enough, to use the comforting language of object relations, close enough to begin repairing the loss, rebuilding lost knowledge.

On our final walk through the pogrom area, Natasha and I stopped to buy water at the little grocery adjacent to the dwelling known as "House Number 13," a place singled out as a scene of violence by Vladimir Korolenko's newspaper reportage in 1904.[10] On my previous visit I had been frustrated not to be able to enter the courtyard of the building, a site described by an Israeli researcher who had visited Kishinev on the one hundredth anniversary of the pogrom.[11] Natasha asked the young clerk if he had access to the courtyard and scribbled the phone number of his boss, the grocery store owner, in her notebook. But we both knew without saying that it was too late. I would have to accept the evidence of the many neighboring courtyards I had already seen. Much as I longed for particulars, I was going to have to be satisfied with the markers of collective, not individual, identity—with approximation. This should not have been surprising. All along I had been able to piece together the Kipnis puzzle, my patrimony, only through the lateral bonds that tied these family members to others of their generation and to the conditions of their emigration, to the collateral domain of what I call the transpersonal. Wasn't that what the museum exhibits were designed to represent, "an average Jewish home" at the time of the pogrom, a community, moreover, that revealed something important about my grandparents by their difference from its rules?

This lesson of the second visit was not lost on me. A door had literally closed—the door to the yard of House No. 13. Gentrification had begun in the pogrom area; more of the old buildings were bound to disappear. The exhibits at the Jewish Cultural Center library would no doubt change again. The monuments to the pogrom and to the Holocaust would remain, but the city would reconfigure its shape and architecture around them. In yet another rescripting of historical borders, the impoverished country of Moldova itself might merge with its neighbor Romania and fly a new flag. As myth, however, Kishinev would linger in the metaphors of the "City of the Killings" and in collective Jewish history.

Would this be my last return? As we headed for the airport at Chisinau, I felt that something had settled in me, the compulsion had loosened its hold. I knew so much more than when I had begun and yet there was so much I would never know. The exertion of the voyage had been absolutely necessary, but so was acknowledging its limits. Still, I've come to relish the pleasures of vanishing knowledge: a photograph of my grandparents taken in a photography studio that no longer exists and a home address, not theirs but that of their friends, friends whose relationship is established, after the fact of their separation, in a handwritten farewell inscribed on the back of yet another photograph taken at another photography studio that no longer exists. Most of the rest of what I wanted to know will take that form of removal—the equivalent of the psychic distance, and yet relatedness, of second cousins—and of puppets.

In a conversation I moderated between Saidiya Hartman, Eva Hoffman, and Daniel Mendelsohn about their memoirs of return, Mendelsohn recalled an event with Leon Wieseltier in which Wieseltier challenged him about the expression "going back." How could you go back to where you had never been? Wieseltier wanted to know. Mendelsohn answered that when you grow up in an immigrant family you constantly hear about "the country of origin. So it does feel like going *back*."[12] In my case, I had not heard enough growing up to feel that I was going back to a specific place in the "old country"—and, in particular, when I visited, on the heels of my first trip to Kishinev, the town in Ukraine where my paternal grandfather and great-grandfather were born (as I had discovered searching through the archive of immigrant papers in New York), I definitely did not feel that I was returning there or that there lay my roots, even though, literally, by bloodline and genealogy, I knew this to be true.

Instead, the second trip to Kishinev persuaded me that this was where I *wanted* to have come from. Through the literary history of the city, the traces of the archive, and the photographs of my grandparents and their stylishly dressed friends, I was moved to an act of "affiliative self-fashioning," a chosen identification created by the journey.[13] Returning to Kishinev had forced me to understand that while this place was the scene of a historical experience that I needed to see, a place where history had happened to the people who came before me, much of what I wanted from the past would continue to elude me. No matter how concrete, how referential, the way a photograph refers to the object in front of its lens, this place of the past lacked the story I was seeking, but it was the origin of the story I would write.

Notes

1. I described this triggering moment in the epilogue to *But Enough About Me: Why We Read Other People's Lives* (New York: Columbia University Press, 2002). A version of this essay appears in Nancy K. Miller, *What They Saved: Pieces of a Jewish Past* (Lincoln: University of Nebraska Press, 2011).

2. For a succinct account of the pogrom, see Edward H. Judge, *Easter in Kishinev: Anatomy of a Pogrom* (New York: New York University Press, 1992).

3. Hayim Nahman Bialik, "City of the Killings," *Songs from Bialik: Selected Poems of Hayim Nahman Bialik*, trans. Atar Adari (Syracuse: Syracuse University Press, 2000), 1–9. The title of the poem is alternately translated as "In the City of Killing" and "The City of Slaughter." Bialik was sent by the Jewish Historical Committee in Odessa to write a report based on victim testimony; instead he wrote a poem. The hero of Zangwill's play is a "pogrom orphan" who is also a talented violinist. Israel Zangwill, *The Melting Pot: Drama in Four Acts* (New York: Macmillan, 1932). Zangwill published a children's story version of his drama as "The Melting Pot: A Story of True Americanism," in *From the Tower Window of My Bookhouse,* ed. Olive Beaupré Miller (Chicago: Bookhouse for Children, 1921).

4. The archive of the experience has been inventoried and canonized in a now out-of-print, door-stopper-size volume, *Jewish Roots in Ukraine and Moldova: Pages from the Past and Archival Inventories* published by Miriam Weiner and her "Routes to Roots" foundation in 1999. I describe my two trips more fully in Miller, *What They Saved.*

5. In this volume.

6. Aleksandar Hemon, *The Lazarus Project* (New York: Riverhead, 2008).

7. Sigmund Freud, *Beyond the Pleasure Principle,* trans. James Strachey (New York: Norton, 1961).

8. Kiran Desai, *The Inheritance of Loss* (New York: Grove, 2006).

9. On the affect generated by visits to the Lower East Side Tenement Museum, see Liz Ševčenko, in this volume.

10. V. G. Korolenko. "House No. 13: An Episode in the Massacre of Kishinev," *Contemporary Review* 85 (February 1904): 266–80.

11. Dan Laor, "Kishinev Revisited: A Place in Jewish Historical Memory," *Prooftexts* 25 (2005): 30–38. As Laor's title suggests, every visit to Kishinev after Bialik's poem, which itself performs a return and an invitation to bear witness, could also be considered a return. But Laor also closely followed the itinerary recorded in Bialik's notebooks of testimony. On the relation of the testimony to the poem, see Mikhal Dekel's "'From the Mouth of the Raped Woman Rivka Shiff,' Kishinev, 1903," *WSQ* 36, nos. 1 and 2 (Spring/Summer 2008): 199–207.

12. In this volume.

13. Term coined by Alondra Nelson, in this volume.

18   Trauma as Durational Performance

A Return to Dark Sites

DIANA TAYLOR

Pedro Matta, a tall, strong man, walked up to us when we arrived at the unassuming side entrance to Villa Grimaldi, a former torture and extermination camp on the outskirts of Santiago de Chile. He is a survivor who, twice a month or so, gives a guided visit to people who want to know about the site. He says hello to Soledad Fallabella and Alejandro Gruman, colleagues of mine in Chile who thought, given my work with human rights groups in Argentina, that I would be interested in meeting Matta.[1] He greets me and hands me the English version of a book he has written: *A Walk Through a Twentieth-Century Torture Center: Villa Grimaldi, A Visitor's Guide.* I tell him that I am from Mexico and speak Spanish. "Ah," he says, his eyes narrow as he scans me, "Taylor, I just assumed . . ." The four of us walk into the compound. I ask if I can take photographs and record the visit—he says of course. I hold the booklet and my camera—Alejandro holds my digital tape recorder. I've come prepared for my "visit."

The site is expansive. It looks like a ruin or a construction site, there's some old rubble and signs of new building—a transitional space, part past, part future. In several ways it's hard to get a sense of where we're standing. A sign at the entrance, Parque Por la Paz Villa Grimaldi, informs visitors that 4,500 people were tortured here and 226 people were disappeared and killed between 1973 and 1979. I take a photograph of the sign, which points to the multivalence of this place—simultaneously a torture camp, a memory site, and a peace park. Like many memory sites, it reminds us that this tragic history belongs to all of us, asks us to behave respectfully so that it might remain and continue to instruct. Lesson One, clearly, is that this place is "our" responsibility.

"This way, please." Matta, a formal man, walks us over to the small model of the torture camp to help us visualize the architectural arrangement of a place now gone: Cuartel Terranova (barrack "new land"). The mock-up is laid out, like a coffin, under a plastic, slightly opaque sunshade. As in many historically important sites, the model offers a bird's-eye view of the entire area. The difference here is that what we see in the model is no longer there. The death space we visit is one that we cannot see and never know except through all manner of mediation. Even though we are there, we will not experience it "in person." So, one might ask, what is the purpose of the visit? What can we experience by being physically in a death camp once the indicators have disappeared? Does the space itself convey the event? Little beside the sign at the entrance reveals the context. My photographs might illustrate what this place *is*, not what it *was*. Still, we are here in person with Matta who takes us through the *recorrido* ("walk-through"). Matta speaks in Spanish; it makes a difference. He seems to relax a little, though his voice is very strained and he clears his throat often.

The compound, originally a beautiful nineteenth-century villa used for upper-class parties and weekend affairs, was taken over by DINA, Augusto Pinochet's special forces, to interrogate the people detained by the military during the massive round-ups.[2] So many were captured that many civilian spaces were transformed into makeshift concentration centers. Villa Grimaldi was one of the most infamous. In the late 1980s one of the generals sold it to a construction company to tear down and replace with a housing project. Survivors and human rights activists could not stop the demolition, but after much heated contestation they did secure the space as a memory site and peace park in 1995.[3] Matta, among others, has spent a great deal of time, money, and energy making sure the space remains a permanent reminder of what the Pinochet government did to its people. Three epochs, with three histories, overlap in this space that even now has multiple functions: evidentiary, commemorative, reconciliatory, and pedagogical.

The miniature extermination camp positions us as spectators. We stand above the model, looking down on its organizational structure. The main entrance to our top left allowed passage for vehicles that delivered the hooded captives to the main building. Matta's language and our imaginations populate the inert space. He points to the tiny copy of the large main building that served as the center of operations for DINA—here the military planned who they would target and how they evaluated the results of the torture sessions. The officer in charge of Villa Grimaldi and his assistants had offices here, and there was a mess hall for officers. The space housed the archives, and a shortwave radio station kept the military personnel in contact with their counterpoints throughout South America. The small buildings that run along the perimeter to the left where the prisoners were divided up, separated, and blindfolded—men here, women there. Miniature drawings made by survivors line the periphery—hooded prisoners pushed by guards with rifles for their thirty seconds at the latrines; a hall of small locked cells guarded by an armed man; a close-up drawing of the inside of one of the cells in which a half dozen shackled and hooded men are squeezed in tightly; an empty torture chamber with a bare metal bunk bed equipped with leather straps, a chair with straps for arms and feet, a table with instruments. The objects reference behaviors. We know exactly what happened there/here. Matta points to other structures on the model. It is clear that the model gives him a sense of control—he no longer needs to fully relive the image to describe it—he can externalize and point to it. The violence, in part, can be transferred to the archive, materialized in the small evidentiary mock-up. He is explicit about the criminal politics and very clear in his condemnation of the CIA's role in the Chilean crisis. He looks at me and remembers I am not *that* audience—an audience but not that audience.

Looking down at the model, I see we are standing on the site of the main building, usurping the military's place. Looking offers me the strange fantasy of seeing or grasping the "whole," the fiction that I can understand systemic criminal violence even as we position ourselves simultaneously in and above the fray. We are permitted to identify without identifying. This happened there, back then, to them, by them . . . The encounter, at this point, is about representation and explication of the facts. The model, made by survivors, stages the evidence. The mock-up or "fake" gives others at least a glimpse of the "truth" of Terranova. I take photographs, wondering how the tenuous "evidentiary" power of the photo might extend the evidentiary claim of the model camp. We know what happened at Villa Grimaldi, of course, but is there anything that Matta (or I, with my camera) can do to make visible the criminal violence? The "other" violence, the economic policies that justified and enabled the breaking of bodies, remains safely outside the frame.

We look up and around at the place itself—emptied though not empty—empty *of* something palpable in its absence. The remains of a few original structures and replicas of isolation cells and a tower dot the compound. With the camp demolished, Matta informs and points out, but he does not seem to connect personally or emotionally to what he describes. The objects have been reconstructed and placed to support the narration—this happened here. I imagine some visitors must actually try to squeeze themselves in those tiny, upright cells. They might even allow someone to close the door. Does simulation allow people to feel or experience the camp more fully than walking through it? Possibly. Rites involving sensory deprivation prepare members of communities to undertake difficult or sacred transitions by inducing different mental states. The basic idea—that people learn, experience, and come to terms with past/future behaviors by physically *doing* them, trying them on, acting them through, and acting them out—is the underlying theory of ritual, older than Aristotle's theory of mimesis and as new as theories of mirror neurons that explore how empathy and understandings of human relationality and intersubjectivity are vital for human survival.[4] But these reconstructed cells have a fun-fair quality to them for me, and I stay away. Following Matta from place to place, it becomes clear that these props don't help me relate. Rather the opposite: the less I actually see intensifies what I imagine happened here. My mind's eye—my very own staging area—internalizes the violence, fills the gaps between Matta's formal matter-of-fact rendition and the terrifying things he relates.

Matta walks us toward the original entryway—the massive iron gate now permanently sealed as if to shut out the possibility of further violence. From this vantage point it is clear that another layer has been added to the space. A wash of decorative tiles, chips of the original ceramic found at the site, form a huge arrowlike shape on the ground pointing away from the gate toward the new "peace fountain" ("symbol of life and hope," according to Matta's booklet) and a large performance pavilion. The architecture participates in the rehabilitation of the site. The cross-shaped layout moves us from criminal past to redemptive future. Matta ignores that for the moment—he is not in the peace park. This is not the time for reconciliation. His traumatic story, like his past, weighs down all possibility of future. He continues his *recorrido* through the torture camp.[5]

Matta speaks impersonally, in the third person, about the role of torture in Chile—one half million people tortured and five thousand killed out of a population of eight million. I do the math. There were far more tortures and fewer murders in Chile than Argentina. One in sixteen. He speaks about the development of torture as a tool of the state from its early experimental phase to the highly precise and tested practice it became. Pinochet chose to break rather than eliminate his "enemies"—the population of ghosts or individuals destroyed by torture, thrown back into society, would be a warning for others. Matta's tone is controlled and reserved. He is giving archival information, not personal testimony, as he outlines the daily workings of the camp, the transformation of language as words were outlawed. *Crimenes, desaparecidos,* and *dictadura* (crimes, disappeared, and dictatorship) were replaced by *excesos, presuntos,* and *gobierno militar* (excesses, presumed, military government).

As we walk, he describes what happened where, and I notice that he keeps his eyes on the ground, a habit born of peering down from under the blindfold he was forced to wear. The shift is gradual—he begins to reenact ever so subtly as he retells. I feel compelled to register the moment—I take a photograph as if I could capture the move inward, into the dark space in which we stand but cannot see. He moves deeper into the death camp—here, pointing at an empty spot: "Usually unconscious, the victim was taken off the *parrilla* (metal bed frame), and if male, dragged here."[6] Maybe the lens will grasp what I cannot grasp. Looking down, I see the colored shards of ceramic tiles and stones that now mark the places where buildings once stood and the paths where victims were pushed to the torture chambers. As we follow, we too know our way by keeping our eyes on the ground: "Sala de tortura. Celdas para mujeres detenidas."

I follow his movements but also his voice that draws me in. Gradually, his pronouns change—they tortured *them* becomes they tortured *us.* He brings us in closer. His performance animates the space and keeps it alive. His body connects me to what Pinochet wanted to disappear, not just the place but the trauma. Matta's presence performs the claim, embodies it, *le da cuerpo.* He has survived to tell. Being *in place* with him communicates a very different sense of the crimes than looking down on the model. Walking through Villa Grimaldi with Matta brings the past up close, past as actually not past. Now. Here. And in many parts of the world, as we speak. I can't think past that, rooted as I am to place suddenly restored as practice. I too am part of this scenario now; I don't need to lock myself up in the cell to be *doing.* I have accompanied him here. My "unarmed" eyes, to adopt

Walter Benjamin's phrase, look straight down, mimetically rather than reflectively, through his down-turned eyes.[7] I do not see really; I imagine. I *presenciar*; I presence (as active verb). Embodied cognition, neuroscientists call this, but we in theater have always understood it as mimesis and empathy—we learn and absorb by mirroring other people. I participate not in the events but in his transmission of the affect emanating from the events. My presencing offers me no sense of control, no fiction of understanding. He walks, he sits, he tells. When he gets to the memorial wall, marked with the names of the dead (built twenty years after the violent events), he breaks down and cries. He cries for those who died, but also for those that survived. "Torture," he says, "destroys the human being. And I am no exception. I was destroyed through torture." This is the climax of the tour. The past and the present come together in this admission. Torture works into the future; it forecloses the very possibility of future. The torture site is transitional, but torture itself is transformative—it turns societies into terrifying places and people into zombies.[8]

When Matta leaves the memorial wall his tone shifts again. He has moved out of the death space. Now he is more personal and informal in his interaction with us. We talk about how other survivors have dealt with trauma, about similarities and differences with other torture centers and concentration camps. He says he needs to come back. The walk-through reconnects him with his friends who were disappeared. Whenever he visits with a group who is interested in the subject, he feels he is doing what he wishes one of his friends had done for him had he been the one disappeared. Afterward he goes home physically and emotionally drained, he says, and drinks a liter of fruit juice and goes to sleep—he doesn't get up until the following morning. We continue to walk, past the replica of the water tower where the high-value prisoners were isolated, past the *sala de la memoria* (memory room)—one of the few remaining original buildings that served as the photo and silkscreen rooms. At the pool, also original, he shares one of the most chilling accounts told to him by a collaborator. At the memory tree he touches the names of the dead that hang from the branches like leaves. Different commemorative art pieces remind us that "El olvido esta lleno de memoria" (forgetting is full of memory). And, of course, the ever hopeful "Nunca Más." He barely notices the fountain—the Christian overlay of redemption was the government's idea, clearly.

After we leave the site, we invite Matta to lunch at a nearby restaurant he recommends. He tells us about his arrest in 1975 for being a student activist, his time as a political prisoner in Villa Grimaldi, his exile to the

U.S. in 1976, and his work as a private detective in San Francisco until he returned to Chile in 1991. He used his investigative skills to gather as much information as possible about what happened in Villa Grimaldi, to identify the prisoners who passed through, and name the torturers stationed there. One day, he says, he was having lunch in this same restaurant after one of the visits to Villa Grimaldi when an ex-torturer walked in and sat at a nearby table with his family. They were having such a good time. They looked at each other and Matta got up and walked out.

Later Soledad tells me that Matta does the visit the same way every time—stands in the same spot, recounts the same events, cries at the Memorial Wall. Some commentators find this odd, as if the routine makes the emotion suspect. Are the tears for real? Every time? Is there something fake about the performance? Is Matta a professional trauma survivor? Am I his witness? His audience? A voyeur of trauma tourism? What kind of scenario is this? Is trauma, like performance, known by the nature of its repeats: "never for the first time"? For me, what's interesting is the way that Matta's performance of trauma is itself part of a much larger evidentiary and commemorative project—one that he fully imagines will exceed and outlast him.

The Parque de la Paz, I have suggested, is a highly practiced place. The violently contested history of spatial practices continues to return and disturb the present. On the evidentiary level, Villa Grimaldi demonstrates the centrality of site in individual and collective memory. What happens to that space is tantamount to what happens to Chileans' understanding of the dictatorship: will people repress, remember, transcend, or forget? The warring mandates about the space rehearse the more salient public options: tear it down to bury the violence; build a commemorative park so that people will know what happened; let's get beyond violence by hosting cultural events in the pavilion; forget about this desolate place, forget about this sorry past. Nowhere is there talk of justice or retribution.

Matta, of course, has been instrumental in building the evidence—he has investigated and helped collect the information of what happened at Villa Grimaldi; he worked to preserve the space as a memorial site. He helped construct the model; he wrote and published the booklet. He has actively participated in creating the external material markers that designate this a "dark site." He has even prepared for a visit without him present—again, investing in the archival and historical aspects of preservation. The book maps out every move; the brutal images in the margins make visible every practice: "Here the torture began." The book, given the nature of print media, tells the same story the same way every time. It outlines the path and numbers the stops—here people were tortured with electricity. The numbers in the book—like a tour guide—align with the map. Actually, it's a double map—one layer shows the torture camp, while a semitransparent layer of onion paper outlines the Peace Park, with the pavilion, the fountain, and the numbered places of interest: "storage of confiscated goods" and "sites for hanging." A red dotted line outlines the *recorrido* exactly as Matta conducts it. This, then, is the trauma in the archive, envisioned by Matta to outlast him and transmit meaning to those who come after to visit the space. It is not an exaggeration to state that future knowledge of this site will only be available through archival practice—the annotated tour, the replicas, the memorial wall, the art pieces. Like my photos, these archival objects might well spark an affective reaction in some visitors. But it's hard for me to imagine that these objects will move someone who has not been involved in the practice, who has never been to the site, or who has no connection to what happened there. The punctum, or the trigger, has to come from someplace in the viewer. Trauma lives in the body, not in the archive.

Being in the site with Matta, however, is a powerful experience—one of a kind for me even if it's a repeat performance for him. But even the nature of the repeats is important in Matta's performance. He returns again to recount the events that took place there, to instruct, to remember those who died, and perhaps even to externalize the pain associated with place. Although different in kind, these various acts all serve to externalize the trauma—put it out there, point to it, and demand recognition. Trauma blurs the lines between inside/outside, past/present, personal/collective. The "never for the first time" of performance mirrors/enacts the "never for the first time" of trauma.[9] We speak of trauma only when the event cannot be processed and produces the characteristic aftershocks. Trauma, like performance, is always experienced in the present. Here. Now.

Memory, we know, is linked to place—one clear reason why that place needs not only to exist but to be marked. For any guide, routine serves a mnemonic function—people can remember certain events by associating them with place.[10] But for a survivor of torture, going back to the site, the *recorrido* is a memory path—through the act of walking, the body remembers. Memory always entails reenactment, even in our mind's eye. The book too is organized as a "walk." Neuroscientists suggest that these paths are physiological as well as material, fixed in the brain as a specifically patterned circuit of neurons. Being in a situation can automatically provoke certain behaviors unless other memory tracks are laid down to replace them.[11] A change in Matta's routine might well change the affect. But routine also protects against unexpected affect—survivors can often recall some aspects of their torment and not others—there are some places (literally and physiologically) where no one dares to go.

For Matta, both victim and witness, trauma is a durational performance. His experience does not last two hours—it has lasted years, since he was disappeared by the armed forces. His reiterated acts of leading people down the paths characterize trauma and the trauma-driven actions to channel and alleviate it. As for the Mothers of Plaza de Mayo, the ritualized tour offers him both personal consolation and revenge. Memory is a tool and a political project—an honoring of those who are gone and a reminder to those who will listen that the victimizers have gotten away with murder. His tour, like the Mothers' march, bears witness to what gets spectacularized—a society in which judicial systems cannot bring perpetrators to justice—and what gets invisibilized—rapacious economic systems that disappear certain populations. Yet the walk-through, like the march, also makes visible the memory paths that maintain another topography of place and practice, not of terror but of resistance—the will not only to live but also to keep memory alive.

What does Matta's performance want of me as audience or as witness? What does it mean about witnessing and the quality of *being in* place? He needs others (in this case me) to acknowledge what happened there and thus complete the task of witness. *To witness*, a transitive verb, defines both the act and the person carrying it out; the verb precedes the noun—it is through the act of witnessing that we become a witness. Identity relies on the action. We are both the subject and the product of our acts. Matta is the witness for those who are no longer alive to tell; he is the witness to himself as he tells of his own ordeal; he is a witness in the juridical sense—having brought charges against the Pinochet dictatorship. He is also the object of my witnessing—he needs me to acknowledge what he and others went through in Villa Grimaldi. The transitivity of "witness" ties us together—that's one reason he's keen to gauge the nature of his audience.

Torture, of course, produces the opposite of witnessing—it breaks personal and social bonds and guts all sense of community and responsibility. Torture isolates and paralyzes both victims and bystanders who are tempted to look away. Percepticide I've called this elsewhere. This is why they continue to practice torture even though they know that they receive no "actionable" information. It's inaction they seek. My job, as I understand it, is to keep those memory paths fresh and do something— acknowledge the violence generated by our governments or write about the place or donate money or bring other people. Trauma-driven activism (like trauma itself) cannot simply be told or known; it needs to be enacted, repeated, and externalized through embodied practice.

I can understand what Matta is doing here better than I can understand what I am doing here. I wonder about aura and worry about voyeurism and (dark) tourism. Is Matta my close-up—bringing unspeakable violence up as close as possible? If so, to what end? This too is multilayered in the ways that the personal, interpersonal, social, and political come together. Walking through Villa Grimaldi with Matta, the oversize issues of human rights violations and crimes against humanity—too large and general on one level—take on an immediate and embodied form. In our everyday lives we have no way of dealing with violent acts that shatter the limits of our understanding. We all live in proximity to criminal violence—and, though some have felt it more personally than others, this violence is never just personal. If we focus only on the trauma we risk evacuating the politics. Standing there, together, bringing the buildings and routines back to life, we bear witness not just to the personal loss, but to a system of power relations, hierarchies, and values that not only allowed but required the destruction of others.

The questions posed by these dark sites extend far beyond the fences built around them. The small model near the entrance is to Villa Grimaldi what Villa Grimaldi is to Chile and what Chile is to the rest of the Americas: a miniature rendition of a much larger project. There were eight hundred torture centers in Chile under Pinochet. If so many civic and public places like villas and gyms and department stores and schools were used for criminal violence, how do we know that the whole city did not function as a clandestine torture center? The scale of the violations is stunning. The ubiquity of the practice spills over and contaminates social life. The guided tour through Villa Grimaldi gives us a condensed experience within the compound walls. But here, within the camp, we know that the violence only appears isolated and bracketed from everything that surrounds it, accentuating the knowledge that criminal violence has spread so uncontrollably that no walls can contain it and no guide can explain it. We might control a site and put a fence around it, but the city, the country, the southern cone, the hemisphere has been networked for violence—and beyond, too, of course, and not just because the U.S. openly outsourced torture. Is the dark site sickening because it situates us physically in such proximity to atrocity made visible and externalized in this small place? Or because, by participating, we internalize the violence? And how can we not participate when we recognize that the ubiquitous practice of torture situates all of us in constant proximity to criminal politics? As I follow Matta deeper down the paths, his experience resonates with me in part because I actually do always know what happened here/there and accept that this, like many other sites, is my responsibility. I do participate in a political project that depends on making certain populations disappear. I am constantly warned to keep vigil, to "say something" if I "see something." Though I shirked responsibility when I first met Matta—the Mexican government had nothing to do with the Chilean coup—there is another layer. After years of my own self-blinding, I realize that the Mexican government under then President Luis Echeverria disappeared thousands of young people about the same age as I was then. Now that I live and work in the U.S., I know my tax dollars pay for Gitmo. For me, the emotional charge of the visit comes from the friction of place and practice—inseparable, though at times disavowed. Something has been restored through the tour that brings several of my worlds into direct contact. As the multitiered space itself invites, I recognize the layers and layers of political and corporeal practices that have created these places, the histories I bring to them, the transparent and flimsy dividers that differentiate them, and the emotions that get triggered as we walk through them in our own ways. I experience the tour as performance, and as trauma, and I know it's never for the first, or last, time.

Matta, the booklet tells us, "feels a strong desire to transform history into memory." He makes the past alive through the performance of his recorrido. Yet trauma keeps the past alive in Matta as well—the future is not an option for him as long as Terranova grips him in that place. The "future" in fact might be a very different project. In the best of all possible worlds, the future would mean turning this memory into history, the testimonial walk-through into archival evidence, Matta's personal admonition into legally binding indictments against perpetrators, and visitors into witnesses, human rights activists, and voters. Someone else, maybe someone who has never been tortured, would lead the tour, with or without Matta's guide. But that future is predicated on a past in which trauma has been transcended or resolved. That future is nowhere in sight, even though the arrow points us toward the fountain symbolizing "life and hope." The tour does not offer us the end of trauma or the end of performance. Looking downward, we follow Matta as he negotiates this transitional space between remembrance and future project.

Notes

1. The research that came out of that project was published (in part) in *Disappearing Acts: Spectacles of Gender and Nationalism in Argentina's Dirty War* (Durham: Duke University Press, 1997).

2. DINA stands for Dirección Nacional de Inteligencia (National Intelligence Directorate).

3. Teresa Meade, in "Holding the Junta Accountable: Chile's 'Sitios de Memoria' and the History of Torture, Disappearance, and Death," writes that Villa Grimaldi was the "only 'memorial' of torture in Latin America" when it was built in 1995. Now "Parque de la Memoria" and ESMA in Buenos Aires also function as memorials. *Radical History Review*, 79 (2001): 123–139, http://muse.jhu.edu/journals/radical_history_review/v079/79.1meade.html (accessed October 24, 2008).

4. See Vittorio Gallese, "The "Shared Manifold" Hypothesis: From Mirror Neurons to Empathy." *Journal of Consciousness Studies*, 8, no. 5–7 (2001): 33–50, http://www.imprint-academic.com/jcs.

5. See Michael J. Lazzara, *Chile in Transition: The Poetics and Politics of Memory* (Gainesville: University Press of Florida, 2006), for an excellent analysis of Pedro Matta's tour and Villa Grimaldi.

6. Pedro Alejandro Matta, Villa Grimaldi, *Santiago de Chile: A Visitor's Guide* (Self-published), 13.

7. Walter Benjamin, "The Work of Art in the Age of Mechanical Reproduction," *Illuminations: Essays and Reflections* (New York: Schocken, 1969), 223.

8. Marcial Godoy-Anativia, "The Body as Sanctuary Space: Towards a Somatic Topography of Torture" (unpublished manuscript, 1997).

9. Diana Taylor, "Trauma Driven Performance," 21, no. 5 (2006): 1674–1677.

10. See Thomas A. Abercrombie, *Pathways of Memory and Power: Ethnography and History Among an Andean People* (Madison: University of Wisconsin Press, 1998).

11. See Vittorio Gallese, "Intentional Attunement. The Mirror Neuron System and Its Role in Interpersonal Relations," http://www.unipr.it/arpa/mirror/pubs/pdffiles/Gallese/Gallese-Eagle-Migone%202007.pdf (accessed October 25, 2008).

19   Pilgrimages, Reenactment,
      and Souvenirs

Modes of Memory Tourism

MARITA STURKEN

In 1995 Binjamin Wilkomirski published a much lauded Holocaust memoir entitled *Fragments* that told the story of his childhood experience in several concentration camps.[1] Poetic and compelling, the book
was quickly translated into many languages and praised by critics for ex-
emplifying both "a child's state of grace" and an experience of the Holocaust "free from literary artifice of any kind at all."[2] Wilkomirski's prose
allowed readers, many of them scholars of Holocaust literature, to feel
they were reading an unmediated account of the Holocaust.

For a few years Wilkomirski became the focus of enormous attention
in the world of publishing and Holocaust studies, receiving numerous
awards and connecting with survivor groups. Then, in 1998, Swiss journalist Daniel Ganzfried accused Wilkomirski of being a fraud, declaring
that he was a Swiss orphan named Bruno Doessekker who had spent the
war in the safety of an orphanage, and later with his adoptive parents.[3]
Ganzfried claimed, and a subsequent report by the publisher concluded,
that the only time Wilkomirski had been to Auschwitz was as a tourist.

It remains unclear whether Bruno Doessekker was calculating or simply delusional, yet the Wilkomirski case received significant attention
because it raised difficult questions about authenticity, memory, origins,
return, and tourism. If Wilkomirski was a tourist, rather than a survivor,

of the Holocaust, then technically one could not call his visit to Auschwitz one of "return." Yet the contemporary landscape of experience tells us that experiences facilitated by media forms often create intensely emotional and personal memories. In a historic moment when authenticity appears always out of reach, memory, *whosever you choose*, appears to provide one of the few sources of comfort available. The Wilkomirski affair thus points to the potentially complex relationship of memory tourism to the status of the "return." What kind of an experience of return is the tourist visit to a site like Auschwitz? What does it mean to be a tourist of memory and to what degree are we all, like Wilkomirski, simply tourists of memory?

In this essay I consider memory tourism as a rite of mediated return through which tourists, some of whom may also be survivors, create an experience of memory. I see memory tourism as falling into several potential overlapping modes including the modes of the pilgrimage, in which the journey undertaken to a site is particularly meaningful; reenactment, in which architectural designs, memorials, and museum displays deploy reenactment strategies to evoke memories; pedagogy, in which sites aim to educate; souvenir consumerism; and kitsch, both in terms of souvenirs and narrative sentiment.

The practices of tourism can allow for a range of intersecting activities at sites of memory. One can, for instance, feel empathy and engage in mourning for others while simultaneously being a tourist at a site of trauma. One might leave a talisman while also purchasing a souvenir. Certain modes of memory tourism may provide visitors with the sense that they have experienced a "return" or allow them to feel they are close to an event. Or, tourist practices may position tourists to feel distance and irony from the memories on display. It is in this shifting terrain of proximity and distance that tourist practices can be charted.

Yet each of these practices raises crucial questions about the politics of the experience of memory. Do we engage with traumatic pasts at sites of memory tourism with empathy and compassion or, as in the Wilkomirski story, with trauma envy? Memory tourism can succeed in opening up a space for necessary and valuable engagement with sites of trauma. Simply put, there are reasons, pedagogical as well as compassionate, to visit Auschwitz. Yet there are also potentially politically disabling aspects of memory tourism that demand our scrutiny, precisely because of the ways in which they can offer a simplified and packaged sense of proximity to and connection with complex and violent histories. How the practices of memory tourism can produce for us a sense of "return" to sites we have not previously experienced is a key factor in the different modes of memory tourism, including the pilgrimage, reenactment, pedagogy, and kitsch consumerism.

The Tourist

The subjectivity of the tourist offers a primary metaphor of our times in terms of the mechanisms we can deploy to screen out or deny the political ramifications of our personal actions. The tourist is a figure who embodies a detached and seemingly innocent pose. As tourists we *visit* sites where we do not live, we are outsiders to the daily practices of life in tourist destinations, and we are largely unaware of the effects of how tourist economies have structured the everyday lives of the people who live and work in tourist locales. As tourists we typically remain distant in the sites we visit, engaging in practices, such as picture taking and souvenir purchasing, that allow us to define ourselves as innocent outsiders, mere observers whose actions we believe have no effect on what we see.[4]

Tourism is a key practice in the experience of modernity, and, as Dean MacCannell argues in his classic study, *The Tourist*, the tourist is a primary subject position available to modern citizens.[5] It is an essential trait of modernity that indigenous groups who have been devastated by modern colonialism have often become the primary objects of modern tourism. Thus visitors to New Mexico flock to purchase Native American crafts without having to engage with the realities of Indian reservations and their poverty, and tourists at sites in Central America such as Guatemala can purchase native crafts at upscale boutiques in ways that obscure the ongoing brutalization of native populations there. In tourist destinations like Hawaii, native rituals are staged for tourists in modes that obscure the ways that tourism is a primary economic factor in the disempowerment of native Hawaiians—it is for this reason that the economic dependencies of tourism have been targeted by indigenous activists and sovereignty movements like those in Hawaii.

The subjectivity of the tourist is thus infinitely tied up with concepts of authenticity and inauthenticity. Tourists visit places that are understood to be authentic in part because they see their own world as an inauthentic, modern one; at the same time, the activity of tourism is usually regarded as an inauthentic activity, one that often must be apologized for. MacCannell writes that most critics of tourism condemn tourists not because they leave home to travel elsewhere but "for being satisfied with superficial experiences of other peoples and other places."[6] There are many different modes of tourism today, and the actual practices of particular tourists can vary a great deal from the modern definition of a tourist. Contemporary tourism, in particular high-end tourism, is filled with tourist experiences that aim to move beyond superficial tourism, such as exotic tourism, ecotourism, extremist tourism, war tourism, "tragic tourism," or the "dark tourism" of visiting places of death and destruction, such as former concentration camps and war sites.[7] Thus many forms of contemporary tourism, including some forms of memory tourism, are guided by self-consciousness about the superficialities of everyday tourism and attempts to travel in ways that take the problematic role of the tourist in account.

Tourism at sites of collective trauma is often about seeking authenticity. By visiting these sites of trauma as tourists we can come to feel we have experienced a connection to traumatic events and to have gained a trace of authenticity by extension. A site like ground zero in lower Manhattan, for instance, embodies competing and powerful meanings of authenticity—the authenticity of a site of violence, a place that contains the remnants of a much photographed building, a place where the dead were not found, a place where iconic images of spectacle took place—just as the ruins and remnants of Auschwitz carry force as physical reminders of its industrialized genocide. Such sites constitute a draw for tourists through the sense that the places themselves embody deep meaning where the traces of these events can be experienced and felt. The specificity of these sites as charged with meaning is often taken as a given—we believe them to be places where the dead can be spoken to, where the dead potentially reside in their absence, and this has, in turn, created complex relationships with those who feel closest to the dead. Yet they are also inevitably contested sites. While many sites of trauma—former concentration or internment camps, sites of massacres—by design exist in remote places, the designation of sites of violence in urban centers as sacred has often been in conflict with other economic and political interests in such places. For example, at ground zero in New York, the new economy of tourism is in conflict with the economic interests of real estate and business for whom the site has significant financial value; the practices of memory tourism that depend on a sense of sacredness at the site are in ongoing conflict with its meaning as a neighborhood and workplace.

Tourism is guided by practices of media. As tourists, we take photographs and videos in order to produce image artifacts of tourist destina-

tions; indeed, picture taking is one of the most universal and central activities of tourism (now fueling online sharable photo albums through
sites like Flickr). Tourism is defined by the activity of taking things away
from the places we have visited, not only photographs but also commodities such as curios, souvenirs, and artifacts. In addition, visitors to sites of
memory often bring objects to leave at collective shrines. These factors—
the search for authenticity, the role of images and media, the practices of
consumerism, and the distanced proximity of the tourist—are key factors
in the ways that tourism can produce a position of innocence.

Yet memory tourism can also provide an experience of return—a return to memories that one might or might not have, yet a return nevertheless. The experience of memory tourism can be a return to a place
that we experienced only previously through photographs and television
images, yet one that we feel we "know" in a certain sense. Through this
sense of return, and its attendant production of memories in retrospect,
memory tourism can be seen as potentially enabling us, like Wilkomirski,
to experience vicarious relationships of "trauma envy." The kitschification of memory can allow not only for a detached sense of innocence but
also for an ironic engagement with history. But it is also the case that
memory tourism can provide a space for people to mourn strangers and
to reflect on the effects of violence. This shifting terrain of modes of proximity—from a sense of empathetic engagement to the prescribed closeness offered by kitsch—and remove from the disengagement of modes of
tourism to distanced forms of irony that allow for critical modes underlie
this experience of mediated return.

The Tourist Pilgrimage

The pilgrimage has been a primary mode of memory tourism.
In its traditional meaning of a religious journey to a sacred site, the term
pilgrimage implies a kind of personal transformation. And it can be said
that people make pilgrimages to sites of tragedy not simply to pay tribute
to the dead but also to feel transformed in some way in relation to those
places. In sites of memory tourism, the practices of sorrowful pilgrimage
and tourism are intermixed and often inseparable.

Such pilgrimages often take place in sites that are nationalized and
thus incorporate aspects of citizenship practices in relation to symbols

of national identity. Lauren Berlant has written about the "pilgrimage" to Washington, D.C. as a mode of infantile citizenship; she writes, "when Americans make the pilgrimage to Washington they are trying to grasp the nation in its totality."[8] The texture of that pilgrimage, as the National Mall in Washington has become lined, over the past twenty-five years, with memorials, is increasingly one of national memory and discourses of national trauma.

At the Vietnam Veterans Memorial, for example, tourists often participate in a set of rituals that evoke the fact that they journeyed there and make connection to the meaningful experiences of "return" that veterans and families of the war dead have when they visit the names listed there. The practices of visitors to the memorial are shaped in many ways by its aesthetics, which encourage the leaving of artifacts and notes at the wall, and the contact of visitors with the names of the dead that are engraved in black granite. The pilgrimage to the Vietnam Veterans Memorial has been understood within a therapeutic culture of healing in which the experience of veterans and the families of the dead has been transferred to all visitors, and this allows all visits to the memorial to be seen potentially as the coming to terms with difficult memories, of a return to and engagement with those memories, by all visitors. The Vietnam Veterans Memorial's capacity to create a space for many different kinds of engagements with the past remains powerful. Its continued relevance as a site on the Mall, one that demands a more complex interaction with the past than the national monuments it sits among, demonstrates that, as a site of pilgrimage, it continues to convey a sense of loss that remains cautionary and unresolved.

Like religious pilgrimages, which display religious devotion through the arduousness of the journey, memory pilgrimages are often about signaling the effort of the journey to a site of memory. Thus, people pay tribute to the dead and to shared loss through the efforts they expend in journeying to these sites. At the Oklahoma City National Memorial, for instance, visitors leave license plates and key rings with the names of distant places on them. They are simple offerings, cheap tourist items made in China and discarded license plates, brought from other places to be left at the fence that serves as a public repository on the edge of the memorial. The offerings seem intended to honor the dead by displaying the length of the journeys that these tourist-visitors took to come to them—*we came here a long distance, we did that for you,* they seem to say. In the case of the

Oklahoma City memorial, the journey is given more meaning because the memorial is one of very few sites of tourism in Oklahoma City or, for that matter, in that part of the country. The pilgrimage codes tourist activity as one in which the journey makes as much meaning as the rituals of the visit itself precisely because of the time it took to make, the labor it involved, and the empathy this labor displays.

The Tourism of Reenactment

Reenactment is a primary mode of memory tourism that can take many different forms, each of which provides a mediated experience of some kind. Docudramas and memory narratives are primary forms of reenactment, and the reenactment culture of historical events, such as Civil War and Vietnam War reenactments, offer means through which people believe themselves to have had experience of particular historical events. Tourist reenactment can also take the form of historical performance; so, for instance, in Colonial Williamsburg, tourists encounter people who are performing identities from the past, in dress, speech, and mannerisms, so as to allow tourists to "experience the life" of colonial times—even the life of slaves. Such forms of historical reenactment follow from a set of codes that provide an experience for visitors of simultaneously "being there" and being in the past.

Forms of reenactment at sites of memory often follow this strategy of creating a sense of being there in the moment of trauma. For instance, the Memorial Center of the Oklahoma City National Memorial, which tells the story of the bombing and its aftermath, begins by placing visitors in an experiential relationship to the event. Relatively soon in the exhibit, groups of up to twenty-five visitors are asked to enter a room that is set up to replicate the hearing room at the Water Resources Building, which once stood across the street from the Murrah Building, where they listen to a recording of the hearing that began exactly at 9:00 AM on April 19, which is the only recording of any kind of the bomb blast itself. At the sound of the bomb going off and people screaming, the lights go out and a wall lights up with photographs of the 168 bombing victims. This reenactment intends in many ways to produce a cathartic and traumatic response in museum visitors; it aims to jolt visitors out of their experience as distanced viewers and into an experience of trauma. Thus the reenactment experience of the bomb is an attempt to place visitors in the subject position of the unexpecting, one could say innocent, public for whom it was, on April 19, 1995, a shocking event, disrupting "a day like any other." Yet it inevitably comes close to a theme park experience of reenactment that allows visitors to feel this mediated experience brings them closer to an authentic encounter with trauma.

Reenactments are intended not simply to provide representations of the past for tourists, but to actually create experiences for them. In this sense reenactment can constitute a kind of mediated return, one that intends to create a sense of proximity to an event, a sense of being there. Reenactments give us memories by design. While many museum reenactments, like the example of the Oklahoma City museum, use media forms to produce a literal experience, reenactments can also take place in the form of generating an "effect" of a past event. Here I am indebted to Ernst van Alphen's concept of the "Holocaust-effect," by which he means the intended impact of artistic engagements with the Holocaust that, rather than producing representations of the Holocaust, aim to produce "effects"—the experience of certain aspects of the Holocaust by "reenacting principles that are defining aspects of the Holocaust." He writes, "In such moments the Holocaust is not re-presented, but rather presented or reenacted. . . . Our access to this past is no longer mediated by the account of a witness or narrator, or by the eye of the photographer. We will not respond to a re-presentation of the historical event, but to a presentation or performance of it. Our response, therefore, will be direct or first-hand in a different way."[9] One of van Alphen's key examples is the work of Christian Boltanski, who takes images of children who might or might not have died in the Holocaust and reworks them with a set of objects that are not from but can evoke the Holocaust, such as archive boxes, to present an "effect" of the Holocaust.

One of the most compelling sites for this particular mode, which I would characterize as a kind of reenactment effect, is the Holocaust memorial (the Memorial to the Murdered Jews of Europe) in central Berlin that was designed by Peter Eisenman (initially in collaboration with Richard Serra, whose lasting influence on the design is evident). The memorial is comprised of a vast field of pillars or concrete slabs in the center of Berlin that change in height and create different kinds of walkways between them. One of the achievements of the Holocaust memorial is precisely the way in which it does not demand of visitors a particular, proscribed emotional response. Walking between the pillars of the memorial, visitors are not encouraged to imagine the events of the Holocaust.

Rather, visitors can feel the shifting terrain, as the pillars change in height and one goes from light to cavernous spaces to undulating stones. If we see others walk into the field of pillars, their heads disappear within it—we know they are there, but they are lost to us. The experience of walking through the memorial evokes an experience of the tenuousness of history, the inescapability of different paths. As one gets deeper into the chasms and loses the city behind, one catches glimpses of others moving through, fleeting and then gone, never to be seen again. Thus, in walking through the memorial, visitors can experience the arbitrariness of life, its tenuousness. The experience of the memorial constitutes a sense of reenactment and return, through which one can, in some way, access the experience of the past. Yet there is nothing in this experience that touches the realm of trauma envy. It is, rather, an experience that demands reflection and a distance that doesn't allow any simple sense of identification. I would not characterize this Holocaust memorial as an empathetic work, creating an experience of closeness, rather, it provides an experience, however abstract, of the ungraspability of being there.

Pedagogy

The Berlin Memorial has an information center, discreetly situated underground beneath its forms, which has a tastefully rendered exhibition about the Holocaust and those who died in it. This raises the question of the relationship of memory tourism to pedagogy. The tourism of memory is to a certain extent about seeking knowledge about history and sites of memory, and the mode of pedagogy intersects with these other modes of reenactment, effect, and consumerism. Eisenman was, not surprisingly, opposed to the inclusion of the information center, since its intent could be seen in opposition to the open-ended effect of the memorial itself. And such an addition has been increasingly the case with memorials that deploy modernist and/or abstract codes to create sites of contemplation, reflection, and effect. So, for instance, the museum at ground zero has become a central focus of the site, one that will likely overshadow the memorial that names the dead. If the funding comes through, the Vietnam Veterans Memorial, which has stood for twenty-eight years on the Washington Mall, will soon be accompanied by an interpretive center that will tell the history of the war and the stories of those Americans who died in the war. Over time, the memorial's simple evocation of loss does not seem to be enough, and the explication of history, even one as fraught as this one, is demanded.[10]

The increased proliferation of explanatory, educational, and informational centers at memorials reflects a broader anxiety about the limitations of memorials (and their effect) as forms of pedagogy, in particular memorials that deploy modern design to provide spaces of contemplation that highlight mourning over historical narrative. It is the case that most memorials are essentially ineffective as forms of political pedagogy. They pay tribute to the dead, but they cannot speak in more than very simple terms to the complexity of history. The Memorial Center of the Oklahoma City National Memorial is emblematic of this tension between memorialization and pedagogy. While the spare design of the memorial, with its field of chairs, allows for a range of responses, the accompanying memorial center and its gift shop combine to reduce the story of bombing to a set of simple narratives about citizenship, heroism, and ordinary people responding to a crisis. The exhibition simply cannot engage in credible ways with the "why" of the bombing. As Erika Doss writes, "Focused on the 'comfort' of survivors and on cultural tourism, the Oklahoma City National Memorial represents a lost opportunity to engage in critically and historically informed public conversations about dissent, violence, authority, loss and grief in America."[11] At sites such as this, the emphasis on sentiment, in the form of comfort, overanalysis, is only heightened by the role of consumerism.

Kitsch Consumerism

The experiences of memory tourism, however they may partake of pilgrimages, reenactment, pedagogy, and effect, are inevitably caught up with the practices of consumerism. The experience of return constructed by memory tourism is thus often conducted through memory objects and souvenirs (many of them kitsch) that are seen as embodying the emotions of a particular site. Thus over the past few decades a particular kind of kitsch consumerism and a kitschification of history have emerged that reveal the tension of proximity and distance in the modes of memory tourism.

In the United States memory kitsch has reached new heights in relationship to national trauma. For instance, in Oklahoma City, the gift shop that sells various kinds of kitsch objects, such as Oklahoma City National

Memorial teddy bears, snow globes of the memorial, post-it pads, T-shirts, and running shorts with the memorial logo, refrigerator magnets, and memorial-branded bottled water. A vast array of memory kitsch has been produced in the wake of 9/11, compared by one commentator to the experience of a "Graceland giftshop," from souvenirs sold at ground zero to innumerable memorials around the nation that deploy prepackaged codes of redemption and innocence.[12] These forms of kitsch operate not only to produce a set of prescribed and contained emotions (from redemption to revenge) but also to provide simplistic notions of comfort that facilitate political acquiescence. Such memory kitsch addresses consumers within a particular and limited emotional realm (including sympathy, sadness, comfort, and the reassurance of cuteness).

Yet memory kitsch can take many different forms and registers, not only in a position of innocence but also as ironic pastiche and bemused recoding of historical icons and objects, thus moving from faux proximity to engaged distance. This has been the case, in particular, with memory tourism that has emerged in relation to the history of communism in both China and Eastern Europe. This kind of kitschification of history raises numerous questions about how kitsch forms and experiences can reshape historical understanding. For instance, the Cultural Revolution has become fodder for a thriving tourist trade in Beijing. Street vendors sell cheap knockoffs of Cultural Revolution objects (bags, hats, flags, etc.), and Mao figurines and paintings proliferate. In Beijing, one can now visit the Red Capital Club Restaurant and stay at the Red Capital Residence, both of which are decked out with Mao kitsch mementos, and Cultural Revolution figurines. One can also go for a tour in the Red Capital limo, one of a few limos used by Chinese officials in the 1970s, where one can snack on caviar and drink champagne while being shown through the capital by a guide dressed in the Red Detachment of Women gear with copies of Mao's Little Red Book on display.[13] Mao memorabilia has also become valued collectibles, with Mao plates, posters, and figurines selling for hefty prices at Sotheby's.

This kind of kitsch repackaging of memories makes them more palatable, though such transformations inevitably render memory in simplistic modes that efface trauma—in this case, the reduction of the terror of the Cultural Revolution, in which millions died, to a cute and laughable figure of Mao. The border between kitsch as ironic engagement and kitsch as trivialization is a key issue raised by this kind of memory tourism. On one hand, the kitschification process can produce engagements that are as cheap as its trinkets; on the other, it can be seen as a device for making history less distant and less sure, a playing with the past that can help open it up to rethinking.

This tension is particularly evident in many parts of Eastern Europe, where an ironic engagement with memories of communism has emerged as a mode of tourism that both engages in nostalgia and simultaneously deploys irony as its primary mode. As one tourist site notes, "Travelers seem to be interested by the Socialist Realist statues, Communist tours and re-enactments. . . . There is a dark paradox in the often nostalgic use of sometimes repressive and brutal regimes to provide kitsch attractions."[14] Grutas Park in Lithuania features discarded statues of communist heroes. Tourists to Krakow and its Nowa Huta district can go on a communist tour in a Trabant, the Soviet Union's classic car model, and witness what, according to the tour guides, life under communism was like.[15]

A central site for cold war kitsch is the former Checkpoint Charlie in Berlin, where a museum that once stood next to the Berlin Wall has been transformed into a site of kitsch artifacts and tourist reenactment. There one can buy key chains and chocolate bars with replicas of the former East Berlin signs reading, "You Are Entering the American Sector"—signs that are now a mere reminder of a time when the city was divided into zones— as well as Russian soldier paraphernalia, Stalin mugs, and other such curios. Tourists can pose with a Soviet "border guard" and an American GI, both collecting fees as photo props at a former guard station. On one hand, this activity produces a kind of ironic humor, a recoding of historical codes and a playing with history through pastiche. Yet there is simply no doubt this kind of playful engagement makes it hard to remember the brutality and violence, the suffering, of this history. Buying Soviet curios and kitchen towels at the gift shop, it is difficult to remember that people lost their lives trying to cross at this site.

What is the status of the memory that we consume at sites like Checkpoint Charlie, and what does it do to people's engagement with history when brutal dictators such as Mao, Stalin, and others are so easily repackaged as amusing curios? To what extent do these practices of memory tourism participate in the kind of experiences (reenactments, effects, secondary experience, mediated experiences) that brought Wilkomirski to invent the actual subjectivity of memory (and return) for himself? In other words, what distinctions could we make, if any, between Wilkomirski and the memory tourist? The facility of playing with these codes of memory at the sites is certainly key to the anxiety that has led to the demand for pedagogy at such sites.

Memories migrate, circulate, and change modalities in ways that can often feel painful and trivializing of past traumas. The "return" that is constructed by these experiences makes clear the complex interrelationship of media and memory experiences—we often feel that we can "return" to pasts that are not our own because we have experienced their effect through modes of reenactment, memorials, and images. These modes of pilgrimage, reenactment, pedagogy, and consumerism provide a range of experiences that allow a sense of proximity and of distance, from potentially faux kinds of closeness to a deep sense of implication and engagement, from the distance position of tourist innocence to the potentially enabling distance of irony. The experience of the return is invariably mediated, layered, and available to many. This requires a critical vigilance, as it allows for histories to be commodified, trivialized, and rescripted. Yet, it is important to note, finally, that sites of memory tourism are places where visitors are asked to situate themselves in relation to historical events of violence, to learn those histories, and, in effect, to mourn for strangers. It is this gesture, embodied in the pilgrimage, that has the potential to show the power of mediation in opening up a space of compassion for others. Sites of memory tourism are inevitably contradictory places where we might mourn while purchasing souvenirs, where violent and brutal histories are rendered as kitsch. Yet if these sites can succeed, even marginally, in allowing us to mourn for strangers, then they demonstrate the potential of a politics of memory.

Notes

1. Binjamin Wilkomirski, *Fragments: Memories of a Wartime Childhood*, trans. Carol Brown Janeway (New York: Schocken, 1995). Two articles published in 1999 were crucial in telling this story to English-speaking audiences: Elena Lappin, "The Man with Two Heads," *Granta* 66 (1999): 9–65; and Philip Gourevitch, "The Memory Thief," *New Yorker*, June 14, 1999, 48–68.

2. First quote is from Julie Salomon, in the *New York Times Book Review*, from the cover of *Fragments*, and the second quote is from Jonathan Kozol, on the back cover.

3. An investigation by Suhrkamp, the German publisher of the book, reached a similar conclusion a year later. The book is now published in the U.S. by Schocken

Books as *The Wilkomirski Affair* with the Suhrkamp report by Swiss historian Stefan Maechler that analyzes its falsity. Stefan Maechler, *The Wilkomirski Affair: A Study in Biographical Truth*, trans. John E. Woods (New York: Schocken, 2001). The book includes the original text of *Fragments* that was translated by Carol Brown Janeway.

4. I have written about this as a particular aspect of American culture in *Tourists of History: Memory, Kitsch and Consumerism from Oklahoma City to Ground Zero* (Durham: Duke University Press, 2007).

5. Dean MacCannell, *The Tourist: A New Theory of the Leisure Class* (Berkeley: University of California Press, 1999 [1976]), 1, 8.

6. Ibid., 10.

7. See John Lennon and Malcolm Foley, *Dark Tourism: The Attraction of Death and Disaster* (New York: Continuum, 2000); and Lucy R. Lippard, "The Fall," in Joan Ockman and Salomon Frausto, eds., *Architourism: Authentic Escapist Exotic Spectacular* (New York: Prestel, 2005), 72.

8. Lauren Berlant, "The Theory of Infantile Citizenship," in *The Queen of America Goes to Washington City: Essays on Sex and Citizenship* (Durham: Duke University Press, 1997), 25.

9. Ernst van Alphen, *Caught by History: Holocaust Effects in Contemporary Art, Literature, and Theory* (Stanford: Stanford University Press, 1997).

10. It's worth noting that Jan Scruggs, the veteran who spearheaded the building of the original memorial, has been a key figure in promoting the education center.

11. Erika Doss, "Death, Art and Memory in the Public Sphere: The Visual and Material Culture of Grief in America," *Mortality* 7, no. 1 (2002): 80.

12. Heather Havrilesky, "The Selling of 9/11," Salon.com, September 7, 2002, http://archive.salon.com/mwt/feature/2002/09/07/purchase_power/index.html.

13. Ron Gluckman, "Driving Mrs. Mao's Car," http://www.gluckman.com/RedCapital.html.

14. John Guzdek, "Communism and Kitsch in Central Europe," *BootsnAllTravel*, January 27, 1999, http://www.bootsnall.com/articles/09−01/communism-and-kitsch-central-europe-krakow-budapest-bratislava-berlin-europe.html.

15. It's worth noting that there has been for some time an extensive tourist industry about former Jewish life in Poland, not simply the Holocaust tourism of visits to Auschwitz and the Schindler's List tour but also tourism to the former Jewish ghetto and kosher restaurants where tourists are encouraged to dress up as Orthodox Jews.

Contributors

NADIA ABU EL-HAJ teaches in the Anthropology Department at Barnard College. Previously, she held a fellowship at the Institute for Advanced Study at Princeton. She is the author of *Facts on the Ground: Archaeological Practice and Territorial Self-Fashioning in Israeli Society* (2002).

ELAZAR BARKAN, Professor of International and Public Affairs at Columbia University, is the codirector of the Human Rights Concentration at SIPA and is founding director of the Institute for Historical Justice and Reconciliation at the Salzburg Seminar. His recent books include *The Guilt of Nations: Restitution and Negotiating Historical Injustices* (2000); *Claiming the Stones/Naming the Bones: Cultural Property and the Negotiation of National and Ethnic Identity* (2003), an edited volume with Ronald Bush; *Taking Wrongs Seriously: Apologies and Reconciliation* (2006), an edited volume with Alexander Karn, and

SVETLANA BOYM is the Curt Hugo Reisinger Professor of Slavic and Comparative Literatures and an associate of the Harvard Graduate School of Design. She is also a writer and a media artist. Her books include *The Future of Nostalgia* (2001), *Architecture of the Off-Modern* (2008), and the novel *Ninochka* (2003). Her book *Another Freedom* (2010) examines cross-cultural conceptions of freedom and the relationship between art and politics.

KEITH CALHOUN and CHANDRA MCCORMICK are both native New Orleanians. A husband and wife team, they have been documenting Louisiana and its people for more than twenty-five years. Their photographs have been shown in major museums, including the Brooklyn Museum, the New Orleans Museum of Art, the Philbrook Museum in Tulsa, OK, and the Smithsonian Institute in Washington, DC. They recently created the L9 Center for the Arts, a gallery space and community center with a residency space for artists.

SAIDIYA HARTMAN is the author of *Scenes of Subjection: Terror, Slavery, and Self-Making in Nineteenth-Century America* (1997) and *Lose Your Mother: A Journey Along the Atlantic Slave Route* (2007). She has published essays on photography, film, and feminism and is currently working on a new project on photography and history. She teaches at Columbia University.

AMIRA HASS is a graduate of the Hebrew University. Since 1989 she has worked on the staff of *Haaretz*, first as copy editor, and, since 1993, as a reporter on Israeli Occupation and Palestinian life. She lived in Gaza from 1993 through 1997, and since then in Ramallah. Her books in English are *Drinking the Sea at Gaza* (2000) and *Reporting from Ramalla* (2003).

JARROD HAYES is associate professor of French and Francophone studies at the University of Michigan. His research focuses on the intersection between queer theory and French postcolonial studies. He is the author of *Queer Nations: Marginal Sexualities in the Maghreb* (2000). His current book project is entitled "Queer Roots for the Diaspora: Ghosts in the Family Tree."

MARIANNE HIRSCH teaches English and Comparative Literature and Gender Studies at Columbia University. Her most recent books are *Family Frames: Photography, Narrative, and Postmemory* (1997); *The Familial Gaze* (1999, ed.); *Teaching the Representation of the Holocaust* (2005, coed.); and *Ghosts of Home: The Afterlife of Czernowitz in Jewish Memory* (2010), coauthored with Leo Spitzer.

EVA HOFFMAN is the author of seven books, including *Lost in Translation* (1990), *Exit Into History* (1994), *Shtetl* (1999), *The Secret* (2002), *After Such Knowledge* (2004), and *Time* (2009). She has lectured internationally on issues of exile, memory, Polish-Jewish history, politics, and culture and has taught literature and creative writing at various universities. Her latest novel, *Appassionata*, appeared in 2011.

MARGARET HOMANS is professor of english and of women's, gender, and sexuality studies at Yale University. She has published widely on nineteenth-century British and U.S. literature and on feminist theory. She is completing a book, "Adoption Narratives," on transracial and transnational adoption, feminism and contemporary literature.

ROSANNE KENNEDY is an associate professor and head of gender, sexuality, and culture at the Australian National University. She is editor, with Jill Bennett, of *World Memory: Personal Trajectories in Global Time* (2003) and is currently editing a special issue of *Humanities Research* on "Postcolonial Testimony."

SUSAN MEISELAS is a documentary photographer and member of Magnum Photos since 1976. She is the author of *Carnival Strippers, Nicaragua, Kurdistan: In the Shadow of History, Pandora's Box* and *Encounters with the Dani* (2003). Meiselas is well known for her documentation of human rights issues in Latin America. Her photographs are included in American and international collections. In 1992 she was made a MacArthur Fellow. Her exhibit Susan Meiselas in History was at the International Center for Photography in fall 2008.

DANIEL MENDELSOHN's first book, *The Elusive Embrace* (1999), was a *New York Times* notable book of the year; his second, a scholarly study entitled *Gender and the City in Euripides' Political Plays*, was published in 2002. In 2006 he published *The Lost: A Search for Six of Six Million*, which won the National Book Critics Circle Award, the National Jewish Book Award, and, in its French translation, the Prix Médicis Etranger. He teaches at Bard College.

NANCY K. MILLER is Distinguished Professor of English and Comparative Literature at the Graduate Center, CUNY. Her most recent books are *But Enough About Me: Why We Read Other People's Lives* (2002), the coedited anthology, *Extremities: Trauma, Testimony, and Community* (2002), *What They Saved: Pieces of a Jewish Past* (2011), and the coedited anthology *Picturing Atrocity: Photography in Crisis* (2011).

ALONDRA NELSON is assistant professor of African American Studies, American Studies, and Sociology at Columbia University. She is coeditor of *Technicolor: Race, Technology, and Everyday Life* (2001) and *Body and Soul: The Black Panther Party and the Politics of Race and Health* (2011).

JAY PROSSER is reader in humanities at the University of Leeds. He is author of *Second Skins: The Body Narratives of Transsexuality* (1998) and *Light in the Dark Room: Photography and Loss* (2005); editor of *American Fiction of the 1990s* (2008); with Laura Doan, *Palatable Poison: Critical Perspectives on The Well of Loneliness Past and Present* (2002); and the coedited anthology *Picturing Atrocity: Photography in Crisis* (2011).

LIZ ŠEVČENKO is founding director of the International Coalition of Historic Site Museums of Conscience, a network of historic sites that foster public dialogue on pressing contemporary issues. She has most recently published "The Making of Loisaida" in *Mambo Montage: The Latinization of New York City* (2001).

LEO SPITZER is the Kathe Tappe Vernon Professor of History Emeritus at Dartmouth College and visiting professor of history at Columbia University. His recent books include *Hotel Bolivia: The Culture of Memory in a Refuge from Nazism* (1998); the coedited *Acts Of Memory: Cultural Recall in the Present* (1998); and *Ghosts of Home: The Afterlife of Czernowitz in Jewish Memory* (2010), coauthored with Marianne Hirsch.

MARITA STURKEN is professor in the Department of Media, Culture, and Communication and codirector of the Visual Culture Program at NYU. She is the author, most recently, of *Tourists of History: Memory, Consumerism, and Kitsch in American Culture* (2007).

DIANA TAYLOR is University Professor and professor of performance studies and Spanish at NYU. She is the author of *Theatre of Crisis: Drama and Politics in Latin America* (1991); *Disappearing Acts: Spectacles of Gender and Nationalism in Argentina's "Dirty War"* (1997); and, most recently, *The Archive and the Repertoire: Performing Cultural Memory in the Americas* (2003). She is founding director of the Hemispheric Institute of Performance and Politics.

SONALI THAKKAR is a doctoral candidate in English and Comparative Literature at Columbia University. Her interests include memory, postcolonial literature, gender studies, and human rights. Her work has appeared in *Women's Studies Quarterly (WSQ)* and in an edited anthology titled *The Politics of Reconciliation in Multicultural Societies.* From 2005–2009 she was a Trudeau Scholar as well as a Doctoral Fellow of the Social Sciences and Humanities Research Council of Canada.

PATRICIA J. WILLIAMS is professor of law, Columbia University, and a contributing editor of the *Nation.* Publications include *The Alchemy of Race and Rights* (1991); *The Rooster's Egg, Seeing a Color-Blind Future: The Paradox of Race* (1998); and, most recently, *Open House: On Family Food, Friends, Piano Lessons and the Search for a Room of My Own* (2004).

Index

Gender and Culture
A Series of Columbia University Press
Nancy K. Miller and Victoria Rosner, series editors
Carolyn G. Heilbrun (1926–2003) and Nancy K. Miller, founding editors

CPSIA information can be obtained
at www.ICGtesting.com
Printed in the USA
JSHW020953110520
5616JS00001B/71